Panorama of the Enlightenment

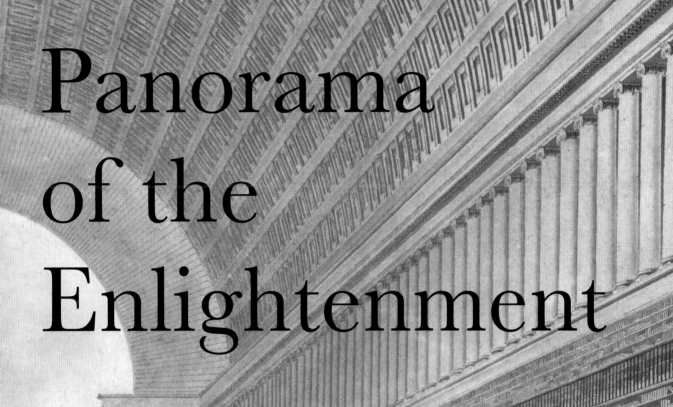

Panorama
of the
Enlightenment

DORINDA OUTRAM

With 387 illustrations, 153 in colour

Thames & Hudson

For Dr L.

Preface

THIS BOOK AIMS TO CREATE a friendship between its readers and the complex sets of ideas and habits which we call the Enlightenment. There are no polemics in its pages, and the reader is not called upon to take sides in any of the very many conscientious disputes which have disfigured the historiography of the Enlightenment. Instead, the book aims to demonstrate for itself the structure of the Enlightenment, not just in the works of major thinkers, but also in terms of those who are in their way representative of the Enlightenment though they may never even have heard of Lock, Kant, Herder or Rousseau. Their chronologies are different from those of the great minds, just as their habits were also.

No rigid order is imposed in this book upon its reader's approach. It is not necessary to read the chapters in the sequence in which they appear. The book is also as much image as it is text. Every picture may be seen as a commentary on the text, often far more succinct than verbal commentary could possibly be. Pictures also enlarge the remarks of the text, and move them from one medium to another.

In every chapter certain themes seemed to demand, and to repay, a fuller visual treatment, and these have been expanded into self-contained 'picture essays' with commentaries of their own. Since they come in a rather random way within the chapters, in order not to confuse the reader they are printed on a tinted paper and distinguished by a different page layout.

DORINDA OUTRAM

Mozart's *Magic Flute* can claim to be the major work of art to be inspired by the Enlightenment. First staged in 1791, it tells a mysterious allegorical story in which the hero and heroine pass through a series of symbolic trials before emerging purified and enlightened. Much of its imagery is derived from Freemasonry and its dominant figure, or 'Grand Master', the high priest Sarastro, was commonly identified with the emperor Joseph II. In 1816 Karl Friedrich Schinkel designed stage sets for a production at the Berlin Opera House which are perfectly in keeping with the atmosphere of the original. This starry sky was the domain of the Queen of the Night.

Introduction

PREVIOUS PAGES
The glowing forge in the background and the extreme contrasts of light and dark give this scene an almost theatrical sense of excitement. The painter was Léonard de France, but it belongs to a new genre, typified in England by the work of Joseph Wright of Derby, of dramatic paintings of industrial and technological processes. Here, most of the characters have their backs to us, which emphasizes their concentration on the forge. The act of demonstration in such scenes also suggests that it is men who understand technical processes, not women, who have to be shown.

The colossal *Hercules* that dominates the park of Wilhelmshöhe at Kassel, Germany (*above*), spoke plainly to the Landgrave's own subjects and to visiting foreigners from all over Europe. In the language of classical mythology, then universally understood, Hercules stood for heroic virtue, strength and power, qualities in which every 18th-century ruler could take pride. Like his ancestor Frederick the Great, the Landgrave Karl saw no contradiction between the ideals of the Enlightenment and those of despotic monarchy. The *Hercules* (*opposite*), made in 1713–17, stands on top of an obelisk rising from a classical octagonal temple. It is a copy of the ancient Roman Farnese *Hercules*, nearly 10 metres (30 feet) high and made of beaten copper.

THE ENLIGHTENMENT IS LIKE AN OCEAN in which great systems of winds and tides pull in different directions. This book tries to represent this interlocking system of opposing directions and seasonal changes. Topics which seem incompatible, or simply unlike previous views of the Enlightenment, are here portrayed side by side. Enlightenment people themselves battled with these contrary ways of knowing and questioning, and in this battle we must join them. If they found it hard to reconcile (say) their era's simultaneous acceptance of slavery and glorification of benevolence, or of religion and reason, we must try to solve what were to them paradoxes and contradictions. This book is not one which looks down upon its subjects as if from a great height, but one which participates in the struggles of Enlightenment people to be enlightened.

'Enlightenment' is a word which both they and we have found to be at once essential and indefinable. This complexity was increased by the way in which the Enlightenment came into being in the first genuinely global era. People, plants, ideas, diseases, furniture, books, tea, gold and silver were sold many times over as they circulated the globe, and global markets and currency exchanges were established worldwide. However much they struggled to keep the word Enlightenment and its surrounding dialectics within the confines of European thinking, Europeans always had the rest of the world clutching at their elbow. What that produced was a pressure for relativism. If Tahitians and Scots were so different, if they were simply incommensurable, how could it be argued that one was better than the other or that the European Enlightenment was a superior form of thought? If the authority of Christian belief based on the Bible was invoked to answer this question, one was immediately confronted with the declining authority of the Bible itself.

All this led to much contemporary discussion and unease about the global application of the Enlightenment and its impact on European and American societies (see Chapter 4). The Enlightenment was born in Europe, yet its meaning became less and less clear the more it tried to incorporate increasing amounts of knowledge coming in from parts of the world beyond its boundaries. Drawings brought back from voyages into the Pacific of tattooed princes, palm trees, outrigger canoes and the lonely giants of Tierra del Fuego, or accounts of the bargaining practices of the Indians of Nootka Sound, caused not only an increased problem with relativism in the European and colonial Enlightenments; they also persistently raised the question: who was the really Enlightened person?

A common mythology

The Enlightenment's struggle for definition in a global age is only one of several overarching themes which organize this book. A second, and no less important, one is that of the use of classical intellectual themes, ultimately drawn from the mythology of Greece and imperial Rome, to illustrate concerns of the eighteenth-century Enlightenment and to establish their legitimacy. This theme is present throughout the book, but perhaps most strongly in the discussion of the imagery of Enlightenment in Chapter 1. But this use of ancient themes and representations was hardly confined to the eighteenth century. For hundreds of years kings and the other elites, to take only a few examples, had likened their strength to that of Hercules, and their power over nature to that of the travels

Wisdom, as appropriate to a monarch as power, was symbolized by the goddess Minerva. This cameo of Catherine the Great of Russia represents her wearing Minerva's helmet decorated with a winged sphinx and a laurel wreath. The original was engraved in 1789 in Siberian jasper; this is one of many copies in biscuit porcelain. The artist was one of the grand duchesses of Catherine's court, Maria Fyodorovna.

of the sun god Apollo. The use and often transformation of classical images served several important purposes: first, that of some kind of propaganda for the prince who was represented as Apollo or Hercules. Before we assume too quickly that this attempt to meld the human and the divine was assumed to be ridiculous, as it would be today, we should realize that for eighteenth-century people the prince who was represented as Hercules was really felt to partake to some extent of the very nature of the cleaner of the Augean stables. Another consequence of the presentation of kings, princes and aristocrats as gods and goddesses drawn from the classical pantheon was to make a common point of reference for those from the middle and upper classes who had been educated in classical mythology. This was one of the major factors allowing the emergence of international elites, so that the Austrian empire could be run by aristocratic bureaucrats from as far apart as Milan, Innsbruck, Prague and Breslau. One of the most important things which linked these men was their education in the classics.

Christian images and narratives, however, were available to all, in a way that classical learning was not. Even simple church attendance, in both Catholic and Protestant Europe, led the believer through a liturgical year designed to familiarize him with the most important biblical narratives, and the most important parallels between Old and New Testaments. Churches were teaching aids, where wall-paintings and sculptures illustrated the lives of Christ and the saints. This meant that even for poorer, non-classically educated readers, a bank of allusions and representations would be available. It is one of the objectives of this book to present a portrait of an Enlightenment which considers not only the middle classes but also looks at the autodidacts, the workmen, farmers, small traders and slaves who learned to read and write, sometimes in conditions of extraordinary difficulty.

Turning points

The third major theme which emerges throughout this text is that of chronology. As there has never been any consensus on the nature of the Enlightenment, so too there has never been any agreement on its chronology. But we can say that contemporaries did recognize certain points in time which for them marked the difference between their own time and before. For some, it was the development by the English cosmologist Isaac Newton, who died in 1727, of new theories of light and planetary motion, ideas which seemed almost to expel God from the universe. But in fact Newton's ideas, expressed in a complex mathematics often overwhelming even to the professional, took a very long time to diffuse themselves, and most encountered Newton's theories only in the popularizations which began to be published in the 1730s.

Many more contemporaries talked about the 'new philosophy' of the French philosopher René Descartes, who died in 1650, as the true opening of the Enlightenment. By the 'new philosophy' most people meant his *Discours de la méthode* (*Discourse on Method*) of 1637. Descartes' teachings spread slowly over Europe, rather than announcing themselves as an overnight wonder. His work has often been described as being an intellectual biography as much as a philosophical treatise. He announced a break with scholasticism, the previous way in which philosophy had been taught, and which accepted the authority of Aristotle. By the seventeenth century scholasticism was strongly linked with

Old dogmas quite rapidly began to be seen
as superstitions. Popular pamphlets of the early
1700s featured a 'Monsieur Oufle' who believed
in everything that people 50 years earlier had
believed in: ghosts, fairies, horoscopes,
divination, magic, etc. But it was inevitable
that in the sceptical atmosphere of the
Enlightenment Monsieur Oufle's beliefs would
be easy to mock, as the pointing fool makes
clear. *Above and left:* the title-page and an
illustration from an edition published in 1711.

efforts by the Church to maintain the truths of revelation. Descartes also accused its followers of settling for answers which were probable rather than true, and having no clear doctrine of the soul. Because of the quasi-autobiographical form of the *Method*, Descartes' philosophy did not appear as a rigid system, but as one which was based on personal experience and which it was left for individual readers to accept. He enjoined on his followers an attitude of permanent doubt, or scepticism, about the world, themselves and their own propositions. He distrusted sense impressions as evidence, so that the famous sentence *cogito ergo sum* (it is only through thought, not sensation, that one can say one has a true existence) expresses a particular form of scepticism. This distrust of sensory knowledge had many consequences for the Enlightenment. It set up problems about the relationship between mind, body and self, which were to last to the end of the century. The break between mind and body also encouraged many women to believe in the validity of their own thoughts, previously denigrated because of the weakness of the female body and the supposed corruption of its perceptions. If the evidence gained from the senses was not valid, then women could *reason* as well as any man.

Descartes also contributed to the problem of the meaning of truth with which the Enlightenment was also concerned. If the evidence of the senses was suspect, Descartes argued that mathematical truth, the only form of truth left after the rejection of the testimony of the body, was self-consistent. Descartes believed that there was no nature, only thought. This left it open for him to construct his method, a way of reasoning which could be theoretically applied by all to obtain a correct result. However, the Enlightenment still had to deal with many unanswered questions about the place of bodily experience.

If Enlightenment people often point to Newton and Descartes as the founders of their world, they often also say that the world of Descartes had been concerned with unseen beings, was 'superstitious' in its belief in an invisible world of angels and the devil, of witches, of spells and magic, charms and incantations – things which, by their own time, were no longer believed or tolerated. They had become enlightened. Before 1700 few except the Dutch Jewish philosopher Baruch Spinoza, who died in 1677, challenged the then-orthodox religious belief that the world was full of spirits and powers, angels and demons, witches and the Holy Ghost itself. Belief in this world view was orthodox in most Churches: how could the works of invisible beings such as God and the Holy Spirit and the angels not be accompanied by those of their opposites? It makes little sense to say that the Holy Ghost works in the world and yet, somehow, the devil does not. Spinoza challenged this view that orthodox belief depends on the unseeable.

In spite of the ferocity with which Spinoza and his followers were attacked by the Churches, it was true that by around the 1730s such a turnaround had taken place. What had been orthodoxy in the 1670s was by the 1730s seen as foolish superstition. A cheap, easily available pamphlet, for example, published in 1710 creates the character of the foolish Monsieur Oufle, who still believes in the invisible world of spirits. Its illustrations have Monsieur Oufle pointedly followed by a fool. The title-page of the pamphlet gives his reading list of books on magic, black magic, demons, sorcerers, wolf-men, incubi and succubi, the witches' Sabbath, fairies, ogres, mad spirits, ghosts and phantoms, dreams, the philosopher's stone, horoscopes, talismans, comets, almanacs, lucky and

Monsieur Oufle patronizes astrologers and geomancers.

unlucky days, eclipses, all sorts of apparitions, divination, spells and enchantments. Monsieur Oufle's more modern-minded family are full of ironies at his expense, all making the same point: that his beliefs arise from nothing but credulity and superstition.

Many of these beliefs and practices had been condemned by the Churches. But that condemnation was founded upon a belief in their reality. It makes no sense to prosecute a witch if you do not believe in witchcraft. It is notable, and an indication of the decline of belief in the world of unseen spirits, that witchcraft trials sharply declined all over most of Europe in this period. The insults endured by Monsieur Oufle are signs of the change from one world view to the next which seems to have occurred in the 1730s. This can definitely be seen as one turning point in the history of the Enlightenment.

However, we should question whether the 'turning points' discussed here, the work of Newton, Descartes and Spinoza, would appear so to the majority of the population of eighteenth-century Europe and its colonies, who probably never heard of any of these names. (An interesting game for historians would be to reconstruct the 'turning points' which *would* be recognized by those outside philosophically aware circles.)

Finally, as I have said, this book does not impose any rigid order. Themes which run between chapters are cross-referenced in the text. What is much more fixed is the relationship of illustration to text. Every picture might, in its positioning, be seen as a commentary on the text, and often a far more succinct one than a verbal equivalent could be. Pictures of course also enlarge the remarks of the text, move them from one medium to another. The title-page of a book, for example, of which many appear in this book, shows what actually faced the reader when he had opened the book and turned the outside cover. Portraits allow the reader to guess at the character of the main personalities. Pictures in fact are the voices that whisper, texts the voices that talk aloud. Both are heard in these pages.

Derision: Monsieur Oufle is mocked by street urchins.

Superstition: Monsieur Oufle visits an alchemist.

Archetypes of the Enlightenment

E VERY AGE CONSTRUCTS its representative characters, human beings who most clearly embody the values of the time and who are held up as models for emulation. For the Middle Ages, the saint and the knight were two such representative figures. Medieval saints, portrayed in sculpture, in sermon collections, in illustrated manuscripts and in the paintings on church walls, were powerful foci for emulation.

The two centuries before the Enlightenment created most of the male representative roles that are still with us. The characters of Don Juan, Faust, Hamlet, Sancho Panza and Don Quixote are still among the templates that we use to identify and analyse behaviour today.

For the Enlightenment, the story was different. Instead of creating a few representative figures of great power, it tended to proliferate the templates for emulation. A whole village of representative characters emerged, such as the technician, the benevolent man, the bluestocking, the reader, the philosopher/ *philosophe*, the bureaucrat, the adventurer, the liberal monarch, the inventor. These images of representative figures, like Cook, Arkwright and the emperor Joseph II, were also circulated far more widely throughout society by new technologies of reproduction such as engraving. Yet, as so often, the Enlightenment seems little different in many respects from the Middle Ages. Pictures of representative men and women served in this century too as ways of focusing emulation, of measuring the gap for viewers between imperfect current reality and the potential future.

Just like the Virgin or the saints, such figures might also mount from earth to heaven supported by clouds and cupids, which marked them out as specially powerful figures for emulation (Cook or Franklin). Hovering over daily life, but no longer part of it, their distance made them all the more strongly the focus for self-fashioning.

Each figure in a portrait represented not only a figure for emulation, but also a potential answer to a particular predicament. It told the viewer something about the technologies of mind and emotion one must possess to carry out a particular project, or to live a particular life. The pictures, for example, of an absorbed reader which proliferated in the Enlightenment indicated the necessary comportment of the serious student – not a matter easily worked out by people who lived, like most people in Enlightenment Europe, in villages and small towns, where they might well be the only person trying self-consciously to live an enlightened life, and thus the only person for whom reading was a central project. It is too easy to focus on such essentially busy urban figures as Diderot and forget the essential loneliness of many others who tried to lead Enlightenment lives. It was this loneliness which gave the pictures of representative men and women, often circulated in engraved form, their peculiar importance. Take another example: What did living as a bluestocking, a learned woman, actually mean? Was the woman in the portrait of the bluestocking happy? Would the viewer also be happy in that role, in that life, so far from the norms of female life represented by marriage and motherhood? This is what reading the book of a picture could help one to decide. What did it mean to be living in an enlightened age? In part, it meant

looking at images of representative people to come to terms with the enlightened age itself.

There were several controversies in the Enlightenment about the problems involved in looking at representative figures. This was the entry point into many debates about the relationship between person and role. This debate reached its climax with acrimonious exchanges between the thinker Jean-Jacques Rousseau on the one side, and Diderot, his former friend, on the other. Rousseau, in his *Lettre sur les spectacles* (*Letter on Theatrical Performances*), argued that theatres and any sort of acting should be forbidden, because they blurred the distinction between reality and illusion. Diderot on the contrary argued that acting was the cement of social life, that it bound people together because it repressed incivility. They and many others debated the inherent theatricality of portraits. Those who followed Rousseau saw portraits as composed of a subject displaying himself to the spectator in the way in which an actor does to his audience.

The Bluestocking. Lady Mary Wortley Montagu's romantic elopement with Edward Wortley Montagu was the prelude to a life spent in writing. Shortly after their marriage, her husband was appointed ambassador to the Ottoman empire. Their residence in Constantinople (modern Istanbul) was the stimulus for her *Embassy Letters*. Her fascination with the Ottoman Empire is well captured by this portrait of her in Turkish costume by Godfrey Kneller (*above*). Like many other bluestockings, she was self-educated and taught herself Latin. Unlike many bluestockings, however, she was married, but the effective breakdown of her marriage in the quarter-century before her death in 1762 made the context of her work similar to that of her unmarried peers. Lady Mary wrote much political journalism and poetry.

The Statesman. Ideally, the thinker, the scientist and the political leader were combined. In Benjamin Franklin the worlds of Enlightenment and Revolution overlap. The student of electricity, of marine currents, of meteorology, of light and of diet, was the same man who stood firm for the rights of the American colonists, and who helped to draft the Declaration of Independence – including in it the characteristically Euclidean phrase: 'We hold these truths to be self-evident.' This allegorical sketch by Fragonard (*right*), in which the *génie* of Franklin casts down tyranny, bears witness to his reputation in France in 1778.

The Reader. Reading as a means to the achievement of an enlightened life is one of the most prevalent images of the 18th century. This is the first era in which solitary silent reading, rather than reading aloud, is at all frequent. When people read aloud in the 18th century, they were reading to someone else. This is why almost all pictures of readers show solitary figures. The reader was an enlightenment hero because it was he or she who internalized through reading the major works of the Enlightenment. In this way, women could also become representative figures. In this 1769 portrait (*left*) by the French artist Jacques-Louis David, Mme Buron looks up briefly from her book, shading her eyes against the light of a candle whose presence may only be deduced by the spectator.

The *Philosophe*. Fragonard's depiction of a wild figure surrounded by heaped open books (*below*) is not a portrait of any particular *philosophe*, the term coined to describe the free intellectuals of the time. Rather, it aims to give a generalized picture of intellectual labour, and is reminiscent of pictures showing divine inspiration given to the writers of the New Testament, especially St John.

The Benevolent Man. Benevolence was one of the central values of the Enlightenment. It was closely linked with 'feeling', that is, sympathy and compassion for the objects of benevolence. This picture of 1785 or 1781 (*left*) by the famous French artist Jacques-Louis David shows the blind Byzantine general Belisarius, once a military hero but now reduced to begging. At its centre is a woman stooping before him to give alms. In the background a soldier stands horrified as he recognizes Belisarius as his former general. Benevolence could indeed have another side: it was a way of marking the distinctions in wealth and status between giver and recepient. Belisarius may have begun as one of the great soldiers of the Byzantine empire, he nonetheless later found himself reduced to beggary. The alms of the woman are a representation of the stability of those who are neither too high nor too low. As such, benevolence is the perfect virtue of the middle class.

The Liberal Monarch. This engraving of Emperor Joseph II of Austria ploughing (*below*) was one of the most widely diffused of its day. So famous was it that it still appeared in school textbooks of the Red Vienna era of the 1920s. Joseph demonstrates his willingness to abandon the ceremonial of the court and to be in touch with poor rural people. This engraving shows something of the change in kingship in the late 18th century away from ceremonial and towards action.

The Bureaucrat. The Spanish government minister, poet and playwright Gaspar Jovellanos is shown here (*above*) by the great Spanish painter Goya looking up towards the spectator, holding a paper whose reading we have perhaps interrupted. The mood, aided by the diffused light and muted colour scheme, is quiet and reflective. Jovellanos himself, his head resting on his hand, looks weighed down with the cares of state. This is one of the few paintings of this period which emphasized the price of office, rather than its splendours. One of the leading ministers of the Spanish reforming monarch Charles III, Jovellanos well fulfilled another Enlightenment archetype, that of the reforming minister. He aided in the regulation of the grain trade.

The Technician. This picture of Friedrich Anton Heynitz, director of the State Academy of Mining in the German state of Saxony (*above*), shows the satisfaction of a senior official. His ceremonial costume carries the marks both of his own status, and emblems of mining and the miners' confraternity. In his hand is a miner's axe, at once emblem and practical tool. This portrait is symbolic, as is that of Arkwright, of the transformation of nature through technology which was an essential part of the programme of reforming monarchs in the 18th century.

The Inventor. Like some medieval saint with his emblematic object, Sir Richard Arkwright is shown here with the mechanism, the Spining Jenny, which he patented in 1769 (*opposite*). This enabled the production of thread of the hardness required to weave cotton, and thus facilitated not only an expansion of the textile industry, but also the widespread adoption for the first time of cotton clothing. It also led to an organization of labour in the textile mills which approximated to the modern factory system.

What Was the Enlightenment?

The image of the sun was the favourite metaphor of the Enlightenment, a movement that saw itself as bringing light – reason and knowledge – to drive out the darkness of supersitition. Apollo's chariot bears aloft Beatrice of Burgundy, ancestress of Carl Phillip von Greiffenklau, prince-bishop of Würzburg, on her way to marry the emperor Frederick Barbarossa. This ceiling fresco is part of a much larger series commissioned from the Venetian artist Giovanni Battista Tiepolo to show the bishop's aristocratic lineage and his connection with the ideals of the Holy Roman Empire. It was painted to be seen from underneath, and this enhances the way in which each picture seems to strive for upward or forward movement. The strong diagonals of the harness on the chariot of Apollo enhance the powerful movement of the horses. Equally the figure of Apollo strives upwards as he emerges from the swirling draperies of the accompanying spirits.

The traveller – symbol of mankind – walks on a twisting road towards the sunrise in the far distance (*opposite*). As was often the case, Enlightenment imagery resembles that of Christianity. This could stand equally well for a depiction of man's life on earth as a pilgrimage towards the light of salvation as it could for a man travelling along a road lit up by the sun's rays, which symbolized Enlightenment. The tiny *Göttinger Taschencalender*, illustrated by Daniel Chodowiecki, was edited by Georg Christoph Lichtenberg, professor of physics at the University of Göttingen, and famous as an aphorist and essayist. Published between 1776 and 1813, the periodical aimed to be easily accessible to educated men and women. Its mixed symbolism of Enlightenment and pilgrimage makes an economical statement that could easily cross national frontiers.

THE ENLIGHTENMENT WAS lived in cacophony and paradox. 'Enlightenment' was a word of power in the eighteenth century, but two people placed in the same room would have produced three opinions about what it actually meant. There was never a stable, universally accepted definition of 'Enlightenment' during the Enlightenment. Even the word itself varied from one region to another. A man in Paris would have spoken of *les lumières*, in Berlin of *Aufklärung*, in Milan of *illuminismo*. These words had come into use at the same time. In France the use of *les lumières*, always in the plural, to designate (among other things) a programme of rational criticism hostile to 'superstition', traditional religion, religious intolerance and abuses such as judicial torture, only dated from around 1750. In the previous century, *lumière* had meant 'natural intelligence' in the singular, and in the plural 'knowledge' or 'cultivation'. If we look at contemporary dictionaries and encyclopedias we can see how long it was before the sense of 'Enlightenment' worked itself into the language. Even the *Encyclopédie* of Diderot and D'Alembert, which began publication in 1751 and is often seen as one of the most powerful engines for the propagation of Enlightenment ideas, contains no entry for *les lumières* and only a brief one for *éclairé* (enlightened). In England, Ephraim Chambers's *Cyclopaedia*, published in 1728, one of the models for the *Encyclopédie*, contained no entry for 'Enlightenment', while the famous *Dictionary* by Samuel Johnson, first published in 1755, begins to provide a definition of Enlightenment only in the later edition of 1775.

In Germany, the word *Aufklärung* came even later. In fact, it was only in the 1780s that the word was accepted into the German language. In 1784, the German-Jewish philosopher Moses Mendelssohn, writing on the meaning of 'Enlightenment', remarked that the word *Aufklärung* was a newcomer, an abstract word, barely understood in everyday speech, and hardly used outside the social and intellectual elite. Further, according to Mendelssohn, *Aufklärung* itself was not really differentiated, even in elite speech, from other newcomers to the language such as *Kultur* or *Bildung*. The very existence of these three overlapping terms shows how difficult it was to define 'Enlightenment'. Surprisingly for us, who today assume that 'Enlightenment' must have been the dominant word of the time, Mendelssohn saw it merely as a subset of *Bildung*, weakly translatable as self-education. Mendelssohn remarked that *Aufklärung* was to *Kultur* as theory is to practice. He connected *Kultur* with eloquence, with poetry and the other arts which contribute to man's social contact with other men. *Aufklärung* had more to do with the sciences and their abstraction. To make his definitions easier to understand, Mendelssohn demonstrated their relevance to national stereotypes. The French have more *Kultur*, the English more *Aufklärung*; the Chinese have a great deal of *Kultur* and very little *Aufklärung*. In this way, by insisting on relating *Aufklärung* to *Kultur* and *Bildung*, Mendelssohn demonstrated how profoundly different the German outlook was.

So words denoting 'Enlightenment' came into different languages at different times. This tells us something about how hard it is to say when the Enlightenment began and ended. That the Enlightenment was not a single, or necessarily coherent programme also makes it difficult for us to estimate a beginning date. Almost all scholars agree that the ideas of the Enlightenment, such as religious toleration and the primacy of reason and nature, survived into the French Revolution and similar movements in the German states, even if the

manner of their implementation, often surrounded with violence and turmoil, was certainly not that which Enlightenment thinkers would have chosen, and certainly often perverted their meaning. Rousseau's concern for equality, for example, and his discussion of the social contract were influential on many revolutionary leaders, and have often been seen as among the factors which led to their use of terror. By the Napoleonic period it is quite clear that the climate of thought and feeling has completely altered, and the attack on the Enlightenment, largely sponsored by the Churches before 1789, has become a state-sponsored campaign, a fierce cultural struggle, not just in France, but in the German and Italian states, and to a lesser extent in England.

It is more difficult, however, to find the point at which the Enlightenment began. As we have seen, words for it seem to have entered languages from the 1750s onwards. But it is clear that recognizably Enlightenment clusters of ideas and concerns, such as the struggle for religious tolerance, are already present before that date. John Locke's work in England from the 1680s, and the publication of Newton's work on optics and gravitation, are often pointed to as signalling the beginning of the new era in Britain, and often of the Continental Enlightenment as well, given the extent to which Locke and Newton were known in Europe. For the German states, the work of the philosopher Christian Thomasius from the 1680s has often been regarded as the starting place. Thomasius called for philosophy to cease being a self-regarding activity, and to work out ways of working on the world: that is, to be practical reason. The German philosopher Leibniz, again active in the last decade of the seventeenth century, has also been regarded as the founder of the Enlightenment in the German states.

Battles like this are hard to resolve. By what criteria does one compare the work of Newton with that of Leibniz? But what does seem to be the case is that it is in the last decade of the seventeenth century that a change in ideas can plausibly be interpreted as opening the era called the Enlightenment. In this decade, for example, Churches were still teaching that unseen beings such as angels, demons and the devil were at work in the world. By the middle of the eighteenth century, no person who claimed to be enlightened could see these beliefs as anything other than 'superstition'. Only what was visible was to be believed. If this example is any indication, then recognizably Enlightenment ideas may have taken over quite quickly from the ideas of the Baroque era, rather than there being a longer process of gradual change.

Contemporaries may well have been far more interested in the way that Enlightenment acted upon the world, and supported new claims to authority by new social groups, than they were about the considerations of chronology which have so exercised historians. Thinking about the meanings of *Aufklärung* could come very near to promoting a social programme for the diffusion of knowledge. Friedrich Gedike, co-editor of the *Berlinische Monatsschrift*, wrote '*Aufklärung* is just as relative a word as is Truth. It is different, and must be so, for different places, times, social classes and between the genders, and not just subjectively, but objectively also. A thoroughgoing equality of the experience of *Aufklärung* is just as little desirable as equality between the social classes.' He argues that a whole nation can be brought Enlightenment only by the middle class. From the middle class, the centre of the nation, the rays of *Aufklärung* would illuminate the aristocracy above, and the workers below. So it is easy to

Simply dressed and, in an age of wigs, wearing his own hair, Moses Mendelssohn looks in this chalk drawing by the Berlin artist Daniel Chodowiecki (*above*) what he really was: a dedicated thinker and worker for religious toleration. In his book *Jerusalem* he tried to bring together Judaism and Christianity in mutual tolerance. This put him at odds with orthodox rabbis, but he was nourished and protected by the concessions granted to the Jews by Frederick II.

Tolerance. From Daniel Chodowiecki's *Taschencalender*, which, like the image on p. 25, mixes Christian and classical elements. Tolerance wears a helm often seen on the head of the goddess Minerva, yet at the same time the radiance of Divine Grace spreads out behind her. Her outstretched cloak recalls many sculptures and paintings of the Madonna extending her blue cloak to cover suffering humanity.

Christian Wolff was another major contributor to debates on the meaning of Enlightenment and truth. His belief that all truth might be reduced to logic gravely offended Christian ideas about the infinity and unknowability of God, and seemed to be an attempt to bind the Creator by mathematical expressions. In this portrait by an unknown artist Wolff's forceful character is well displayed. His carelessly tied cravat shows his truly scholarly disdain for worldly appearance. Wolff's ideas led to his exile from Prussian territories, ordered by King Frederick William I, the father of Frederick II. Immediately after his accession in 1740, the latter recalled Wolff and gave him a chair at the University of Halle. Yet again, Frederick demonstrated his unorthodoxy in religious matters. Wolff argued for the necessary self-consistency of truth, against contemporaries like Christian Thomasius, who thought that it could contain contradictory elements and yet still remain truth.

see here how discussion of *Aufklärung* and its modalities could be turned into a claim for the importance of a particular social class. In the German lands, the aristocracy still in fact unquestionably dominated society. Knowing this, we can understand some of the implications of Gedike's firm pronouncement that Enlightenment was the preserve of the middle class. He was claiming cultural dominance for a class of men who were fighting to define themselves as different from the peasants below them and from the aristocracy above them, against whom they fought for their place in society. Claims to know about Enlightenment were one weapon in that fight. Gedike's opinion also of course challenged the idea that truth must be a unity, and steps straight into the debate between Christian Wolff and Christian Thomasius about the nature of truth. It also challenged the Christian claim that God is truth, and therefore cannot be relativized.

When historians ask what 'Enlightenment' meant to its contemporaries, they often forget that the term did not suddenly emerge in the eighteenth century. In the eighteenth century, the word still carried a weight which had been acquired when it had a spiritual meaning. Two famous encyclopedias, published at the opposite ends of Europe and at different times, demonstrate this very clearly. Dr Samuel Johnson's *Dictionary*, in the 1775 edition, gives five senses to the word 'Enlightenment'. The first and second concern the optical sense. The third is closer to our own expectations, in the way it links Enlightenment to one of its core eighteenth-century values, the use of reason. 'To instruct, to furnish with an encrease [*sic*] of knowledge': 'This doctrine is so agreeable to reason that we meet with it in the writings of enlightened heathens.' Johnson illustrates the third meaning with a quotation from the well-known contemporary magazine *The Spectator*. This example firmly links Enlightenment with reason, seen as the common property of men, whether Christian or heathen. Johnson's fifth meaning, however, comes from an older source. It is 'to illuminate with divine knowledge'. This is a description not of rationality as a way to knowledge but of revelation. It goes back to discussions by St Augustine about the way that the light of God can be perceived by the inner, spiritual eye. These two meanings, so different in every way, co-existed in the eighteenth century. Enlightenment was a word of power: it was also one which still carried residues from quite different spiritual understandings.

The competition to define Enlightenment: Berlin, 1784

In December 1783, a Berlin pastor, Johann Friedrich Zoellner, published an article in the city's leading intellectual journal, the *Berlinische Monatsschrift*. Zoellner complained in a footnote – one of the most fruitful footnotes ever written – that he had never seen a satisfactory definition of 'Enlightenment'. It was, he continued, almost as important for his own times to be able to define 'Enlightenment' as it was to define 'truth'. The resonance of this throwaway remark by an obscure pastor writing on matrimonial law was such that only nine months later, in September 1784, the Berlin Academy of Sciences placed an announcement in the *Berlinische Monatsschrift*, offering a prize for the best essay answering the question *Was ist Aufklärung?* (What is Enlightenment?) This competition has often been seen as one of the defining moments of the Enlightenment, a moment when its different and often contradictory meanings were brought into an otherwise rare confrontation. Yet such a judgement is embedded in irony. The Enlightenment has often been seen as centred on France. Yet the fullest contemporary discussion of the meaning of its defining term came from the other side of Europe, and from a region where the word *Aufklärung* was still, according to contemporary testimony, confined to intellectuals and upper-class people. These complexities, incongruities and ironies teach us more about the real life of Enlightenment ideas than could any smoothly unproblematic collection of essays. Pastor Zoellner was right. At the end of the century which contained the diffuse, self-contradictory, yet easily recognizable intellectual, social, artistic and scientific movement labelled 'the Enlightenment', contemporaries were as little able to define the age they had lived through as they had been at its beginning. However, this situation arose from something more than the normal human attributes of limited knowledge and infinite capacity to tolerate contradiction. It reflected the reality that the Enlightenment comprised (at the most minimal definition) many different paths, varying in time and in geography, to the common goals of progress, of tolerance, and the removal of abuses in Church and state.

In spite of this diversity, one contribution to the essay competition has had an extraordinary resonance and overshadowed most other attempts to define Enlightenment. Frequently anthologized, often taught, often misinterpreted, it has come to represent, not only all the other very diverse essays submitted in this competition, but to stand in as a description of the Enlightenment in general. This is the essay by Immanuel Kant. Kant's reputation as one of the great philosophers of his time and later, and the dramatic opening of the paper, have undoubtedly contributed to the making of its canonical status. He opens with the famous statement that Enlightenment is 'man's throwing off his self-incurred immaturity'. Immaturity he defines as the inability to exercise one's intelligence without the guidance of another person. He then uses the well-known Latin motto, *sapere aude!* – 'Dare to know! have the courage to follow your own understanding!' Kant's definition of Enlightenment thus seems highly optimistic. Yet he soon emphasizes the force of the human cowardice and laziness which stand in its way. He points to people who take little initiative with their own lives, those who let their doctor decide their diet, their pastor supervise their conscience, and their books provide their opinions. Indeed, leading a life of such passivity, they have no need to think at all. For this reason, Kant says, there are only a few people who have been able to free themselves and recover the use of their own judgement.

This is difficult to do. Kant describes how from every side one hears cries of 'Don't reason!' 'The soldier is ordered, Don't think, get on parade! The tax-official orders, Don't argue, pay! The pastor orders, Don't think! Believe!' Kant continues that only one ruler in the world (Frederick II) says, 'Think what you like, about whatever you want, only obey!' Everywhere there are limitations on freedom. But what sort of restrictions prevent Enlightenment, and which can even promote it? It is only the public use of reason which can bring Enlightenment. Kant's definition of public and private are very different from our own. The private use of reason must be very narrowly restricted. Kant explains the public use of reason by giving the example of a learned man in relation to the world of readers (*Leserwelt*). Kant's equation of the public with the world of readers is interesting, and will be explored further (see Chapter 2). Private reason, however, refers to the exercise of an office or

Samuel Johnson's short-sightedness and his extraordinary powers of concentration are both captured in this portrait painted around 1775 by the fashionable portraitist Sir Joshua Reynolds. The strong tonal contrast increases this impression. Reynolds was selective in his sitters, and was already well known in addition for his lectures on aesthetics. In 1768 he had become the first president of the Royal Academy of Arts. Johnson's origins were humble. He had worked his way through university, and earned a living as a journalist and pamphleteer. His own journal, *The Rambler*, like the *Göttinger Taschencalender*, was aimed at an educated, well-meaning middle-class audience. Johnson's main fame, then as now, lay with his *Dictionary*. This was among the first attempts to list and define ordinary English words, and the last to be compiled by one man alone.

profession. Here, freedom cannot be allowed. All must obey, or government and society will not function. An army officer must obey his superiors' orders, even if he believes them to be pointless, incompetent or unreasonable. In his capacity of a learned (thoughtful) man, however, he cannot be stopped from pointing out the mistakes of the army command and laying them before the 'world of readers'. In the same way, a clergyman must preach the doctrine of the Church which he serves. But as a learned man, he should have complete freedom to criticize the theology or organization of the same Church to the public of readers.

Kant then asks the famous question: Do we live in an enlightened age? The answer is, No, but we live in an age of Enlightenment, that is, one in which Enlightenment is growing. There is still a long way to go before all are able to reason without the intervention of another person, but the obstacles to this freedom are becoming fewer. Finally, Kant, whether ironically or not, dedicates the century of the Enlightenment to his own monarch, Frederick II. He praises Frederick's religious toleration, helping exactly to free his subjects from immaturity and restore their freedom of choice in religious matters. He thanks him too for his tolerance of the expression of opinions in his subjects' public roles, and calls Frederick an example to the rest of the world, who has left all men free to use their own reason in matters of conscience. Frederick's Prussia is an example to other rulers of how freedom may exist without jeopardizing harmony and unity in state and society. Kant also emphasizes how religious matters are thus litmus tests for the level of Enlightenment in any given state. Yet only that ruler who disposes, as Frederick did, of a large and well-disciplined army to keep the public peace can afford to be so tolerant. Only such an army maintains the peace in which the display of private reason can flourish without society collapsing into a welter of violent controversy, particularly over religious matters. Here Frederick, Kant and their contemporaries would have remembered the violent religious wars of the preceding century, wars fought with outstanding brutality on all sides, which had devastated much of Germany. Frederick's objective, probably more than any other contemporary ruler, was at all costs to contain religious controversy and keep the different Churches in parity. 'Argue as much as you like, about whatever you like, but obey!' Kant concludes by pointing out a final paradox (and, as an aside, that in human affairs nearly everything is paradoxical). A high degree of civil freedom seems advantageous to a people's intellectual freedom, yet it also sets up an insuperable barrier to it, by destabilizing the surrounding state and society. Conversely, a lesser degree of civil freedom gives intellectual freedom enough room to expand to its fullest extent. Once this has happened, Kant sees the development of maturity as fairly easily attained.

It is easy to see that once the first pages of Kant's essay, with their rousing calls to self-liberation, are left behind, his ideas become far more problematic. They were not greeted with wholehearted approval by Kant's contemporaries. Shortly after its publication, Kant's essay was attacked by Johann Georg Hamann. Hamann was a well-known conservative satirist, who now had Kant in his sights for the second time. He had already written a satire on Kant's *Critique of Pure Reason*, as well as on *Jerusalem*, Moses Mendelssohn's major work of 1783 in favour of religious toleration. This experienced and effective critic of the Enlightenment took care to strike into the heart of Kant's circle. It was to

Three portraits of Immanuel Kant demonstrate the very different ways in which the philosopher could be viewed by contemporaries. They correct the temptation to see him only as he was at the time of his *Aufklärung* essay.

The 1801 caricature by Hogeman (*above right*) seems drawn from life, portraying Kant with friendly amusement, yet at the same time relates well to the strong German literary and visual tradition of mocking professors. It also captures Kant's eccentricity. After seeing this picture, we can believe in his delight in eating mustard from the pot. The engraving by Hans Veit Schnorr von Carolsfeld (*above*) leaves a very

different impression. He portrays Kant with a gentle expression, thus meeting the public expectation that true scholars would be other-worldly, objective, disengaged. The 1808 bust by Johann Gottfried Schadow (*right*) shows yet another view of Kant. The year 1806 witnessed a disastrous defeat for Prussia at the hands of the French, and Schadow's work as an artist became fully part of the movement for national revival that followed. It is no wonder that he chose to portray an iconic Kant, a symbol of the excellence of the national culture. The bust shows Kant unclothed. In so doing it connects him to the phrase 'the naked truth' (*die näckte Wahrheit*).

Frederick II of Prussia is represented in the portrait (*opposite*) of 1769 by J.G. Ziesems as indifferent to the ceremonies and symbols of monarchy. The crown of Prussia lies inconspicuously on the lower edge of the picture. For him power is validated by war (the plans of fortifications under his left hand, and the general's staff held in his right) and by internal reforms. The king is wearing the order of the Black Eagle (*Schwarzen Adler*), which he founded in 1740 to reward bravery.

A Wedgwood cameo issued around 1780 (*above*) shows Frederick II as he would have appeared at the time of the Berlin competition to define Enlightenment. He again wears the star of the Black Eagle, and again appears simply dressed. Here the continuities end. The life and intelligence that animate Ziesems' portrait have been replaced, in years which had seen the near-disintegration of the kingdom during the Seven Years' War, by a withdrawn and weary expression.

Christian Kraus, Kant's favourite pupil and close friend, that he sent an apparently light-hearted, ironic letter explaining his disagreement with Kant's essay. Challenging the most famous lines in Kant's work that Enlightenment means man's liberation from his self-incurred immaturity, he pointed out that weakness and immaturity were not crimes, but rather an inevitable part of the human condition, which it may be both folly and hubris to think that we can free ourselves from. Further, he thought that Kant's assumption of neutrality was deceptive. Kant's claims to know what Enlightenment really was only showed that in reality Kant had appointed himself to the role of what Plato's *Republic* calls a Guardian, a teacher of mankind. As a Guardian figure, Kant set out to discipline his immature readers, but refused to acknowledge his human equality with them. This was an important hit for Hamann. It drew attention directly to the leadership roles claimed by Enlightenment intellectual elites who had yet to integrate themselves fully into the surrounding society. It also pointed to the internal contradictions of an Enlightenment defined as universal yet claimed as the property of an elite group of writers and theorists. We have mentioned this point before, but it becomes clearer than ever here how much writing about Enlightenment, or claiming participation in it, was a way of asserting authority claims. It allowed access to membership of a new elite, one not of wealth or of noble descent, but of verbal and intellectual skills.

Hamann next questions the all-pervasive use of images of light as a metaphor for Enlightenment, of light chasing away darkness and ignorance. He called attention to the biblical injunctions which in fact connect virtue with darkness, instancing Matt. 11.11. Continuing his satire on images of light, he expresses sympathy for the unenlightened immature person, suddenly dragged willy-nilly into the full light of day. Imposed Enlightenment is self-contradictory. Guardians and immature persons, rather than being strongly differentiated, might in fact not be able to exist without each other. Challenging another point, Hamann draws out the consequences of Kant's split between public and private. Hamann does not believe that men can be divided into public and private selves, nor that discussion either can or should be confined to elite professional groups. He says that it is all very well to speak of freedom and reason, but of little use when in public life one is still enslaved. Kant's arguments, he deduces, are not really aimed at the renovation of society. His own three daughters, Hamann jokes, would not tolerate being called immature, or accept their exclusion from the private exercise of reason, or rather from Kant's division between public and private persons. This is just as illogical as St Paul's command that women should be silent in church when there is no impediment to their chattering to their heart's content outside it. Charging Kant with political naivety, he questions too whether the armies of the king of Prussia would always be used to protect Enlightenment. Under another monarch, might not their cannon face in a different direction? Even more disturbing – Hamann calls it comical – is Kant's splitting of individuals into two, the public and the private person, two roles with completely contradictory demands for the individual. One can speak with freedom, the other is constrained. One can criticize injustice and irrationality, the other has to stay mute. Where is the moral centre of such a person, a centre that can hold moral judgement and responsibility? Is there any space for the possession of a soul? Or are such divided people doomed to hypocrisy in both roles?

Grosses vollständiges
UNIVERSAL
LEXICON

Aller Wissenschafften und Künste,

Welche bißhero durch menschlichen Verstand und Witz
erfunden und verbessert worden,

Darinnen so wohl die Geographisch=Politische

Beschreibung des Erd=Creyses, nach allen Monarchien,

Käyserthümern, Königreichen, Fürstenthümern, Republiquen, freyen Herr=
schafften, Ländern, Städten, See=Häfen, Vestungen, Schlössern, Flecken, Aemtern, Klöstern, Ge=
bürgen, Pässen, Wäldern, Meeren, Seen, Inseln, Flüssen, und Canälen; samt der natürlichen Abhandlung
von dem Reich der Natur, nach allen himmlischen, lufftigen, feurigen, wässerigen und irrdischen Cörpern, und allen
hierinnen befindlichen Gestirnen, Planeten, Thieren, Pflantzen, Metallen, Mineralien,
Saltzen und Steinen rc.

Als auch eine außführliche Historisch=Genealogische Nachricht von den Durchlauchten
und berühmtesten Geschlechtern in der Welt,

Den Leben und Thaten der Käyser, Könige, Churfürsten

und Fürsten, grosser Helden, Staats=Minister, Kriegs=Obersten zu
Wasser und zu Lande, den vornehmsten geist=und weltlichen
Ritter=Orden rc.

Ingleichen von allen Staats=Kriegs=Rechts=Policey und Haußhaltungs=

Geschäfften des Adelichen und bürgerlichen Standes, der Kauffmannschafft, Handthierungen,
Künste und Gewerbe, ihren Innungen, Zünfften und Gebräuchen, Schiffahrten, Jagden,
Fischereyen, Berg=Wein=Acker=Bau und Viehzucht rc.

Wie nicht weniger die völlige Vorstellung aller in den Kirchen=Geschichten berühmten

Alt=Väter, Propheten, Apostel, Päbste, Cardinäle, Bischöffe, Prälaten und

Gottes=Gelehrten, wie auch Concilien, Synoden, Orden, Wallfahrten, Verfolgungen der Kirchen,
Märtyrer, Heiligen, Sectirer und Ketzer aller Zeiten und Länder,

Endlich auch ein vollkommener Inbegriff der allergelehrtesten Männer, berühmter Universitäten,
Academien, Societäten und der von ihnen gemachten Entdeckungen, ferner der Mythologie, Alterthü=
mer, Müntz=Wissenschafft, Philosophie, Mathematic, Theologie, Jurisprudentz und Medicin, wie auch aller freyen und
mechanischen Künste, samt der Erklärung aller darinnen vorkommenden Kunst=
Wörter u. s. f. enthalten ist.

Mit Hoher Potentaten allergnädigsten Privilegiis.

Anderer Band, An — Az.

Halle und Leipzig,

Verlegts Johann Heinrich Zedler,

Anno 1732.

How well does Kant's essay really represent the Enlightenment? How far can it really be seen as the paradigmatic account of Enlightenment programmes? It can be argued that Kant was profoundly different from other Enlightenment writers who, like Rousseau, stressed the value of the integrity and autonomy of the individual. Kant divides the individual between roles which seem virtually irreconcilable. He takes reason as his highest value, like many other Enlightenment thinkers, yet differs greatly from them in imposing limits on its operation. Thought must not be pursued to its conclusion if it seems to damage social order, or the state – a new idea that undercuts his battle cry of *sapere aude!*, which was itself in any case in use several decades before the Berlin competition, and cannot be associated exclusively with Kant's essay. On the other hand, the struggle for religious toleration plays a role in his essay certainly commensurate with its centrality to the Enlightenment in general.

We could prolong indefinitely such an accounting exercise. Deeper themes emerge when we take Kant's essay as a way of working out the very difficult practical position of the Enlightenment. It did depend on the power of princes for its survival. That the power of reason was not pursued to its limits was due not only to efforts of kings such as Frederick II to maintain order, but also (paradoxically) to the social fears of the thinkers themselves. These contradictions, so characteristic of Enlightenment thought in general, restricted the use of reason. Kant deals quite realistically in this sense with another serious problem. In the German lands, where there were far fewer free intellectuals than in France, and where nearly everyone who participated in enlightened discussion was involved with the support structure of state and monarchy (aristocrats, soldiers, bureaucrats, pastors, teachers), the separation of public and private reason was both highly necessary and disturbing. This tells us that Kant's essay is unusually sensitive to the way in which the need for security and stability in state and society can have a strong effect on thought.

Johann Georg Hamann opposed Kant's view of the Enlightenment. For him, it did not free men from weakness and immaturity, but rather subjected them to an intellectual elite.

The Universal Lexicon of Johann Heinrich Zedler, first published in 1732, was at once recognized as the most important repository of learning in the German-speaking world. Zedler was a printer in Leipzig working with a team of collaborators. This title-page (*opposite*) spells out its claim to take in all human knowledge, 'all learning and all arts [i.e., technologies as well as painting, sculpture and so on] which are the result of human reason and wit'. Though it contains many articles about theological teachings, Zedler treats them like any other area of knowledge. The *Lexicon*, in 68 volumes, drew to completion in 1754, three years after the *Encyclopédie* of Diderot and D'Alembert began publication in 1751. The appearance of these works shows the enormous appetite among the middle classes in Britain, France and Germany, part of the emerging elite who were the most eager consumers of written material, for facts and information about the visible world in the Enlightenment.

The Language of Light

The chariot of Apollo, or *quadriga*, was a favourite theme in Roman decoration, appearing both in mosaic and as statuary, not to mention on small domestic items (*above*). The chariot is orientated as if following the sun's course from east to west. Around Apollo's head are stylized rays of the sun that recall those around the head of the Statue of Liberty. The visual vocabulary of Apollo and his chariot has enjoyed extraordinary longevity.

Rulers, great or small, did not forget this solar imagery in the 18th century. Frescoes commissioned in 1744 from the famous Italian painter Giovanni Battista Tiepolo by Carl Phillip von Greiffenklau, prince-bishop of tiny Würzburg in southern Germany, were as full of solar imagery as any emperor's (*opposite*).

WHEN THE FRENCH MATHEMATICIAN and *philosophe* Condorcet wrote that 'The time will come when the sun will shine only on free men who have no master but their reason', he was not using unduly romantic language or inflated rhetorical expressions. In fact, he was employing what was the most banal and predictable metaphor, both verbal and visual, of the Enlightenment: light. Enlightened people moved as a matter of course among words and images of radiance, of sunlight, illumination, clarity. Exploring the meaning and origin of such images is a way into the issues and problems of the era. The aesthetic qualities of visual images of light were just as important as the polish of verbal argumentation in ensuring their acceptance.

Visual images of light were beautiful. At the same time, they were far easier to understand, retain and internalize than the material in printed books and pamphlets. It was easy to show with a single picture how light could shine into dark corners where abuses, stupidity and ignorance might still lurk. It could take hundreds of words to make the same point, and every line of those words could be subject to interpretation and misinterpretation. Words often seemed better at spreading discord than capturing the reader's attention. Images, on the other hand, acted as a homogenizing force. They enabled the wider diffusion of Enlightenment concerns. It was far easier to become interested in, even attached to, a representation of some quality such as 'benevolence' or 'toleration' than it was to read disputatious books or pamphlets on the same topics. Just like the images of the saints so familiar to Enlightenment peoples from previous ages, images concentrated thinking and promoted attachment.

However, the Enlightenment did not itself create the visual language of light that played such a large part in identifying it and in spreading its message. Someone who saw a picture of the sun, the central image of the Enlightenment, was not confronted by a novel image. The allegorical images of light that formed the visual language of the Enlightenment had been shaped by the mythology of the classical world and its Christian successors. For the Romans, Apollo the sun god crossed the skies once every day. For Christians, God created the world with a joyful cry of 'Let there be light!', and St John's Gospel (John 8.12) described Christ as 'the light of the world'. In the end, Enlightenment images brought together both Christian and Roman strands.

The meaning of the image of the Roman god Apollo is complex, and not all of it is connected with his role as the sun god. Apollo was the god of learning and of science. He was associated with rational thinking. He accompanied the Nine Muses, and himself played the lyre. As the sun god, travelling in his chariot, he traced the course of the sun from east to west, beginning at dawn and ending with twilight. Once a day, his rays illuminated every part of the world. It was this that made it easy for many later rulers to use Apollo's cosmic journeys as the foundational image behind claims to universal monarchy.

The association between the sun god and assertions of worldwide power survived the centuries between the classical world and the Enlightenment. Louis XIV covered his vast palace at Versailles, completed in 1682, with solar emblems. It was orientated so that the first rays of the morning sun entered the king's window. Louis's architects here recalled the Roman idea of the *oriens*

In the same decade that Tiepolo laboured on the frescoes in Würzburg, a far greater ruler, Frederick II of Prussia, turned to them for inspiration in planning his new palace of Sans Souci. A visitor to the park surrounding the palace would come upon a hauntingly beautiful trelliswork pavilion studded with golden sunbursts, which sheltered *The Praying Boy*, a statue of a young man holding both hands up to the sun, as if waiting for them to be filled with sunlight.

The Praying Boy, a Hellenistic figure, had been discovered in the 16th century during work on the fortifications of the island of Rhodes. It came into Frederick's possession in 1747. The statue is unlikely to have had any original connection with the sun. That it was placed under the trellis hows how Frederick II interpreted it as part of the solar imagery relating to the strength of rulers.

A century before the park at Sans Souci was laid out, Louis XIV of France had participated in court masques on themes from the mythology of Apollo. The king wears starbursts all over his costume, which look very like those which adorn the pavilion of *The Praying Boy*. Such continuities are characteristic of the solar imagery whose use stretches back to the ancient world. Louis ceased to dance in his early thirties.

Augusti, which had identified the rising sun with the emperor's power. The great reception room in the palace was called the *Chambre d'Apollon*. Louis took the title roles in court ballets, such as that of the rising sun in the 1653 *Ballet de la nuit*, or of Apollo in the 1654 *Marriage of Peleus and Thetis*. In his autobiography, Louis gives a detailed account of his insistent use of this solar symbolism. Solar imagery was compelling. He wanted his subjects to perceive him, like the sun, as constantly in motion, yet always at the centre of the world. As the sun, the bearer of ineluctable light, he would penetrate darkness, and give fructifying warmth to all living beings. As the sun, it was his light which both nourished the world and made it transparent to his all-seeing, monarchical eye.

Yet the images of light available to eighteenth-century people were not all so neatly aligned with the classical heritage of the myths of the passage of the sun god. At the end of the Roman world, much of this imagery had been absorbed and reformulated by the new Christian religion. The radiance of Apollo became a metaphor for divine grace, and then transmuted into the haloes of the saints. Light itself was changed from being something which came from outside into a metaphor for inner spiritual experience. Zedler's widely diffused multi-volume *Universal Lexicon*, part of the furniture of every aspiring German middle-class home in the Enlightenment, begins its entry on light with a discussion of the word's optical meanings, then goes on to contrast this light, perceived by the body, with spiritual light, perceived by the eye of the soul. Zedler uses Jesus' question in the Gospel of John (11.9) to demonstrate the easy flow from optical light to spiritual light: 'Are there not twelve hours in the day? If any man walk in the day, he stumbleth not, because he seeth the light of this world. But if a man walk in the night, he stumbleth, because there is no light in him.' On this quotation Zedler bases his description of a light which is both natural and supernatural and spiritual, and which exists to drive away darkness from the soul, to chase away evil and its children, and to illuminate the reason and will of man, so that they can live as children of light and, through the light of belief, come to eternal life.

It is obvious how close the visual language of the Enlightenment came both to the solar imagery of the ancient world, and to its Christianized derivatives. It was powerful and compelling precisely because it mobilized both of the major referents used by educated Enlightenment people. These were the two poles between which the Enlightenment oscillated. However, the way in which this particular classical imagery of Apollo was used began to change in the Enlightenment. A visual language of sunlight to convey the power of monarchs was still in use in the 1740s, as the Würzburg frescoes and the grounds of Sans Souci demonstrate. Yet from around the mid-century we begin to see it used less often, and reflecting a changing meaning for the self-images of the monarchs. Frederick II of Prussia, however much he used solar imagery, had never identified himself with the sun. In England, solar imagery had never been used by monarchs after its brief adoption by Richard II. In France, it faded gradually after the death of Louis XIV and died out completely after the accession of Louis XVI in 1776. No French monarch after Louis XIV publicly identified himself with the sun. The imagery which in 1740s Würzburg had seemed so compelling appeared to have gradually faded from use in regal circles.

It was just at this time that the imagery of sunlight and radiance began to be increasingly adopted by the thinkers of the Enlightenment. They recast it as a secularized visual language, while still drawing heavily on the tropes of Christian light images. The convergence between the two was actually very strong. Enlightenment was meant to refer to the transformation of the present world and the creation of a better future state. So was Christian belief. It was this very syncretism that made its use so compelling.

In this tapestry from the palace of Versailles (*opposite*), strongly ordered solar and cosmic symbols are used to the same end. Full of arms and armour, the tapestry quickly establishes the theme of military grandeur under the sun image near the top. Louis's crown is above the sun (a piece of hubris), and the scales of justice intervene. Justice, so central to kingship, is here strongly connected with the cosmological balance symbolized by the globes held by cherubs in the top corners.

Suns and stars, globes and Apollo's chariots drew to Louis XIV something of the majesty of the orderly cosmos. This was the imagery which was to be inseparable from Louis' name in the future. This medal (*above*) from 1661 may be one of those ordered by Louis from the Académie des Médailles et des Inscriptions as part of his personal propaganda. The centre is taken up by the sun god driving the *quadriga* across the heavens. On the rim, 'Assiduitas' is used as a motto. Apollo is assiduous because he drives his chariot every day across the sky, without resting or ceasing – like the king. On the bottom rim is a cartouche containing the fleur-de-lys, the symbol of the Bourbon dynasty. Across the sun king's path runs a band of astrological figures in the ascendant at the time of Louis' birth.

The view from France

France was far removed intellectually and socially from Prussia, yet Enlightenment agendas, particularly those concerned with toleration, seem to have been surprisingly broadly shared between the two. In France, dominated by a rich and powerful Catholic Church claiming the allegiance of the vast majority of its inhabitants, the struggle for tolerance was near the heart of that agenda – the struggle often went hand in hand with attacks on organized religion. Voltaire's 1758 novella *Candide* was inspired by the devastating earthquake and tidal wave which had killed tens of thousands in Lisbon three years before. He also used the story to satirize the *Theodicy* of the famous philosopher Leibniz, who had attempted to solve the age-old problem of the existence of evil in a world supposed to be ruled by a beneficent God by 'proving' that this world was the best of all possible worlds, and that the cruelty and injustice so visible in it were part of a scheme by God, of which inadequate human understanding could decipher nothing.

The plot of *Candide* sets out to refute Leibniz, and to question the benevolence of God. The rapid-paced narrative has the naive Candide and his strangely assorted companions, of several different faiths, travel the globe only to encounter injustice, suffering and intolerance at every turn. Shipwreck, tidal

This image of Voltaire in old age vividly conveys his humorous and ironical outlook on life (*above*). Houdon's bust also shows Voltaire with naked shoulder and chest, implying that he uttered the 'naked truth'.

The real, unglamorized Voltaire is shown in this painting by Jean Huber from around 1759 (*right*). We see Voltaire beginning his day's work dictating to his (decently clad) secretary while hopping into his breeches from his skimpy nightshirt. The long skinny legs and shallow chest are left undisguised. Voltaire is not only indulging in self-satire here, but is also validating his satires against the highly placed, and against social and governmental evil, by his employment of the 'naked truth'. The monarchy is also satirized here. Voltaire's rapid and inelegant rise-and-shine is in satirical contrast with the Apollonian *levée du roi*.

waves, earthquakes, war, murder, rape, burning at the stake, flogging, mutilation, disfigurement and forced prostitution are only a few of their trials. Voltaire narrates these disasters with a speed normally reserved for the action of a farce, and with a light, easy, cynical tone that somehow manages to turn into high comedy a narrative full of grotesque disasters. This whole work thus ridicules the different Churches' inability to deal with the problem of evil. If all the Churches are equally incompetent, no one Church has any monopoly on truth, and thus no claim could be made that one Church should impose its views on others. The only response to the problem of evil is religious tolerance, the work seems to be suggesting.

Conclusion: authority, revelation and reason

In spite of such defensive measures, the Enlightenment found itself under heavy criticism. The Göttingen physicist Georg Christoph Lichtenberg, now famous for his aphorisms, thought that Enlightenment would fail unless it considered its audience: 'People talk a lot about Enlightenment, and want more light. My God, all the light they want won't help when people either have no eyes, or close those that they have.' Lichtenberg realized that Enlightenment, for all its images of transcendent light, need not necessarily immediately compel others by its truth. It had to be understood as a process, an opening of the eyes, not as an instantaneous bolt of light. Other criticisms were far broader. Pastor Zoellner wrote of the destructiveness of the Enlightenment, calling it a movement which devoted itself to undermining the basis of morality, to denying the value of religion and turning heads and hearts away from God. Opponents both Catholic and Protestant also argued that the Enlightenment was too concerned with the visible world. The images of light served only to illuminate this world, not the unseen world of spiritual life. In fact, for the

Candide, **Voltaire's brilliant satire** on Leibniz's optimistic view that 'all is for the best in the best of all possible worlds', is his most famous work. The German edition (*above centre*) was illustrated by Chodowiecki. One engraving (*above right*) shows Pangloss, the embodiment of optimism, standing in front of the baron, Candide's benefactor. On the right is Candide, who is in love with Cunégonde, the baron's daughter. When this is discovered, Candide is thrown out by the baron, and the action of the novel begins. The attribution to Ralph (*above left*) is a false authorship attached to shelter Voltaire from the French censorship.

Cesare Beccaria's only book was the *Dei delittie dei pene* (*Of Crimes and Punishments*). Written on themes discussed with his friends the major Enlightenment figures Pietro and Alessandro Verri, it quickly achieved international fame. It argued for the abolition of the use of judicial torture, for more equal punishments between the social classes and between crimes, and less agonizing forms of capital punishment. It both helped to create a strong current in the late Enlightenment for judicial reform, and encouraged pre-existing movements in that direction. This symbolic engraving shows Justice rejecting capital punishment and the use of torture, whose instruments are displayed here.

Enlightenment, such commerce with the invisible world of angels, spirits, demons and apparitions, though the orthodoxy of a generation before, was pure 'superstition'. If nothing else united them, both Catholic and Protestant believed that Enlightenment was their enemy. It not only hacked away at theology and Church organization, not to mention questioning the great economic power of the Church, but also supported toleration. The Jesuit order repeated these claims in its *Journal de Trévoux*, the war engine of the anti-Enlightenment (see p.284). Religion was also at the centre of Enlightenment concerns for another reason. Religious belief gave authority to knowledge gained from revelation rather than from sense impressions, calculations or logical deductions. It was orientated on an unknowable, unpredictable future state of heaven or hell. Nothing could be further away from Enlightenment ideas. Religion became thus a battleground for control of authority. That is why works such as David Hume's *On Miracles*, which attacked the authority of the accounts of Christ's miracles given by the apostles as proof of his divinity, were important. Hume pits sense impressions and our normal expectations of human behaviour against miracles, which offend against the laws of nature. To talk about religion was to take part in a struggle for authority between revelation and reason.

So, where does this leave us? It may seem that the whole concept of the Enlightenment has simply exploded. It may seem that 'Enlightenment' itself has next to no stable meaning, that the term has become nothing but a catch-all for the very diverse thoughts and practices of the eighteenth century. But the Enlightenment was far from being just a thing of semantic differences and regional variations. It was the focus of energies, needs and desires. Its aspirations, such as the eradication of superstition, the achievement of toleration, the abolition of judicial torture, the belief in human progress, the critique of Church and state, the remaking of the family, acted as spaces where men and women could validate their status as members as the new elite of thought and word. Enlightenment ideas spread though Europe and its colonies. Whatever the regional differences, the accelerated distribution of ideas in this period meant that all (among the educated) who wanted to could participate in debates, and that a global enlightened consciousness could emerge which would homogenize ideas in spite of variations at local level. The Enlightenment was a project to harmonize the cacophony of the world, and to explore the paradoxes of human needs and passions. It is the project of this book to accompany the men and women of the Enlightenment in their search for definition and redefinition of the values of their time. It is also its project to show how complex, how controversial and how ironical it could be either to think Enlightenment thoughts or attempt to live an Enlightenment life.

The German philosopher Georg Christian Lichtenberg was fond of calling himself 'the little man'. Almost a dwarf, he still managed to marry twice and become famous as a physicist and also as an aphorist. Most of his short and pithy sayings remained in manuscript until his death. But those printed had already established him as a major commentator on science and politics. The peculiarities of his physical appearance were caught in this caricature (*left*) by the Göttingen scientist G.H.W. Blumenbach, who was particularly interested in the connection between physical features and intelligence.

Lichtenberg's life-size statue by N. Dushki stands in the middle of Göttingen today (*above*). A more modernist portrait sculpture stands at the door of the Department of Physics of the University of Göttingen. Of all the famous intellectuals who have lived in Göttingen, it is Lichtenberg who has been adopted as its *genius loci*.

The Encyclopédie,
Engine of the Enlightenment

I N April 1767, Voltaire wrote to his friend Vermes: 'I write in order to act.' In saying so, Voltaire could have stood for most Enlightenment writers who, very differently from their Romantic successors, saw the written word as necessarily acting on the world. The great compilation of knowledge that was the encyclopedia edited by Diderot and D'Alembert was brought together with the same belief in mind. What they produced was not just for recreation or reference; it was an engine through which they hoped to change the world.

The complete *Encyclopédie* was published between 1751 and 1765. It contained 17 volumes of text and seven of plates: 71,818 articles and 2,885 engravings. Its history had hardly been smooth. The first two volumes were published in 1751. Such was their impact that in 1752 the Paris theology faculty, the Sorbonne, condemned them to be publicly burnt. It was only after intense lobbying at court, with the Church authorities and with the royal bureaucracy responsible for book censorship, that the authors' licence to publish was restored. It has often been remarked that this lobbying, which saw the Sorbonne, the *Parlements* (the Appeal Courts) and the monarchy, the old conservative bodies, ranged against liberal court factions, such as that of Malesherbes, who was in charge of the bureaucracy for the censorship of books, revealed all too well the divided, factional nature of old-regime society.

It was only Malesherbes's protection that allowed the publication of volumes III to VII between 1753 and 1757. In 1759, however, the *Encyclopédie* was again prohibited. Pope Clement XIII condemned the work, and D'Alembert left the editorial team. Several contributors followed suit. Alone, Diderot published

Denis Diderot, one of the editors of the *Encyclopédie*, is portrayed here (*above*) by the French artist Jean Fragonard. Although the portrait was widely praised, Diderot himself greatly disliked it, and almost had it destroyed because it drew on representations of inspired poets and writers. This was anathema to Diderot, who instead wished to portray Enlightenment life as something calm and reasonable.

Reason pulls away the veil from Truth (*opposite*), while clouds withdraw to open up the sky to light. Below Truth may be seen the Nine Muses and other symbolic figures bearing the emblems of the arts, sciences, fine arts and technologies which would feature in the work of which this is the frontispiece, the *Encyclopédie* of Diderot and D'Alembert. It was engraved by B.L. Prevost after a drawing by Charles-Nicolas Cochin. The title-page of the 1772 edition (*left*) follows up many of themes of the frontispiece, emphasizing in particular the practical arts of navigation and printing, along with easel painting.

ENCYCLOPEDIE,
O U
DICTIONNAIRE RAISONNÉ
DES SCIENCES,
DES ARTS ET DES MÉTIERS.

volumes VIII to XVII, a feat not only of literary gunmanship, but also of political courage. Diderot remained in sole charge of the *Encyclopédie* until 1772. He died in 1784. The work had a shadow prolongation when the rights were bought by the large commercial publisher Pancouke. Pancouke issued several further volumes of a supplement in 1776 and 1777, plus an index to the Diderot and D'Alembert *Encyclopédie* and two further volumes of plates.

Diderot and D'Alembert's original plan, to publish a plain translation of the Englishman Ephraim Chambers' *Cylopaedia* (still in existence today), had quickly been abandoned in favour of a far more grandiose project, discussed in the prospectus to the first volume and in the article 'Encyclopedia', written by Diderot.

Both begin by emphasizing the novelty of the *Encyclopédie*. It was the first encyclopedia to be written by more than one person. Even the last substantial works that in any way resembled it, Pierre Bayle's *Dictionary* of 1696 or Chambers' *Cyclopaedia*, were still the work of one man. In the article 'Encyclopedia', Diderot points out the impossibility, in their age of what we would now call 'information overload', of having all articles over all fields of knowledge written by one man. Instead such a work had to depend on a whole team of contributors, who would produce the text as rapidly as possible, 'bound together only by the general interest of humanity, and the sense of mutual good-will'. This was also one of the main tasks shared by Diderot and D'Alembert: the co-ordination of the work of the contributors.

After this, Diderot goes on to discuss the global objectives of the *Encyclopédie*: 'to assemble knowledge scattered across the earth, to reveal its overall structure to our contemporaries, and to pass it on to those who will come after us; so that the achievements of past ages do not become worthless for the centuries to come, so that our descendants, in becoming better informed, may at the same time become more virtuous and content,

Charles Panckoucke aux Auteurs de l'Encyclopedie

Editors and authors feature in this engraving (*above*) from Pancouke's edition. The large portraits are of D'Alembert and Diderot, the smaller ones of other authors. Voltaire and Rousseau are top of the left-hand column, Buffon and Necker of the right.

Madame de Pompadour was one of the *Encyclopédie*'s influential defenders in its battles with Church and state. In a well-known portrait by Van Loo (*opposite*), she is shown with one of its volumes on her left.

A prospectus outlining the scope and purpose of the *Encyclopédie* was issued in 1745 (*far left*), promising coverage of all sciences, human and divine, and including articles translated from the English encyclopedia of Ephraim Chambers. The first two volumes appeared six years later, in 1751 (*left*), again stressing the inclusion of foreign authors.

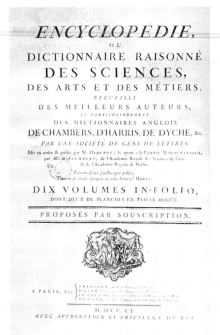

ENCYCLOPÉDIE,
OU
DICTIONNAIRE RAISONNÉ
DES SCIENCES,
DES ARTS ET DES MÉTIERS,
RECUEILLI
DES MEILLEURS AUTEURS,
ET PARTICULIÈREMENT
DES DICTIONNAIRES ANGLOIS
DE CHAMBERS, D'HARRIS, DE DYCHE, &c.
PAR UNE SOCIÉTÉ DE GENS DE LETTRES.

ENCYCLOPÉDIE,
OU
DICTIONNAIRE
UNIVERSEL
DES ARTS ET DES SCIENCES,
CONTENANT
L'EXPLICATION DES TERMES ET DES MATIÈRES COMPRISES SOUS CE TITRE,
SOIT DANS LES SCIENCES DIVINES ET HUMAINES,
SOIT DANS LES ARTS LIBERAUX ET MECHANIQUES;
LA DESCRIPTION

TITLE PAGE OF THE 1745 PROSPECTUS

and so that we do not leave this earth without having earned the respect of the human race.'

But what structure of knowledge did these objectives imply? On what principles was the vast amount of information gathered by the collaborators to be arranged? Diderot tried to solve this problem: 'There is an infinite number of points of view by which both the real world and the world of ideas can be represented, and the number of possible systems of human knowledge is as great as the number of such points of view … why should we not introduce man into our work, as he has been placed in the universe? Why not make man the central focus? This what made us decide to locate the general organization of our work in the principal faculties of man … [memory, reason and imagination] … man must be the unique point of departure, and the point to which all must lead back, if you wish to please, interest and affect people … Everything must be examined, everything investigated, without hesitation or exception … We have come to see that the *Encyclopédie* could only be undertaken in a philosophical age, such as has now arrived.' It was for this philosophical age that the *Encyclopédie* was written.

A second account of the purpose of the *Encyclopédie* was given by its other editor, D'Alembert, who wrote the general introduction to the work. For D'Alembert, the *Encyclopédie* was both a collection of facts and the laying out of a philosophical system of knowledge. He describes the different intellectual faculties of man (the soul is not discussed except as that which distinguishes man from animals), which interact dynamically with each other. D'Alembert in fact puts forward the revolutionary idea that knowledge does not come from revelation, but only from reason. He looks at what he calls the genealogy of ideas, and argues that understanding works with three faculties: memory, reason and imagination. Memory produces history, reason produces philosophy, and imagination produces poetry.

To carry out its objectives, the text of the *Encyclopédie* introduced several innovations. First was the use of the cross-reference. As D'Alembert wrote: 'Cross-references to things clarify the subject, indicate its close connections with other subjects that touch it directly, as well as its more remote connections with still other matters that might otherwise be thought irrelevant, and they suggest common elements and analogous principles … the connections that each special branch of knowledge has with its parent tree and they give to the whole *Encyclopédie* that unity so favourable to truth and its propagation … Finally there is a kind of cross-reference which I would like to call satirical or epigrammatic … [where the reader can easily be led to suspect] that it is wise to read the article with the utmost precaution and with attention to the weighting of every word.'

These cross-references were one of the most effective ways in which the *Encyclopédie* could make its point without having to include a specific article on every subject. There were also large volumes of plates, keyed to articles in the text. Such subjects as architecture and military fortifications were, most importantly, accompanied by plates representing industrial processes. It was one of the innovations of the *Encyclopédie* that it regarded technical and technological knowledge as equal in status with written knowledge such as history and philosophy. Just as importantly, when Diderot and D'Alembert were planning their work, much trade knowledge was still secret, as was much

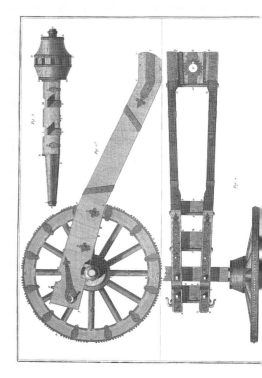

It was the diagrammatic plates that made the *Encyclopédie* such an innovative enterprise and so vital to the diffusion of new knowledge. Here typical pages explain the manufacture of cannon (*opposite*) and of wheeled sedan chairs (*below*).

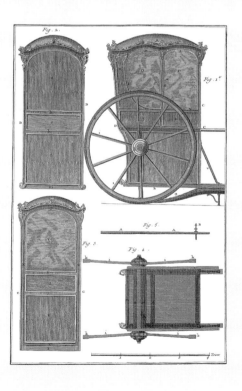

pharmaceutical lore. Families or guilds engaged in particular trades often kept secret the most vital processes of manufacture. This restraint on knowledge prevented industrial development. Diderot, D'Alembert and many of their collaborators went to workshops and saw the trade processes for themselves. The *Encyclopédie* was not simply a collection of information. It also involved direct experience and observation, and the bringing of one form of knowledge into contact with another.

Factors such as these may account for the wide diffusion of the *Encyclopédie*. More than four thousand people subscribed to this massive work which cost the very high price of 874 livres, about twice the annual income of a skilled worker. This number of subscribers is even more remarkable when one remembers the numerous gaps in publication and the papal condemnation. The price of the *Encyclopédie* clearly excluded most ordinary workers and much of the middle class from subscribing to it. For practical purposes, readership was confined to the richer aristocracy, the higher clergy, senior bureaucrats and successful doctors and lawyers. The writers of the articles in the *Encyclopédie*, usually professional commercial writers drawn from the middle class, such as the Chevalier de Jaucourt, Jean-Jacques Rousseau and the Abbé Morellet, were thus of a very different social standing from their readers, and probably could not have afforded to buy the *Encyclopédie* themselves. It was only in the 1770s, with the publication of cheaper revised editions at 384 livres and 225 livres by Pancouke, that wider diffusion could take place. By 1780, 24,000 copies were circulating in Europe – an eloquent indication of the increasing wealth of the middle and upper classes towards the end of the eighteenth century.

Different countries, however, were exposed to the *Encyclopédie* to different extents. Russia and Poland were hardly touched by it, whereas in Germany there was strong demand. Italy ordered many copies, Spain and Portugal hardly any. In England and the Netherlands, demand was less, and the readership quite different from that of France. The higher middle class rather the aristocracy was the social point of diffusion of knowledge and ideas in these two countries. In France, however, 11,000 copies of the *Encyclopédie* were sold, more north of the Loire river than south of it, and more in administrative and cultural centres possessing universities or learned academies than in industrial towns. These figures have often been interpreted as showing the geographical limits of the Enlightenment. They may, however, simply be a measure of the overall wealth of the elites in each region and of the penetration of the French language.

The programme of the Enlightenment is nowhere better revealed than in the pages of the *Encyclopédie*. A thread that runs right though all the articles dealing with theological matters is an outright attack on the Catholic Church, which the *encyclopédistes* saw as nothing more than a priestly fraud, a set of superstitions (see the Introduction on Monsieur Oufle) designed to make the poor patiently endure the misery of their lot on earth in return for the promise of future reward in heaven. Any such attack on the Church, at a time when the Church was intimately bound up with the state and the monarchy, was bound to unleash a storm of hostility. In this period, the king was known as the eldest son of the Church, and swore in his coronation oath to extirpate heresy from his lands.

Religious intolerance was thus institutionalized in France as it was in many other Catholic states. The major religious minorities in France, Protestants and Jews, were seen as disruptive of the links between Church and the state. An attack on the Catholic Church was thus an attack on the monarchical state. In the article entitled 'Intolerance', written at the time of the Calas and Sirvin trials, Diderot made a veiled attack on the intolerant practices of Christian Churches and of the French Catholic Church in particular. Such a position was entirely in keeping with Enlightenment programmes (see Chapter 1) and values. It also brought down upon Diderot personally, and the *Encyclopédie* in general, the publishing difficulties and papal condemnation that afflicted the project. It is not too difficult to see why this happened when Diderot writes: 'Every practice tending to stir up the people, to arm nations and soak the soil with blood, is impious … In any intolerant state, the prince would be simply a torturer, under the sway of the priest.'

The corresponding (anonymous) article on 'Toleration' makes these points even more strongly. Toleration and religious prejudice cannot co-exist. A tolerant society must be founded on humanity, justice and the free exercise of reason. Contractual theories of the relation between ruler and ruled served as a protection against the social and political breakdown caused by the violent emotions typical of religious intolerance.

However, on other subjects, particularly those relating to taxation and the state, that is, monarchical power, the attitudes of the *Encyclopédie* were far from unified and reflected the complexity of responses to the growing political crisis in France. Some articles upheld the traditional conception of the king's power as essentially paternal; others, like those by the *philosophe* D'Holbach, demanded a contractual state. No conception of a democratic state appears in the pages of the *Encyclopédie* – not entirely surprisingly, since even those most critical of the regime did not demand such a thing in the eighteenth century. As for the theory of a contract between monarch and peoples being the basis of society, the articles in the *Encyclopédie* tend to support the idea of such a contract as a submission by the people to the ruler, rather than, as in Rousseau's case, a 'contract of association'. Criticism of the monarchy and its institutions remained muted. However, most articles remained hostile to the *Parlements*, the independent Appeal Courts, which had played a large role in the banning of the *Encyclopédie*, but which by the 1770s were, confusingly enough, among the main political opponents of the monarchy.

The one opinion on which all contributors to the *Encyclopédie* agreed was that man was a rational being and could be guided towards progress and mild reform. It was probably this consensus that led in 1758 to Rousseau's break with the *Encyclopédie*: for him, man's search for his lost liberty was of greater importance than his use of rationality. Rousseau accused the writers of the *Encyclopédie* of showing little interest in the opposing interests of rich and poor. Even their interest in technical knowledge demonstrated how the poor worked for the benefit of the rich.

It was the very contradictions in the *Encyclopédie* that contributed to its success. Nearly every point of view was represented in its pages. In spite of its frequent timidities, it therefore also became an engine for the change in opinions in the years before the French Revolution. Its upper-class readership may paradoxically have absorbed more of its ideas than it realized.

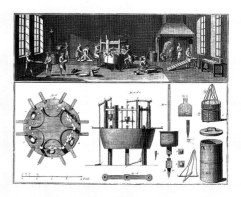

To mass-produce the humble pin required almost incredibly elaborate machinery, all explained in words and pictures in the *Encyclopédie* (*above*). The great advantage was that the machine could make thousands of pins in the time it took a manual worker to make one. Interesting from the point of view of social history is the careful delineation of rank: the higher class of artisans wear more formal clothes.

The tools needed for the manufacture of vices are explained and illustrated (*opposite*). Such pages as this could have had only a limited readership, but are typical of the way Diderot and D'Alembert promoted technology as the equal of other intellectual disciplines.

The ornamental aspects of industry are not neglected. This image (*below*) shows how moulds were used to apply decoration to cannon.

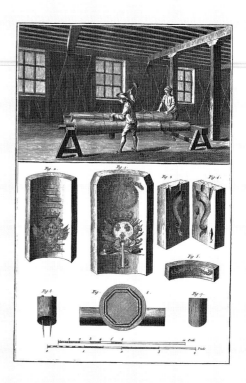

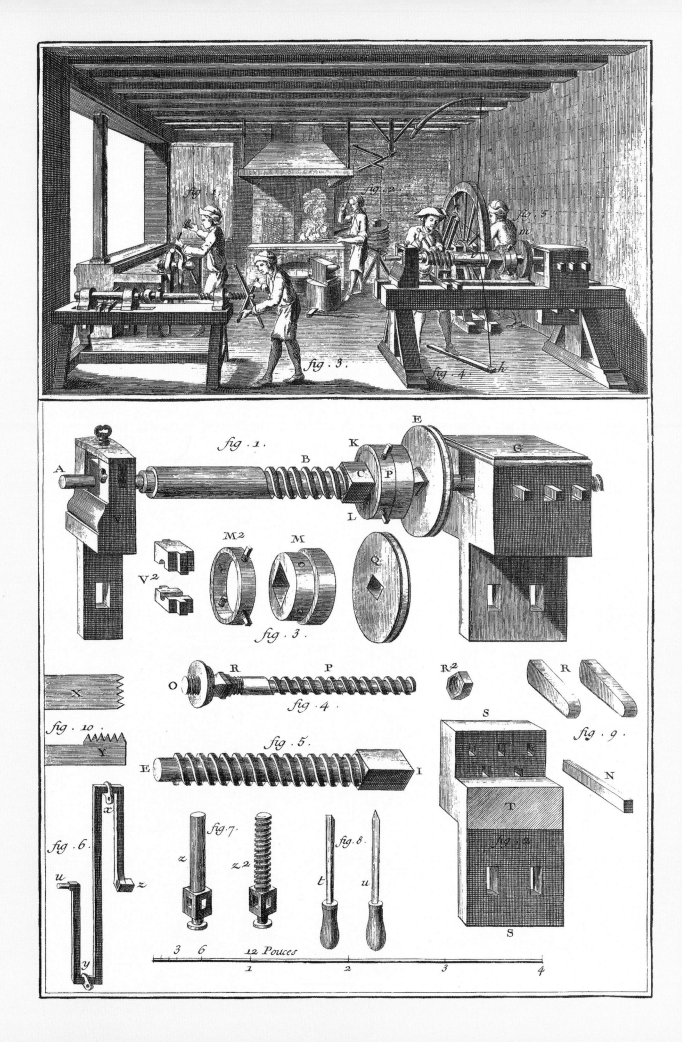

The Sociable
Enlightenment

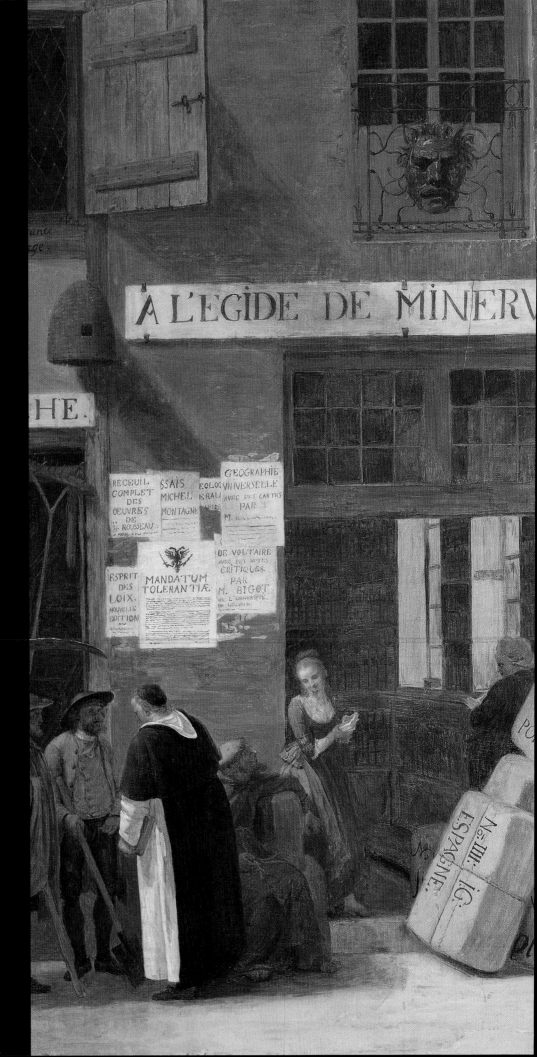

À L'EGIDE DE MINERV

RECEUIL
COMPLET
DES
OEUVRES
DE
J. ROUSSEAU

SSAIS
MICHEL
MONTAGNE

EOLOG
ERAL

GEOGRAPHIE
UNIVERSELLE
AVEC DES CARTES
PAR
M.

ESPRIT
DES
LOIX.
NOUVELLE
EDITION

MANDATUM
TOLERANTIÆ

DE VOLTAIRE
AVEC DES NOTES
CRITIQUES
PAR
M. BIGOT
DE L'UNIVERSITE
DE LOUVAIN.

HE.

Nᵒ. IIII.
ESPAGNE.

had a purely intellectual movement, which is what the Enlightenment was, made a difference to the lives of ordinary people. In the Middle Ages scholasticism was the preserve of theologians. In the Renaissance the classical revival was confined to an elite who could read Latin. Even the scientific revolution of the 17th century had been above the heads of most educated men and women. But by the 18th century several factors had united to create a new, much more broad-based popular culture. One was the spread of literacy among all classes. That promoted a huge increase in the printing of books, which in turn led to new literary forms – not only periodicals, newspapers, travel writing and fiction (can one talk of the novel before 1700?), but also serious works on all subjects aimed at a non-specialist public. The Enlightenment was the age of reading. Reading fed discourse, so it was also the age of conversation. Coffee houses arose to meet the need for places where people could come together and talk. So did bookshops. This animated scene by Defrance de Liège takes place outside a shop called 'The Shield of Minerva' (the goddess of wisdom) and shows parcels of books arriving from all over Europe and a group of well-to-do intellectuals discussing, no doubt, the latest contributions to knowledge and ideas.

The enlightened nobleman was expected to be a connoisseur of the arts, a classical scholar and also to be acquainted with the latest discoveries in exploration and science. Part of his education was undertaking the Grand Tour to see the treasures of Italy. Here (*opposite*), in a portrait by Pompeo Battoni of 1766, the Russian Count Razumovsky displays his appreciation of classical sculpture in the Vatican: the *Apollo Belvedere*, the *Laocoön*, the *Antinous* and, in the foreground, the *Ariadne* (then called *Cleopatra*). Razumovsky was not just an amateur of art. He had studied mathematics in Germany, served in a government post in the Ukraine and been instrumental in bringing Catherine the Great to the throne. From 1746 to 1765 he was president of the St Petersburg Academy of Sciences and an influential patron of architecture. Yet there is nothing pompous about this casual, gentlemanly pose.

How was one to become an enlightened person? Overwhelmingly the answer to that question was: from reading and writing and the sociable experiences of conversing and corresponding, of listening to music and viewing pictures. One was enlightened in virtue of one's participation in these activities. Being enlightened also meant being comfortably apart from the lower classes or the less refined. As the famous essayist Joseph Addison, one of the setters of enlightened values in England, wrote in his *Spectator* magazine: 'A man of polite imagination is let into a great many pleasures that the vulgar are not capable of receiving. He can converse with a picture and find an agreeable companion in a statue. He meets with a secret refreshment in a description, and often feels a greater satisfaction in the prospects [distant views] of fields and meadows, than another does in the possession. It gives him, indeed, a kind of property in everything he sees, and makes the most rude uncultivated parts of nature administer to his pleasures: so that he looks upon the world, as it were, in another light, and discovers in it a multitude of charms, that conceal themselves from the generality of mankind.' Enlightenment had a considerable amount to do with using culture to define class. Those class outsiders who attempted to become enlightened had an uphill path to climb. Even one of the greatest of Enlightenment writers, Denis Diderot, himself the son of a mere master-cutler, could write that: 'There are some readers whom I don't want, and never shall: I write only for those with whom I could talk at my ease.'

Talking at one's ease in the polite and enlightened world could happen in many different places. Probably the most important was the new institution of the coffee house. Present from the late seventeenth century in European capitals such as London, Paris, Amsterdam, Vienna and Leipzig, coffee houses fulfilled a variety of functions. There, one could read newspapers, fall into conversation with a complete stranger whom social prejudice might have prevented one from meeting elsewhere, play cards, watch chess tournaments, engage in political discussion, even have a cup of coffee. Coffee houses, such as the Turk's Head in London, were famous for their political debates. It was in a coffee house that Bach began to compose his 'Coffee Cantata'. Coffee houses, as contemporary pictures make clear, were open to all who could pay for a cup. The customers were heterogeneous in the extreme. Even women could enter. The coffee houses can be regarded as one of the places of informal education on which the Enlightenment, with its treatises on philosophy or the sublime, relied so heavily for the circulation of its ideas. In contradiction of the views of Diderot, coffee houses were places where different classes, genders and nationalities could mingle and exchange ideas. These were places where the reading so crucial to enlightened status could take place as well as in the home. As Addison remarked in one of his *Spectator* essays: 'I shall be ambitious to have it said of me, that I have brought philosophy out of closets and libraries, schools and colleges, to dwell in clubs and assemblies, at tea-tables and in coffee houses.'

Each of these places was a public area, where people conversed and exchanged views on the issues of the day. Conversation was a medium for establishing oneself as enlightened whose importance can hardly be overestimated. It was a performance medium. The 1740 'Essay on Polite Behaviour', for example, advised its readers: 'A man must be master of himself and his words, gestures and his passions, that nothing offensive may escape

PREVIOUS PAGES
The *salon*, epitome of the sociable
Enlightenment, reached its peak in mid-18th-
century France. The most famous was that of
Mme Geoffrin in Paris, a gathering of the best
intellects of the country and a venue for the
circulation of the latest ideas. This painting by
Charles Lemonnier records a meeting in 1755.
In the centre is a bust of Voltaire, then living in
exile. An actor is reading from his *L'Orphelin de
Chine*, a play performed in that very year and
based on an ancient Chinese work transmitted
to France by the Jesuits. Voltaire was attracted
to it by its Confucian philosophy of purely
secular morality. Mme Geoffrin herself, on
the right in a blue dress, sits between the Prince
de Conti and Fontenelle (98 years old and
apparently asleep). In the left foreground,
leaning back, is Buffon, with Réaumur behind
him. To the right of the table are D'Alembert
and (in blue) Helvetius. On the extreme right,
leaning forward, is Montesquieu. Behind the
standing lady in the yellow dress, Rameau turns
to address Rousseau.

It was the ambition of Joseph Addison (*left*)
'to bring philosophy out of closets and libraries
… to dwell at tea-tables and in coffee houses'.
In his *Spectator* essays (1711–14) he introduced
a whole generation to Enlightenment values:
urbanity, toleration, civilized manners, learning
lightly worn and *politesse*.

The Art of Pleasing in Conversation
(*opposite*) offered similar advice to the France
of Louis XIV. Such self-conscious cultivation
of the art of polite conversation was partly
responsible for the sort of artificiality mocked
by Molière.

THE

SPECTATOR.

VOL. I.

LONDON:

Printed for *S. Buckley*, at the *Dolphin* in *Little-
Britain*; and *J. Tonson*, at *Shakespear's-Head*
over-againſt *Catherine-ſtreet* in the *Strand*. 1712.

him, to give others just occasion to complain of his proceedings.' Conversation
was a theatre of self-control. The conversationalist must be able 'to hear
disagreeable things without any visible tokens of offence or displeasure … to
hear pleasurable things without bursts of joy and frantic distortions of the face'.
The diarist Anna Larpent found it hard to follow such advice, and wrote: 'One
must conform to the world… let me hit the medium, neither be too forward
nor too reserved nor too good-humoured, but cautious and prudent, cheerful
and easy, know when to show a proper contempt and when to hide it: when
to encourage and when to avoid… I will do everything with the intention of
doing right. I will endeavour to please all. Converse with the men unaffectedly,
without flirting with the women, with good humour, attention and kindness.'

The salon institutionalized conversational exchange. Great salon hostesses
such as Mme Geoffrin, or her protégée Julie de l'Espinasse, the lover of
Diderot, gathered around them, through humour, charm and brilliance, both
the rising wits and authors of the day and those whose standing was already
firm. Women, though to a far lesser extent, could also become members of
salons. *Salons* were not identical. Each had its own different style and field of
interests. Some were hosted by aristocratic ladies such as Mme d'Houdetot,
others by middle-class hostesses such as Mme Riccoboni. Some interested
themselves in philosophy, others tended towards literature. But whatever their
leanings, they all functioned as places to exchange ideas through conversation.
Often, authors would also read aloud from their works while in the course
of writing them, soliciting opinions from fellow *salon* members, to an extent
which made some Enlightenment pieces of literature collective rather than
individual works.

Getting Together:
Coffee Houses and Conversation

Getting together, chatting, drinking cups of tea and coffee and reading newspapers in a sociable environment were all part of the life of the Enlightenment. Sociability was key to the Enlightenment. It could take the form of dances, of concerts, of public lectures, of drinking parties or public chess performances. Most important of all, however, it was centred around the tea, coffee and chocolate houses which sprang up all over western Europe from the 1680s onwards. By 1760 Vienna alone had at least 60 coffee houses. London and Amsterdam had many more. They were open to anyone who had the price of a cup of coffee, and thus established themselves as a place where discussion could take place, in a temporary suspension of hierarchy.

The sociable Enlightenment was sustained, in its turn, by the growth of global trade (see Chapter 4). Tea and coffee came from India and the Americas, chocolate from South America, sugar from the Caribbean. Books were traded internationally. All this shows how the sociability of the Enlightenment, though superficially varying from coffee house to coffee house, was in fact underpinned by the same international markets. Institutions of sociability themselves looked surprisingly similar across Europe and into the American colonies of Britain and France.

Contemporaries also realized that this new sociability was dependent on the growth of luxury trades and towns. The Scots philosopher David Hume argued in his *Essay on Luxury* that the increasing sophistication of society leads to increasing sociability: 'Curiosity allures the wise; vanity, the foolish; and pleasure both. Particular clubs and societies are everywhere formed ... it is impossible but that they must feel an increase in humanity, from the very habit of conversing together, and contributing to each other's pleasure and

Coffee never lost the allure that belonged to its Eastern origins. It was probably introduced from Turkey in the early 17th century. By the 18th it had become the fashionable beverage of all classes and a whole ritual had evolved around drinking it. Soon coffee houses were flourishing in all the capitals of Europe as meeting places for professional men and gentry and those with leisure enough to indulge in relaxed conversation. A leaflet of 1702 (which preserves a certain Turkish ambience) emphasizes its suitability as a setting for debate (*above*).

The Rococo style eagerly adapted itself to the magical East. *Far left:* a textile from Lyon featuring tea- and coffee-pots. *Left:* a Meissen coffee service, jug, cup and saucer and sugar box, of 1730–35. *Opposite:* Sèvres designs for coffee cups, 1788.

entertainment. Thus industry, knowledge and humanity are linked together by an indissoluble chain, and are found, from experience as well as reason, to be peculiar to the more polished and what are commonly denominated the more luxurious ages.' In this extract we see how he connects material advances which made pleasure possible with the making of particular clubs and societies. Hume knew that ideas cannot be passed sociably without a certain form and direction of economy, and that people have little incentive to come together without it. Luxury and civility lead straight to inquiry.

We are fortunate enough to have records of actual conversations which went on in coffee houses. James Boswell, later Dr Johnson's friend and biographer, enjoyed the coffee houses of London as young Scot trying to make his way in the world of the English capital. His favourite haunt was Child's Coffee Shop

In such a setting Boswell would meet his friends or just sit to overhear amusing conversation to record in his journal. More sober and civilized than the tavern but equally convivial, the English coffee house embodied the world of Addison and Steele. (Note the boy's stylish method of pouring coffee in the centre of the image, *above*.) Foreigners were impressed. They were places, as an Italian visitor wrote, 'where one can hear everything that is believed to be new, be it true or false', and in two hours 'one pays only for what one has drunk'.

In the Strand, a long-established business already noticed more that 30 years before in Addison's *Spectator*. Reading the papers or drinking tea and coffee could be as easily undertaken here as in any other coffee or tea shop. What drew Boswell to it, however, was the conversation. Child's was 'quite a place to my mind, dusky, comfortable and warm, with a society of citizens and physicians, who talk politics very fully and are very sagacious and sometimes jocular'. Boswell records in his London journal for 1762–63 long dialogues on the fate of the British army, for the Seven Years' War was in progress. On another topic entirely, he talks about genius and poetry with the banker Robert Dodsley and the then virtually unknown Oliver Goldsmith. They compare the poetry written in the previous century with that of the modern age:

> DODSLEY: I think those [poems] equal to those of Dryden and Pope.
> GOLDSMITH: To consider them,sir, as villages, yours may be as good; but let us compare house with house, you can produce me no edifices equal to the *Ode on St. Celia's Day, Absalom and Achitophel*, or the *Rape of the Lock*.
> BOSWELL: And what do you think of Gray's *Odes*? Are they not noble?

It was, however, the idea of equality that lay behind all this. The coffee houses were open to anyone who had three pennies in his pocket. Cheap books could be easily bought, art exhibitions were often free. Writers themselves began to conceptualize a new 'virtual' collective, the 'Republic of Letters'. In 1780 the editor of the literary survey the *Histoire de la république des lettres* wrote: 'In the midst of all the governments that decide the fate of men; in the bosom of so many states, the majority of them despotic … there exists a certain realm which holds sway only over the mind … that we honour with the name Republic, because it preserves a measure of independence, and because it is almost its essence to be free. It is the realm of talent and of thought.'

By 1780, these ideas had become commonplace. The notion that writers had a power that was as formidable as those of organized governments, the idea of equality between all those involved in the Republic of Letters, the values of cosmopolitanism, were all very much to the fore in the Enlightenment. This was important, as were all ideas and experiences of equality before the French Revolution. But it had little to do with the actual situation of writers. For every Diderot or Voltaire, world-famous and the companion of monarchs, there existed a thousand who lived by writing pot-boilers on anything from the deeds of the Chevalier Bayard, to children's books, to rehashes of accounts of voyages of exploration. Nonetheless, the ideal of the Republic of Letters was a powerful

In Germany the average price list included many other drinks besides coffee, but that comes top of the list. A great deal more is going on than coffee-drinking in this image (*right*).

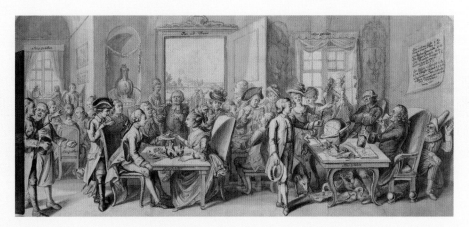

one, because it pointed to the united potential strength of the Republic to shape opinion and thus events. Again, no one had to pay to be a member.

Throughout Britain and Europe, Masonic lodges flourished. Their (supposedly secret) membership vowed to cast aside social distinctions and occupy themselves with key Enlightenment ideals such as rational benevolence. The lodges, some of which were open to women, became centres of debate where members tried to understand the world in ways which were often tinged with mysticism, and which sought the moral regeneration of mankind without reference to any religious doctrine. Mozart's opera *The Magic Flute* (1791), which uses Masonic imagery, is the highest artistic expression of their ideals.

In all, the Enlightenment flourished as much through the spoken as it did through the written word. No wonder conversation could become highly stylized, or that conversationalists could be as highly prized as good authors, or that Diderot chose to set his philosophical novel *Le neveu de Rameau* (*Rameau's Nephew*) in a coffee house.

France too soon had its fashionable coffee house – the Café du Caveau in the Palais Royal (*below*).

Relaxed, communing with nature, while holding a manuscript of Rousseau – Sir Brooke Boothby is the epitome of the enlightened gentleman (in particular the *English* gentleman. What Frenchman would want to be portrayed lying on the ground?). Rousseau wrote his *Dialogues* in 1772. In them he split himself into two, and imagined one self, 'Rousseau', defending his other self, 'Jean-Jacques', against his detractors. Suspicious of his French friends, he gave the manuscript to Sir Brooke for publication, who commemorated the event by commissioning this portrait from Wright of Derby.

Reading: transmitting Enlightenment

Becoming enlightened could also be a profoundly private experience. The newspapers were often read aloud in the coffee houses, but serious reading was done alone. Readers knew the importance of intensive and extensive reading to confirm their status as enlightened people. As a result, their relationship with books was extraordinarily strong. Enlightenment people often talked about 'devouring' their reading material, literally making it one with themselves. The functions of reading were described with extraordinary clarity by Mme Roland, the French political hostess who was to be guillotined in 1793. Her reading of Rousseau's novel *Emile* 'made me pleased with myself, taught me to accept myself, and always gave me the desire to be better, and the hope to be able to become so'. In another place, she comments again on the novel's effectiveness as a modelling device. Not only was it able to give her acceptance of herself, it also showed her how to be the heroine of her own life. In a letter, she remarked that she had just 'devoured' Rousseau's novel for the fourth or fifth time, to the extent that she felt that she 'could have lived with its characters, and that they would have found us to their taste, just as they are to ours'. Writing to her husband, she avowed that in reading a novel or a play, she always identified with the hero, and that she had never been able to read of an act of courage or virtue without feeling that she too could perform such acts. (*'Je l'avoue à toi qu'en lisant un roman ou un drame, je n'ai jamais été éprise du deuxième rôle: je n'ai pas lu le récit d'un seule acte de courage ou de vertu que je n'aie osé me croire capable d'imiter cet acte dans l'occasion.'*) Reading extended Mme Roland's sense of herself: she not only became the heroine of her own life, but also, by the novels which she read, was given a whole repertoire of actions through which to prove that heroism in the world. Reading for her was not *simply* a modelling device. It was the occasion for the internalization of identities and possibilities, a means of living in another, heroic world.

Reading was also a business, and an increasingly large and profitable one. The famous Frankfurt and Leipzig bookfairs doubled in size in this period. In 1764 the bookfair catalogue included five thousand titles of newly published books. By 1800, the number had risen to twelve thousand. Similar trends are discernible in France and in British North America. As far as we can tell from such evidence as library catalogues, wills and censorship records, books written in vernacular languages instead of Latin became far more numerous, and novels, accounts of exploration and works about natural history began to dominate the lists. In particular, this was the period when the novel began to become the normal choice for relaxation reading. It was also the major vehicle by which ordinary readers encountered ideas and information. Many Enlightenment novels are as concerned with conveying factual information and ideas, and summarizing contemporary controversies, as they are with character and plot. Copies of the *Encyclopédie* were sold from Paris to Moscow as part of a highly organized market in books. This expansion could not have taken place without an increasing penetration of book-reading throughout the social classes. Wills even quite low down the social ladder began to mention books. A series of books, called collectively the *Bibliothèque bleue* (the Blue Library), were printed in a small, cheap format aimed at the urban and rural poor, and sold all over France from pedlars' packs. Often retelling folktales and fairy stories, these little

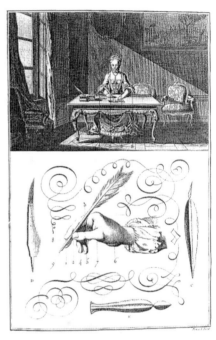

Writing manuals provided instruction in attaining a fine hand. A page from the *Encyclopédie* of 1763 illustrates both the required strokes of the pen and a typically elegant correspondent (*below*).

The popularity of letter-writing gave rise to a literary genre peculiar to the 18th century, the epistolary novel. *Pamela* by Samuel Richardson was one of the first to be written in this form. Richardson had earlier composed a manual of letter-writing, imagining various difficult situations where the writer might need guidance. Pamela herself is a virtuous servant girl pursued by her licentious employer. She bravely defends herself and he eventually marries her. The story is told in letters to her parents. Here (*left*) 'Squire B' interrupts her as she is writing: one of a series of illustrations by Joseph Highmore.

books also often managed to convey Enlightenment ideas such as benevolence or trust in reason by giving these old tales a slightly new moral. We know from his autobiography that journeymen craftsmen like the Frenchman Louis Menetra read, and discussed what they read, as well as visiting the cheap vaudeville theatres. Books and reading were not entirely reserved for the middle and upper classes. But it was only at the higher social levels that intensive reading was vital for the establishment of an enlightened persona.

Books and printed media of all kinds, not surprisingly, became a highly profitable trade. They became part of what some historians have called the 'growth of a consumer society', a society where objects for purchase became plentiful and where the ability to discriminate between objects became a part of the status of their purchasers. The book trade also began to expand at precisely the moment when the division of labour began to affect all forms of production. Even the ideas contained in books became part of the consumer society. The Scottish economist Adam Smith remarked: 'In opulent or commercial society, besides, to think or reason comes to be, like every other employment, a particular business, which is carried on by a very few people, who furnish the public with all the thought and reason possessed by the vast multitudes that labour. Only a very small part of any ordinary person's knowledge has been the product of personal observation or reflection. All the rest has been purchased, in the same manner as his shoes or his stockings, from those whose business it is to make up and prepare for the market that particular species of goods.' Very much the same remarks were made by Diderot and D'Alembert in their preface to the *Encyclopédie*, which observed that in their time the amount of knowledge had become so great that no one person could any longer pretend, as many had in the Renaissance, to be in command of it all. Knowledge had to be divided among experts, just as the making of an object had to be divided among artisans who were experts in each production process. Books, prints, reproductions of paintings, sheet music, pamphlets and newspapers were all part of the increasing volume of consumer goods made and sold. They were ideal commodities. They could be easily transported and sold in large numbers, and could often cross linguistic, geographical and cultural boundaries. The ever-increasing practice of translation was both vital to their portability and a testament to it. The degree to which Enlightenment ideas were uniform across many very different European states and their colonies is evidence of this increasing circulation of books and hence of ideas. This global exchange broke down barriers between cultural systems, religions, genders and geographical areas. It promoted a new kind of equality between the consumers of culture, all of whom might buy the same book or picture. This contributed to the increasing homogenization of the world, in spite of the criticisms to which this tendency was subjected at the end of the Enlightenment. Europeans, as the philosopher Herder pointed out, wish to 'extend our own ideal of virtue and happiness to each distant nation'. Cultural homogenization may have contributed to the almost uniform collapse of highly variable indigenous cultures throughout the European colonies (see Chapter 4).

Commercial and financial considerations favoured the production of increasingly homogeneous media for the conveyance of ideas. Smaller, cheaper books were printed, just as at exactly the same time clothes began to be made from cheap replaceable cotton, rather than more expensive damask brocade or

The postal service played a vital role in the Republic of Letters. Correspondence between men of science and culture was brisk and operated across national boundaries. *Below:* an office of the *petite poste* of Louis XV. Letters are being sorted, with postmen's bags hanging on the wall or near at hand.

silk. Physical access to printed material thus became easier for many people. The growth of cheap commercial lending libraries allowed many people to read voraciously (another word related to eating and digestion) who did not possess the financial resources to build up their own collection of books. Coffee houses, as we have seen, offered newspapers, journals and some of the latest books for the enjoyment of customers. Booksellers' shops also sometimes offered light refreshment and a small borrowing library for the use of patrons.

A 'Republic of Letters'

Changes in the economics of bookselling and book production, as well as in the nature of knowledge, could hardly fail to have an impact on the social status of authors. Very few enjoyed the friendship of crowned heads or the elevated status and financial security of a Voltaire or a Diderot. Many lived in semi-poverty, on 'Grub Street', grinding out commissions from booksellers (who then were almost all publishers as well) for inadequate rewards. Yet there was some recompense to be had, in their membership of the idealized 'Republic of Letters'. Writers of all countries were often described as belonging to this mythical union. A passage from the *Histoire de la république des lettres* of 1780 has already been quoted (p. 65) in which the editor makes this very point – how literature and philosophy, 'the realm of talent and of thought', maintain their own intellectual freedom and independence.

An improved postal system made communication easier. This lavish title-page to a history of the post from Roman times to the 18th century was published at Jena in 1747. The illustration shows the series of new milestones marking distances between the post stations in Saxony. It bears the emblem of the post-horn that is still the symbol of the German post. Mercury, winged messenger of the gods, presides.

Trade in books kept pace with the increase in literacy. At first there was no distinction between printer, publisher and bookseller, but by the 18th century it was normal to go to a shop where customers could not only choose their books but order their own binding, as seems to be happening in this Dutch print of 1760 (*left*). Most countries had a system of licensing but Amsterdam (*below and opposite*) was an important trade centre where books banned in other countries could be bought easily.

By 1795 the bookshops were a vital element in cultural life. Standards of book production had risen spectacularly in the last hundred years. Illustrated books were now plentiful.

LIBRAI. de FRAN. L'HONO.   LIBRAI. de JAQ. DESBOR.

Devant de la Bourse d'Amsterdam

Reading: The Making of the Enlightenment

Nearly everyone could read. It was no longer an accomplishment of the privileged classes – a development that was almost as critical to intellectual history as the invention of printing. The consequences were twofold. On the one hand, information and ideas could spread with unprecedented rapidity, so that the Enlightenment was essentially a matter of debate in print. On the other hand, there was a literary 'dumbing down': new forms of reading – from popular science to travellers' tales, from newspapers to novels – were aimed at a popular readership who in previous ages would have been illiterate. Two engravings from the 1750s (*opposite and above*) show German and French peasants, one reading a weekly paper, the other a book of poems and songs.

OVERLEAF
Solitary reading was the foundation of everything that the Enlightenment stood for (and it could be argued it still is). François-Xavier Vispré's portrait of a young man, John Farr, reading Horace's *Odes* quietly evokes this whole cultural revolution. Vispré moved to England around 1760 and was a member of the Society of Artists.

WITHOUT DOUBT, reading was the quintessential Enlightenment experience. It was not an accident that Mme Roland (see Chapter 3), writing shortly before her execution, remembered her reading not only as an intellectual or emotional experience, but also as akin to the even deeper bodily intimacy of digestion, the very fabric of her being. Her account of reading the century's best-seller, Rousseau's *Julie ou la nouvelle Héloïse*, has already been quoted: 'I have just devoured *Julie* for the for the fourth or fifth time … it seems to me that I have lived with the characters of the novel as if they were real people.'

Like many eighteenth-century novel readers, Mme Roland connected herself with novels in the most intimate ways, so much so that she expected their characters almost to walk out of their pages and become her companions. Such high levels of identification were probably the reason that eighteenth-century people were able to read, often several times, novels like *Julie* or *Pamela* which now strike us as impossibly long even for a single reading.

Novel-reading changed Mme Roland's self-perception in another way. Again writing to her husband, she confessed that her identification with the characters of the novel enabled her to see herself as a perpetual heroine: 'reading a novel and a play, I've never wanted a secondary role. I read them as tales of heroism or virtue that I would not have the courage to emulate in actuality.' Later, she described reading as a 'dream without an awakening'. We need not go as far as some modern literary critics have done, equating erotic acts with reading and writing, to realize the extent to which, for Mme Roland and many other eighteenth-century readers, reading broke down barriers between intellect and sensibility, affect and action, and became imbued with physical messages and responses.

Such deep identification with the beautiful or virtuous actions and emotions of others, whether written or real, was an important part of the eighteenth-century cult of sensibility which emerged in the 1740s. This was aided by the advent of the European 'best-seller', including Richardson's *Pamela* (1740) and *Clarissa* (1747), Goethe's *The Sorrows of Young Werther* (1774) and Rousseau's *Julie* (1761). Throughout Europe, readers, both male and female, read the same novels in the same state of emotional exaltation which true sensibility demanded. It is not surprising that the patterns of behaviour which both male and female readers discovered in fiction were deeply internalized and re-emerged in the autobiographies of the period.

Novels, however, were not the only books intensely studied in this period. Middle-class family life began to be permeated by advice books. Previous eras had seen the publication of many books of advice, usually moral advice, for parents and children. But the Enlightenment was the first to compile detailed manuals of infant care, the 'baby books' of the eighteenth century, which went into minute details about the physical care of the child. The rise of paediatrics as a special branch of medicine also occurred at this time.

The reading habits of the Enlightenment were embedded in wider changes.

Without an extension of the trade in books, the experience of mass reading would have been impossible. Books and pamphlets could be easily sold in large numbers, were portable, and could cross boundaries of all kinds – linguistic, cultural, geographical – better than almost any other medium of culture and ideas. Changing habits of literacy contributed to a rapid rise in the number of readers, and global trade routes (see Chapter 4) diffused the best-sellers written in Europe to colonies in India and the Americas. The global exchange of ideas broke down barriers between cultures, eroded religious divisions and gender differences. It promoted a new kind of equality between the consumers of culture – the reading public, who could pay for the same novel, play or book of poetry or non-fiction. It is no wonder that Kant in his famous essay (see Chapter 1) should have characterized the 'public' as the 'world of readers', the *Leserwelt*. The increase in the numbers of books and pamphlets printed is clear from such sources as the records of the Frankfurt and Leipzig bookfairs. All the other sources that we have, point too an increase in the numbers of books, newspapers and pamphlets printed and purchased in this period. Increasing numbers of libraries were open to the public. Wills left by private individuals more often mention books among the deceased's possessions, even at quite low social levels. All these indications are fragmentary, and it is hard to make comparisons between different parts of Europe and its colonies. Nonetheless, all the indirect indicators point in one direction: that more books were being printed than ever before, and that familiarity with print media was spreading throughout society. It was this that contributed to the Enlightenment's homogeneous agenda. Through books, the same ideas and problems could be diffused over widely differing geographical areas.

It is thus important to find out how and to what extent the printed word was received in the Enlightenment. As always, most of most direct sources for the history of reading relate to the upper classes. Historians find great difficulty in estimating the numbers of those who could read or write among the lower social classes. Few historical sources bear directly on this problem. Most of the data that historians use to estimate literacy levels are thus indirect indications. For example, how many wills were signed with a cross and

Women for the first time began seriously to influence the publication of books. *Right*: the artist's wife, 1758, by Donat Nonnotte. *Below*: Anna Dorothea Therbusch was a German artist who painted this self-portrait in 1776 on her admission to the French Academy. Bravely defying both convention and vanity, she depicted herself as short-sighted, wearing the eyeglass that she needed for reading.

A reading heroine. Serena is the main character in a now-forgotten poem, 'The Triumphs of Temper' by William Hayley (1781), here painted by the poet's friend George Romney. A lady 'of constant sweetness and good humour', Serena is rewarded with a happy marriage.

how many with a name has often been used as an indication of literacy rates. But it has been pointed out that neither signatures nor crosses indicate anything real about the ability of the signers to read and write. Some people could only write enough to sign their names and so cannot be called by any stretch fully literate, for example. Literate wives would often sign with a cross in order not to shame illiterate husbands. From this example, it is easy to see the sort of problems involved in literacy research.

The history of reading faces similar challenges. The German historian Rolf Engelsing argues that a 'reading' revolution took place in the eighteenth century. Around 1750, people ceased to read 'intensively' (that is, read a few books over and over) and began to read 'extensively' (by which Engelsing means reading many printed works once only), with reading also becoming more of a solitary, silent and introspective activity, rather than one connected with reading aloud. This presents an attractively simple picture, well able to explain the origins of our own reading habits, as well as to make more comprehensible the *Lesewut*, or 'reading fever', which swept through the Enlightenment Europe of the best-sellers and the pamphlet wars. However, it is easy to point to evidence which simply does not fit Engelsing's picture. Mme Roland reading *Julie* four or five times is an example of highly intensive reading well into the 1780s. Of the other major European best-sellers, none, except *Werther*, remarkable for its brevity, was read intensively by upper-class people.

At the same time we also have to wonder how well Engelsing's ideas fit the world of lower-class reading. One of the primary reading materials of peasants and poor workers in the towns was the so-called *Bibliothèque bleue*, a collection of small-sized, cheaply produced and crudely illustrated books created for the semi-literate. Sold in large numbers at country fairs and cheap booksellers, these books included almanacs with weather predictions and farming advice, devotional works, accounts of sensational trials, biographies of famous criminals, condensed versions of recent novels, and retellings of medieval romances such as the deeds of Roland or the Chevalier Bayard.

Literary historians have seen the *Bibliothèque bleue* in contradictory ways, some as being purely escapist, others as in convergence with the Enlightenment lived by the upper and middle classes. In any case, we know that the small volumes, often the only reading material available to the peasants and poor workers, were read aloud, and read intensively. It seems difficult to fit the *Bibliothèque* into Engelsing's thesis. It is clear, however, that reading was a part of life for all social classes, whatever it was that they actually read (or in many cases had read to them). It is also clear that intensive and extensive reading, far from competing with each other in the 1750s, co-existed throughout the century. It is also clear that, for many readers, reading was part of the project of making the self (see Chapter 5). Reading a book was an act of information-gathering, of experience and imitation, of intimacy and self-fashioning.

BIBLIOTHEQUE
DE
CAMPAGNE,
OU
AMUSEMENS
DE
L'ESPRIT ET DU COEUR.

Nouvelle Edition rectifiée & augmentée.

a. Philippe de Prétot.

TOME PREMIER.

A LA HAYE,
Et se débite à GENEVE,
Chez les FR. CRAMER & CL. PHILIBERT.

M. DCC. XLIX.

Circulating libraries (*opposite*, an English print of 1782) were the means by which the great mass of the people obtained their books. It meant that a new novel would be read by many more than might be guessed from the sales figures. The most successful of these libraries, such as Mudie's in England, could also exercise a potent influence on literature; they could make or break a potential author. And since novels in three volumes were the most profitable, authors were obliged to write to that length. The *Bibliothèque de campagne* of 1748 (*left*) was a poetry anthology running to eight volumes. *Below:* a portrait of Susanna Oakes, keeper of the circulating library of Ashbourne, Derbyshire. Readers of Jane Austen will remember her heroines' dependence on the libraries for the latest novel, and the intense competition between them to borrow it first.

By the 1780s, such notions had become commonplace. The idea that writers as conveyors of knowledge and makers of opinion exercised a sort of power which was as formidable as that of organized governments or aristocracies, the idea of equality between all members of the Republic of Letters, or that knowledge and its producers acted across political boundaries, were all very much to the fore in the Enlightenment. Germinating within them was the notion of an association of equals which was to cast a long shadow forwards to the French Revolution.

Another great change in the lives of writers had begun to mature earlier in the Enlightenment. For centuries, almost all writers had gained the greater part of their income from personal commissions from patrons highly placed in the Church, the royal courts or the aristocracy, who often regarded artists and writers in their employment as little more than skilled craftsmen. Such relationships had involved a high degree of personal dependence, even subservience. In the later years of the eighteenth century, moreover, they were still very much in being. Haydn wore the livery of the Esterhazy family which employed him, and Mozart for some time, in spite of his Europe-wide reputation, was a dependant of the archbishop of Salzburg. The transition from personal patronage to writing for the market was clearly incomplete by 1789. Nonetheless, the transformation was gathering momentum, so that writing for the market would soon become the rule and writing for a personal patron the exception. It was widely felt that this situation was becoming the rule for all producers of culture, but perhaps especially for writers. In the 1740s, for

Books could be bought in the street from itinerant pedlars or at open-air auctions. *Below:* a seller of broadsheets in Berlin (1786). *Bottom:* a similar tradesman, Thomas Carr of Lincoln, 'the well-known dealer in almanacs', represented in 1804. *Right:* a book auction in London about 1700: 'Ne'er cry you don't the subject understand.'

The printseller (*opposite*) is satirically given a complete costume of pictures, numbered and catalogued in an attached caption; a print made in Augsburg, *c.* 1730. At the bottom, left of centre, for instance, is Erasmus, with Adam and Eve above him.

Ausruffungen von Berlin.

Come Sirs, and view this famous Library,
Tis pity Learning should discourag'd be :
Here's Bookes (that is, if they were but well Sold)
I will maintain't are worth their weight in Gold :

THE COMPLEAT AUCTIONER

Then bid apace, and break me out of hand :
Ne'er cry you dont the Subiect understand :
For this I'll say - howe'er the Case may hit,
Whoever buys of me. - I teach 'em Wit.

THOMAS CARR of LINCOLN, *August 1804.*
The well known Dealer in Almanacks &c has borns born at Heathorpe near Doncaster, and was christened the 19th of October 1716.

example, D'Alembert, the future co-editor of the *Encyclopédie* and a famous mathematician, had to argue passionately for the independence of men of letters from personal patronage. Such independence was necessary, he argued, if original work was to be produced by writers and thinkers, and also to maintain a real-life equality among the members of the Republic of Letters. By the 1750s, Denis Diderot, D'Alembert's co-editor, could point to the existence of a group of independent men of letters writing for the market, which alone, he remarked, made possible the appearance of large collaborative works such as the *Encyclopédie*. However, it is questionable whether dependence on the market made writers any freer or more equal than dependence on a personal patron. The Republic of Letters offered a promise of equality, rather than its reality. In the same way, its promise of civility between equals was always more honoured in the breach than the observance. Quarrels between writers were routine, as each tried to capture the favour of the market or manifested his envy of the small elite who were still backed by important patrons, such as Rousseau or Voltaire, the friend of Frederick II of Prussia.

This thread of equality and inequality which weaves itself through the history of men of letters in this period also existed in relation to gender. Much

of the struggle for equality has its roots in Enlightenment thinking about gender (see Chapter 3). There were many female members of the community of Grub Street, and even women who belonged to social elites, and who wrote and pursued ideas, such as Voltaire's own companion, the Marquise de Châtelet. But at the same time there were attacks by many male writers on the capacity of women in general to contribute to the store of ideas. Why was this attack on women's rationality, their very capacity to think, so strong a feature of the allegedly egalitarian Republic of Letters? Part of the problem may have arisen because of the insecurity of writers and thinkers, which the move towards market production did nothing to alleviate. Still completing the transition from hired dependent to autonomous intellectual producer, the members of the Republic of Letters laid claim to be a force acting on public opinion in a way which in theory obeyed the dictates of reason, impartiality and humanity. The autonomy of these producers of knowledge was a crucial issue by the middle years of the century. Women, almost all eighteenth-century people believed, were not autonomous or rational beings. Family duties removed autonomy, and anatomy dictated that emotion rather than reason governed their lives. The participation of women could thus be seen as reducing the legitimacy of the Republic of Letters as a whole. Their equivocal position as novelists, translators, playwrights, writers of conduct manuals and theological works, political tracts and travel literature, in fact virtually every literary genre that was never truly accepted into the Republic of Letters, demonstrates how, in spite of its universalism, the Enlightenment often seemed to devote as much energy to designating entire social groups, such as women or peasants or the poor, as deaf to the voice of reason, as it did to constructing a better world.

Equality and inequality run like Ariadne's thread throughout the story of the sociability of the Enlightenment. If the Republic of Letters was obsessed precisely with the equality which its members lacked, and the coffee houses gave a temporary equality to all who patronized them, other institutions too, far

Voltaire and Frederick of Prussia could meet as equals in the 'Republic of Letters' (*above*), though it was clear to everybody that this was no more than a figure of speech. Frederick went out of his way to be gracious to the great genius of the Enlightenment (and he was not alone among European monarchs). Voltaire was his guest at Potsdam for nearly three years (1750–53), but in the end he succeeded in offending the king and was expelled.

The power of the press truly began in the 18th century. Newspapers were not confined to the literate. Here (*opposite*) the *Gazette* is given a public reading to a group of old men in France: an engraving of 1780.

The French Revolution was flooded with print, eagerly bought and sold in the streets of Paris. In 1791, 'Year Three of Liberty', the *Almanach Nationale* is dedicated to the 'Friends of the Constitution' (*left*).

Societies of like-minded intellectuals were a defining feature of the Enlightenment. The most characteristic of all was the English Society of Dilettanti, founded in 1732 by a group of young men who had been on the Grand Tour and wished to promote interest in antiquities and the arts. They actively encouraged research in their subjects by providing funds. Joshua Reynolds painted the occasion in 1777 when Sir William Hamilton was introduced (*right*). He is seated in the centre pointing to a volume illustrating one of his famous Greek vases. The others are drinking his health.

Academies served much the same purpose, with less conviviality. In 1750 the Academy of Dijon offered a prize for an essay on 'whether the Arts and Sciences have contributed to purify manners' (*below*). The winner was 'a citizen of Geneva' – i.e., Jean-Jacques Rousseau.

more carefully regulated, also revolved around the idea of equality being part of cultural life. The claim to sociability was one of the defining characteristics of Enlightenment, particularly in France and Italy. Learned academies were founded in many provincial towns in this period, often with some resemblance to the royal academies founded in France, Russia and some Italian states. The academies were formally organized bodies, often with constitutions defined by royal charters, and possessing their own meeting hall and library. Membership was open to all those who could pay a fee, which in practice meant that membership was open to the local elites, people who headed their social or professional group but would have had little communication with each other in the normal course of events. The aristocracy, the higher members of Church and royal bureaucracies, the commercial elites, wealthier doctors and soldiers were normally divided by prejudice, and in fact very different income levels. A successful doctor might earn more than an impoverished aristocrat, but be despised by the latter as earning money by his own labours. In the academies such distinctions, theoretically, were obliterated. Topical and learned papers were presented and commented upon by academy members, local intellectual life was encouraged by the formation of a publicly accessible library and the organization of prize competitions. The prize essays were capable of mobilising public opinion far beyond the confines of academy membership. Furious public debate broke out, for example, on the subject of capital punishment after the prize competition at the Academy of Metz in 1784, or on the social role of the arts after an equally renowned competition at Dijon in 1750. Often the prizewinners, such as Rousseau, the winner of the 1750 competition, were people who would otherwise have had no way of being included in the elite bodies who offered the prizes. Such institutions, as their historian Daniel Roche has said, performed not only valuable intellectual roles, but also helped to bring together the social elites of each region and connect them to public opinion.

Emphasis on equality was carried even further in the case of Freemasonry. Masons vowed to cast aside social distinctions and unite in pursuing the practical social fulfilment of key Enlightenment ideas such as rational benevolence, without reference to established religions. Membership was secret, which also had the effect of promoting equality between members. Masonic lodges became centres of debate where members tried to understand the world in ways which were often tinged with mysticism. Mozart's opera *The Magic Flute* (1791), with its extensive use of Masonic imagery, is probably the highest artistic expression of its values.

Yet to some, all this cultural creation and struggle was far from seeming a straightforward good. Rousseau's 1750 prize essay had in fact argued the reverse – to such an extent that the Scots philosopher and historian David Hume felt compelled to write in favour of a sociable Enlightenment. In his essay 'Of Refinement in the Arts' (1752), he remarked: 'The more [the] refined arts advance, the more sociable men become; nor is it possible, that, when enriched with science, and possessed of a fund of conversation, they should be contented to remain in solitude, or live with their fellow citizens in that distant manner, which is peculiar to ignorant and barbarous nations. They flock into

The Order of Freemasons, founded in the early 18th century, related uneasily to the Enlightenment. On the one hand, it embraced science, especially geometry, and promoted the idea of universal brotherhood. But it was also a secret society, deeply committed to belief in God (though not to any institutionalized religion) and expressed its principles in deliberately obscure symbolism. *Above: A Freemason Formed out of the Materials of his Lodge*, an English satirical print of 1754, including the sun, compasses, the Bible, the triangle (plus Pythagoras's theorem), the two pillars, an apron and a mallet. *Below left:* a new apprentice, blindfolded on the left, is received into a French lodge in 1742. On the right is the Grand Master and in front of him a tracing board bearing symbols of the order.

cities; love to receive and communicate knowledge; to show their wit or their breeding; their taste in conversation or living, in clothes or furniture … Both sexes meet in an easy and sociable manner; and the tempers of men, as well as their behaviour, refine apace. So that, besides the improvements which they receive from knowledge and the liberal arts, it is impossible but they must feel an increase in humanity, from the very habit of conversing together, and contributing to each other's pleasure and entertainment … if we consider the matter in a proper light, we shall find, that a progress in the arts is rather favourable to liberty, and has a natural tendency to preserve, if not produce, a free government.'

Mozart was a Mason and his opera *The Magic Flute*, an allegory of man's quest for moral purity, is full of Masonic symbolism. *Opposite:* the frontispiece of a contemporary edition of the libretto. *Below:* a set design by Angelo Quaglio of 1793.

Opposing views of the Enlightenment were held by David Hume and Jean-Jacques Rousseau. Hume (*right*) saw it as encouraging the social virtues. Rousseau (*above right*) believed that man in a state of nature was innately good and that civilization only corrupted him.

3

Marriage, Children and Gender: The Enlightenment Family

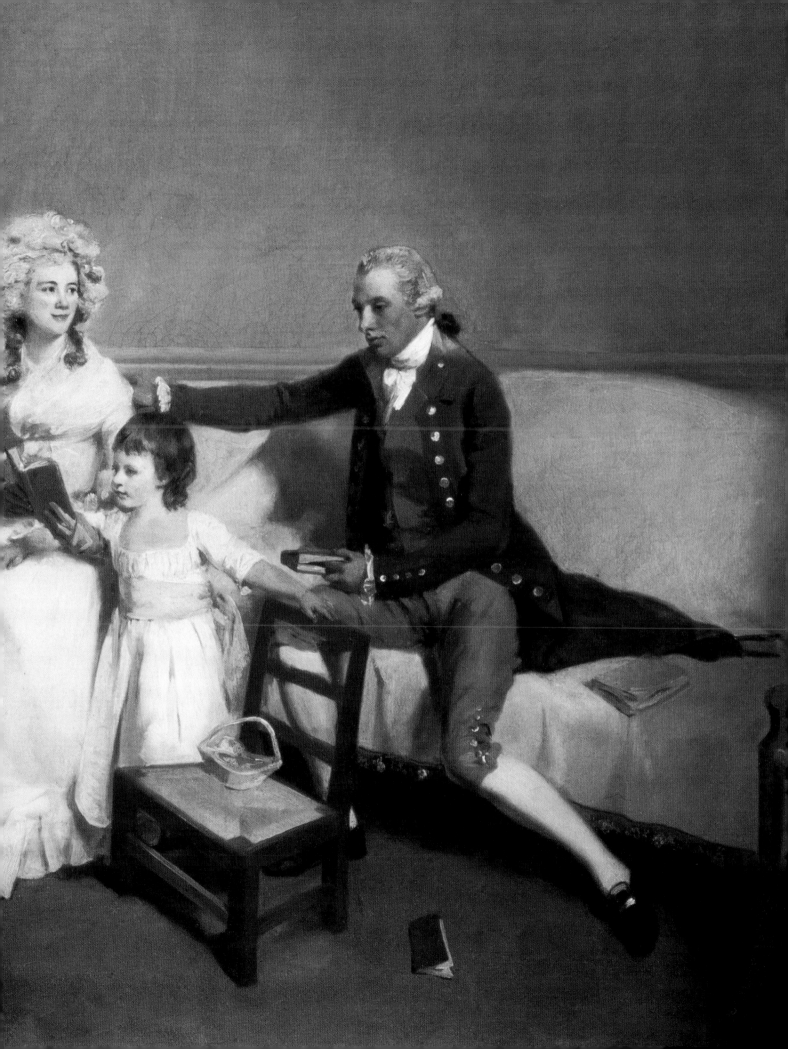

THERE WAS NO ENLIGHTENMENT FAMILY. There was only a myriad of families each living its triumphs and disasters. No one story can fold this complexity into a single history. No single walk across this field can take us satisfactorily to the other side. Our way into understanding this complexity must be brutally arbitrary.

Working-class families were very different from middle-class families. The world inhabited by children was different from that of adults, yet in all social classes interlocked with it. Families were surrounded often by a penumbra of poor relations, servants, neighbours and pet and working animals, and lived in more diverse households than the 'nuclear'-family structure composed only of parents and children and often taken for granted in the modern West. The Enlightenment was a time when the nature of marriage came under enormous debate, and new forms of middle-class marriage emerged. Educationalists also played an increasingly prominent role in the shaping of the family. Controversial works on child-rearing, such as Rousseau's *Emile*, challenged conventional thinking about the family, and the roles of women within it. Children themselves played large parts in philanthropic social experiments closely linked to discussions of the nature of man and society. In the eighteenth century too, the state took an increased interest in the regulation of sexual relations and the shape of the family. Sexual and gender identities were equally in the process of change. Both Enlightenment debate and eighteenth-century realities found a focus in the family.

If what we mean by the history of the family is an astonishingly varied list of topics, so too is the evidence we use to approach it. State papers stand alongside the diaries of children. Painters give us powerful images of children, husbands and wives and mothers; at the same time artists such as Stubbs and Oudry represent the role of pets and horses who lived side by side with their human masters. The educational philanthropists, their buildings and the regimes they bought into being stand alongside the resolutely individualistic educational ideology of Rousseau.

Rousseau, *Emile* and the enlightened family

This is the time when the modern speciality of pediatrics was founded, when efforts to reform society were linked with efforts to create the perfect person through education. The English philosopher John Locke was one of the first to write on the nature and education of the child in his 1693 *Some Thoughts Concerning Education*. This book became one of the most widely known works on the subject of the entire century. Locke's major innovation was to argue that a child comes into the world as a *tabula rasa*, a blank slate, on which the impressions of the world and its own ideas and imagination have yet to be written. He argued that there was a strong connection between the formation of ideas and the child's processing of sense impressions. In doing so, he opposed those who still believed that each child was born already implanted with 'innate ideas' such as shame or the knowledge of good and evil. Locke also believed in encouraging the union of mind and body through exercise and out-of-door activities and Spartan training. 'Keep the body in strength and vigour, so that it may be able to obey and execute the orders of the mind … A sound mind in a sound body, is a short but full description of a happy state in this world; he that has these two has little more to wish for; he that wants either of these will be but

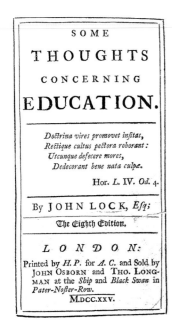

Patterns of family life varied almost as much as the families themselves. One of the most egalitarian marriages – almost a textbook example of enlightened partnerships – was that of the scientist Antoine Lavoisier and his wife, Marie-Anne, seen here (*left*) in a double portrait by Jacques-Louis David (1788). Lavoisier was one of the most brilliant minds in France; he made several crucial discoveries in chemistry and physics, Marie-Anne acting as his assistant. But because he was involved in the infamous tax system, the *Ferme Générale*, he fell victim to revolutionary hatred and was guillotined in 1793 at the age of 51.

A revolutionary family: Michel Gérard was the deputy for Rennes after 1790, and in this portrait by David (*below*) he presents himself as a man of the people, wearing a peasant blouse. Incongruously, however, his sons and daughter do not keep up the same image.

A bourgeois family (*opposite*) in 18th-century Germany engages with the issue of child-raising. The husband, as we can deduce from the pictures on the wall, the pair of pistols and the way he is encouraging his sons to play at soldiers, is a military man, and perhaps also a man with scientific interests. But there is a gentler undercurrent, perhaps due to the wife: the lute behind the door, the girl with the shuttlecock racquet, the canary and the little dog. The artist is W. J. Laquy and the date 1790.

More conventional is this portrait by Philip Reinagle of 1782 of Mrs Congreve and her children in their London drawing room (*above*). Her husband, Captain William Congreve (later ennobled), is absent, but the painting of him with their son hangs prominently behind her. One little girl holds a book, the other a squirrel, but the baby boy (who rose to be a more eminent military man than his father) plays with a cannon.

Spontaneous rapport between mother and daughter was given supreme value by Rousseau (which makes it all the harder to forgive him for putting his own children in an orphanage). No painter caught these ecstatic moments better than Joshua Reynolds in his portrait of Georgiana, Duchess of Devonshire of 1784 (*right*).

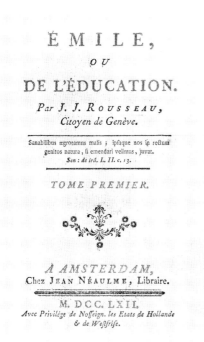

little the better for anything else.' While part of his training programme was of course about the development of rationality in the child, Locke took Juvenal's famous injunction seriously. Hoping to produce a sort of 'sensory rationality', the English philosopher would have his pupil learn riding, dancing and fencing, but also a trade involving manual work. He summed up his teachings as: 'Plenty of open air, exercise and sleep; plain diet, no wine or strong drink, and very little or no physic; not too warm and strait clothing; especially the head and feet kept cold, and the feet often used to cold water and exposed to wet.'

A generation later Rousseau's *Emile ou de l'éducation* was being widely debated, the more so perhaps because copies of it had been burnt (for its religious views) in a Paris city square by the public hangman. In the German-speaking lands, too, experimental educational institutions sprang up, and gained public visibility far outside their homelands, as well as princely support. This century, in addition to all its other names, may well be called the century of the child.

Emile was undoubtedly the most controversial as well as the second-most influential piece of writing about education in the century. Rousseau's novel recounts the education of Emile, its child hero, at the hands of his tutor. (Contemporaries were not slow to point out the irony that Rousseau had placed five children of his own in orphanages.) It carries over Rousseau's hatred of human society as presently constituted, full of corruption, falsity and inauthentic desires, from his *First* and *Second Discourses*. It presents a whole interlocking sequence of reflections on education, on human nature and on the nature of the child in a rich texture surrounding its central 'story'. The novel

Emile by Jean-Jacques Rousseau (*above*) was (after Locke's book) the most influential book on child-rearing of the whole epoch, but one whose precepts were not easy to follow in practice. 'Nature' was Rousseau's guide. He held strongly that the mother should breast-feed her baby. But when it came to education the child was subject to a sophisticated regime designed to make him (it was never 'her') discover the great truths of morality for himself. The portrait of Rousseau (*right*), of about 1755, is by Maurice-Quentin de la Tour.

The close-knit family became a domestic ideal long before Rousseau. François Boucher painted *The Breakfast, or Morning Coffee* in 1739 (*opposite*). The little girl is plentifully supplied with toys.

'**Nature displays** to our eyes all her magnificence.' Rousseau's Emile learns to admire sublime landscapes by discovering them for himself (*opposite top left*).

A woman's education should be aimed solely at making her a good wife and mother. Here, Emile's bride, Sophie, in order to be of practical help, learns to use a plane (*top right*).

Emile learns about private property by planting beans in someone else's garden (*bottom*). The gardener, however, has planted melon seeds there, which the beans destroy, so he has a perfect right to tear out the beans. So 'each respects the work of the other, to ensure that his own labour is safe'.

thus follows Rousseau's central idea, that man's best hope is to return to nature and to follow its example in the teaching of children. As he says at the very beginning of the book: 'we are born weak, and we need to grow strong; we have nothing and we need help; we are born stupid, and we need to acquire judgement. Everything that we need is given to us by education. Education is given to us by nature.'

Rousseau goes on to argue that a child is not a miniature man, and should not be treated as such. Here he directly contradicts such contemporary advice books for young people as the *Letters* of Lord Chesterfield written for his illegitimate son, Philip Stanhope, with the precise intention of fitting him for the adult world. Instead Rousseau argues that a child has to be treated less in relation to his future adult life than to his present happiness, happiness being defined as living in the moment, in a balance between the child's wishes and abilities. The child should not be bothered by purely verbal lessons, but should live within the realm of things. No complex reasoning should be offered him. In teaching, only his own experience should be called upon, even if this means he will make slow progress. By experience, particularly painful experience, the child learns about life. If, for example, he freezes in a room in which he has broken all the windows, he will learn to control his temper. Seeing his neighbour pilfer from his garden, he will acquire the notion of private property.

The object of education is ignorance. It is a mistake to put books into the hands of a child, or to exercise his memory. He should not be made to memorize fables, especially those of La Fontaine, which are dangerous in point of morality, and in any case inaccessible to the intelligence. Rousseau in any case, seemingly unaware of his self-refutation, exclaims that he hates books, which are only good for learning how to talk about things of which one has no direct knowledge. In the novel Emile learns to read and write only at the time when he begins to show a personal interest in literacy. The teacher should take care to make his pupil strong and alert, and familiarize him with physical exercises appropriate to his age. By the age of 12, Emile is interested in plants and animals, at which point the project of keeping him ignorant, the famous 'negative education', is abandoned. Rousseau emphasizes that one must never substitute the sign for the thing, the star map or the picture of the plant for the night sky and the plant itself. Looking at the sky by day and by night, Emile will learn cosmology; as he walks, geography. Emile is expected to make his own scientific instruments. He should leave books completely to one side – except *Robinson Crusoe*, which Rousseau persisted in seeing as the novel of natural man, in the sense of nature as that part of the external world which human beings understand, master and make their own. This is exactly what Crusoe does to the nature of his island, domesticating its goats and learning to eat its foods. Thus, Rousseau's teaching continues, Emile, without being taught, would know things in a lasting way because he had learned them at a time appropriate for him, rather than at a time dictated by a school curriculum.

It is at around this epoch in his life that Emile also begins to learn a trade, even though he is rich. The upheavals of life can quickly change that condition. The story continues through to Emile's adolescence, a notoriously stormy period when new passions and desires emerge. His tutor concentrates on developing piety, benevolence and gratitude, and begins to teach him history, which Rousseau regards as morality in action. History shows Emile that there

l'Education de l'Homme commence à sa naissance;

are such things as good and bad, and he hears the voice of conscience. At 18, the time has come to reveal to him that there is a god. Rousseau does this by inserting the famous 'Confession of Faith of a Savoyard Vicar', which summarizes the arguments for the existence of God from the design and harmony of nature. Rejecting the contradictory arguments of philosophers and theologians, the Savoyard vicar thinks of faith as an inner voice, conscience, which reveals to us the existence of God. This version of faith is called deism, which Rousseau calls a 'natural' religion, better than all the 'revealed' religions which depend on the acceptance of the authority of events, such as the miracles, which have to be 'revealed' to believers, because they cannot be proved by reason or logic.

Adolescence of course also introduces Emile to the notion of love. Emile's preceptor has to guide his passions, enable him to define his ideal companion and keep him apart from the social world with its distractions, such as the theatre, always for Rousseau a threat to the authentic, natural, man. Instead, Emile should retire and read the classic authors, and live in a small house, white with green shutters, away in the country. The fifth and final part of the novel is dedicated to Emile's search for a wife. Full of disquisitions on the nature of women, this section includes the famous saying that 'the male is a male only at certain moments; the female is female her whole life … Everything constantly recalls her sex to her … A perfect woman and a perfect man ought not to resemble each other in mind, any more than in looks.' Rousseau describes how a young girl, Sophie, is deliberately raised as a future mate for Emile. Later on, meeting as if by chance, they fall in love and, after a barrage of virtuous stipulations by Emile's preceptor, are allowed to marry.

Rousseau's portrayal of the absolute character of male and female difference is famous. It also puts him at one with much contemporary thinking. The concern of Rousseau and others like him was to define the female as 'natural' and hence as both right and ineluctable. Natural is one of the key words of the Enlightenment. For Rousseau it was vital that Emile stay natural (i.e., ignorant) for as long as possible. Natural could mean many other things. It could mean 'not socially defined', 'not artificial' or 'based on the external physical world'. Natural was used, often in a mixture of all these meanings, to describe and legitimate arrangements which we in the twenty-first century would see as socially created, and hence susceptible of criticism and capable of change. Calling something natural, in other words, was a very good way to argue for points of view that were in fact often novel and always highly prescriptive. Mme Roland fought hard to maintain her 'natural' capacity to breast-feed.

Arguments for the 'naturalness' of female roles could thus, because of the ambiguity of the term, gain force from biological propositions about created nature, and at the same time from repeated Enlightenment polemics against 'artificiality' in society, by which was meant social practices which were held to be at odds with the true structures of human 'nature'. This is one of Rousseau's favourite arguments, dating from his 1750 *Discours sur les sciences et les arts* (*First Discourse on the Arts and Sciences*). Thus women could be defined as closer to nature than men, as well as being more determined by 'nature', meaning anatomy and physiology. Because of their closeness to 'nature', it was often argued, and not just by Rousseau, that women were emotional, credulous and incapable of objective reasoning.

'That's the law of nature. Why go against it?' Rather than fill the child's mind with philosophical ideas, Rousseau believed that 'ignorance is the only way to avoid error'. 'The childhood of children,' he wrote, 'must be allowed to ripen.' These engravings are from the edition of *Emile* of 1785.

Rousseau, the man of nature. Here, as an older man, he brings a gift of flowers (wild flowers, of course) to a young mother, who is following his own precept and breast-feeding her baby – as, incidentally, the sheep is too.

Enlightenment Animals

The Enlightenment family was not simply composed of parents and children. It was a household, containing not only humans but animals. It is difficult to realize today how closely animals were intertwined with the life of human beings in the Enlightenment. It was still true in many parts of rural Europe that farm animals were housed with only minimal separation between them and their owners. Almost all agricultural labour power, apart from that of humans, was provided by animals – oxen, horses, even dogs. Animals were of course raised not only to work but also to be eaten. For the upper classes throughout Europe, animals such as horses and hunting dogs functioned as status symbols. Horses, more practically, were the only means of locomotion faster than a man could walk – just as they had been under the Roman empire.

By the end of this period, the household pet had emerged, giving not only status to its owner, but also emotional comfort. How strong these links might be is made clear in the poet Christopher Smart's celebration of his cat:

> *For I will consider my cat Jeoffry.*
> *For he is the servant of the living God duly and daily serving him …*
> *For when his day's work is done his business more properly begins.*
> *For he keeps the Lord's watch in the night against the adversary.*
> *For he counter-acts the powers of darkness by his electrical skin and glaring eyes.*
> *For he counteracts the devil, who is death, by brisking about the life.*
> *For in his morning orisons he loves the sun and the sun loves him …*
> *For he will not do destruction, if he is well-fed, neither will spit without provocation.*
> *For he purrs in thankfulness, when God tells him he's a good cat.*
> *For he is an instrument for the children to learn benevolence upon.*
> *For every house is incomplete without him and a blessing is lacking in the spirit.*

Smart sees his cat Jeoffry as an individual in all that he does, loved by God and, being a cat, without necessary links to humankind; but yet also as a link between God and the household that owns him. He is a moral instrument through which the children of the house will learn to practise that prime Enlightenment value, benevolence.

Domestic pets had moral value. But animals were also seen in quite different ways in the Enlightenment. Great energy was invested in two quite separate enterprises: naturalists competed with each other to find the best way of classifying animals; and

Pet animals go back at least to the Middle Ages (nuns were reprimanded for keeping little dogs), but only in the 18th century did they become a regular part of the normal middle- and upper-class household, to be treated with understanding. A charming scene on a piece of Sèvres porcelain of 1764 (*left*) shows a little girl stretching up to feed sweets to her pet parrot.

The infant duke de Montpensier was painted by Boucher in 1749 surrounded by his toys and with his kitten in his lap (*opposite*).

An unexpected pet is the goat on which a princess of France (Marie Adelaide, later queen of Sardinia) sits, accompanied by her brother Charles Philippe (later Charles X). The artist is François-Hubert Drouais, the date 1763.

Equine nobility. The genealogy of horses was almost as important as that of the gentry, and they take their place in family portraits as the equals – sometimes, one suspects (at least in the eyes of the English painter George Stubbs), the superiors – of their owners. In this sensitive study of the Wedgwood family (*below*) it is largely the horses who convey the tacit claim to aristocratic status. Josiah Wedgwood, however, was not an aristocrat but a prosperous potter, and the setting is the grounds of his Staffordshire estate, Etruria. Stubbs had worked for him decorating some of his porcelain.

practical farmers vied with each other to produce new breeds of horses and cattle. The naturalists viewed animals in very complex ways. Buffon, for example, published an *Histoire naturelle*, a multi-volume work which was an instant best-seller, and was used for generations in French schools as a model of style. Buffon's articles on quadrupeds were arranged by the closeness of the animal to man. Dogs and horses thus took pride of place.

Buffon's article on the horse became famous. It argued that the horse's skeleton, in spite of outward appearances, resembles that of man. Buffon praised the horse, not just as a domestic and agricultural animal, but also as one that was vital to the winning of wars. The horse, he wrote, 'shares with us the fatigues of war and the glory of combat. The horse accompanies us and carries us; we travel with him and by him.' Buffon's representation of the horse as close to man resembles that of the centaur, the half-man, half-horse of Greek mythology.

Even more, the horse was an instrument of the human domination of nature, just as the cat Jeoffry was the image both of himself and of divine order. Taxonomy, the science of classification systems, absorbed much of the energy of naturalists in this period, who struggled among themselves to find the best representation of the structure of nature. Yet such fascination with taxonomy did not prevent a naturalist as eminent as Buffon, who was superintendent of the king's botanical gardens, from considering the emotional relationship between humans and animals. As he wrote, the horse is 'a creature which renounces its own individual being, and only exists by the will of another [person] … Yet the horse is so close to man that he dares to look at him face to face.' The horse seems to put himself above his position as a quadruped just by lifting his head; in this noble attitude he looks man in the eye. Looking at man face to face, he becomes his mirror, his alter ego.

This period also witnessed, as evidence of man's dominion over animals, the rise of selective breeding practices. Oxen and bulls in particular were bred for massive form and strength. Pigs were developed to enormous size by present-day standards to produce a fatty, heavy pork meat. Horses began to be specifically bred either for speed or for strength. From 1786, as the historian

Harriet Ritvo has noted, 'stud books' were regularly kept in England, which traced the genealogy of horses and cattle. Just at the same time the famous reference volumes of the genealogies of the English peerage, by Debrett and Burke, also began to be published. It is tempting to ally, as many historians have done, these two developments, and to see the coincidence as a sign of the strengthening of the aristocracy, and its alter ego, the horses and oxen they reared.

Household animals, such as the dog, cat and horse, had complex relationships to their human owners in this period. Their presence, as Christopher Smart's poem suggests, could have a powerful impact on the life of the family, both in its emotional structures and in the signs and symbols of its prestige.

An unusual pet is the choice of the boy in John Singleton Copley's portrait of 1765 (*above*). A squirrel would never have been domesticated before the 18th century, but it seems to show a touching desire to draw closer to nature and to feel kinship with a wild creature.

Beneath the charm of pets, as Goya was well aware, lay the world of untamed nature, a world of cruelty and death. The young Don Manuel Osorio de Zuniga is teaching his pet bird to pick up a card (*opposite*). The three cats, however (one almost invisible in the background), have other thoughts not very favourable to the bird.

The king of Spain's niece, little Maria Teresa de Borbón and Vallabriga (later the Countess Chinchón), was painted by Goya in 1783 (*right*). He must have relished the precocious dignity of the princess next to the unkempt indifference of the little dog.

The word 'natural' allowed Rousseau to maintain that only breast-feeding was 'natural' and to hurl anathemas against selfish mothers who refused to practise it. Early in *Emile*, he charged that mothers who cease to feed their own babies will try to get rid of all the other onerous duties of motherhood too. He argued that wet-nursing was a major cause of depopulation, and that corruption brought about by contraception, knowledge and technology, not to mention philosophy, would soon bring about the depopulation of Europe. Woman should accept the particular style of life which motherhood enjoins upon her. Woman, he continued, in the fifth part of *Emile*, needs 'a soft sedentary life to suckle her babies. How much care and tenderness does she need to hold her family together! … The strictly rigid duties owed by the sexes is not and cannot be the same.'

Mme Roland: the philosophy of motherhood

We are lucky to have the autobiography of Mme Roland, a leading supporter during the French Revolution of the Girondin faction, purged from power in 1793. In great detail she recounts her struggles to follow the teachings of Rousseau. Historians have often connected the rise of this middle-class ideal of companionate marriage with that of a warm, nurturing family life, centred around feeling, sentiment and the relationship between mother and child. They allege, erroneously, that this style of family life was in sharp contrast to the previous attitude, which emphasized property and financial and economic links between husband and wife, and paid less attention to love relations or feelings between parent and child. This, like all such clear-cut contrasts, gives a false impression. There is no reason why the one sort of marriage should preclude the other. Like much else, the idea of companionate marriage and of the family as a haven in a heartless world may well be a construct of historians. It is, however, an important construct because it projects onto the family many other

Husband and wife were rarely equal partners but companionate marriages brought them closer. Typically, in a fashionable silhouette of 1790, the husband reads a book while the wife pours the tea.

concerns of the Enlightenment, such as the relative places of feeling, reason and the nature of the genders.

As a young woman Mme Roland married the far older Jean-Marie Roland. Roland, a member of the progressive middle classes of eighteenth-century France, was an expert in industrial processes, a factory inspector, and the author of a multi-volume encyclopedia of manufacturing. He was one of those who took up the idea in Diderot's *Encyclopédie* that knowledge about the precise ways in which products were manufactured was as valuable as knowledge about literature, history and theology. Mme Roland was his destined helpmeet. She had, however, become a mother during the production of Roland's encyclopedia. These dual roles of wife and mother were difficult to reconcile. As wife, she was defined largely as an assistant in her husband's labours and companion to him; as mother, by intense attachment to her child. These two roles were not only incompatible, they also reflected a split between mind and body. In a letter to Roland shortly after the birth of their daughter, Eudore, she described herself as writing a contribution to his encyclopedia with one hand, while with the other she supported the perpetually suckling baby on her knee: 'This is such a scrawl – I've only got one free hand and I can only look in one direction, the little one is on my knee, where she spends half the day. She's at my breast for sometimes as much as two hours at a time, having little naps broken by sucking. If I take the breast away, she cries and chews her fingers.'

Few texts could make clearer the burden of being both companionate wife and tender mother. Mme Roland's scrawl echoed the way these roles ground

Mme Roland and her much older husband, Jean-Marie, enjoyed a companionate marriage. She was his assistant in publishing an encyclopedia of manufacturing, during the production of which she gave birth to a daughter, Eudore. As a progressive, enlightened woman she tried hard to follow the precepts of Rousseau.

Using a wet nurse or feeding one's child oneself was a major source of disagreement in Enlightenment circles. George Morland's painting of about 1788 *Visit to the Child at Nurse* reflects the situation with perceptive accuracy. One of the things which Rousseau and his disciples found unacceptable was that the child could become more attached to its nurse than to its mother, and that is the case here, where the baby turns away in fear from the fashionable lady it hardly knows – and who is followed by an older child equally in the fashion. The nurse has two other young children in her care, but is shown as conscientious and kindly.

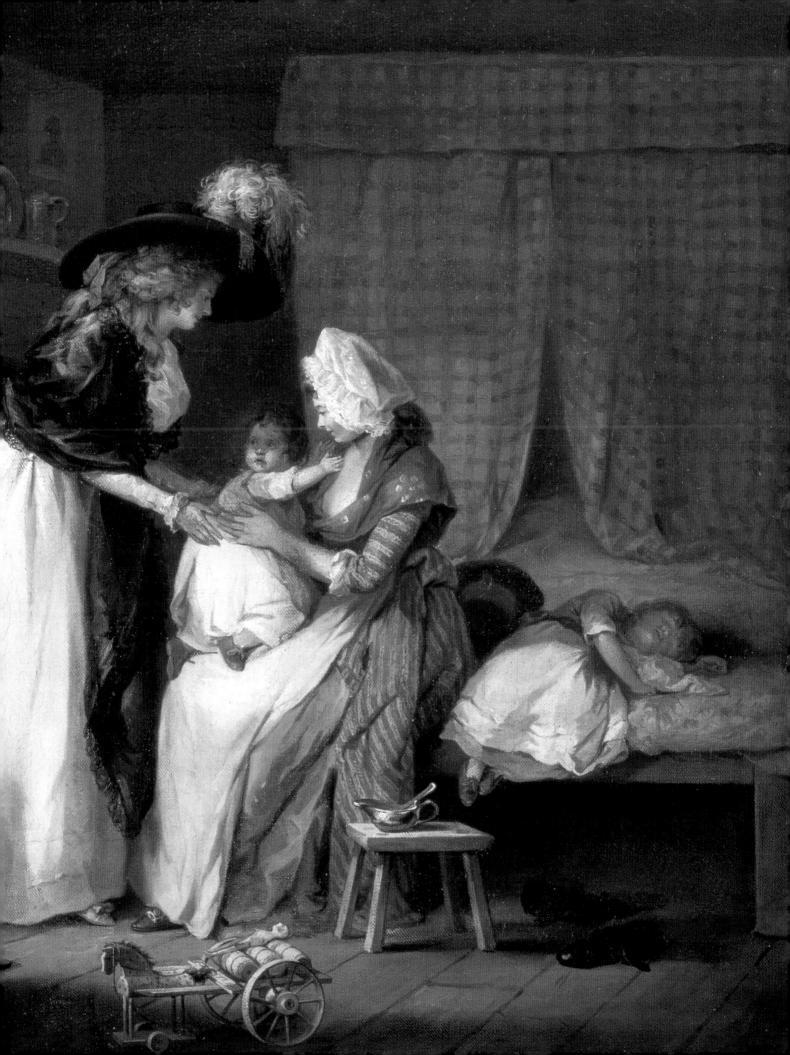

Breast-feeding was unpopular in high society. Satirists made fun of the way it had to be reconciled with contemporary crazes in costume. *Above: Modern Nursing,* by John Kay, a Scottish engraving of 1796. *Opposite: The Fashionable Mama, or The Convenience of Modern Dress* of the same date, a caricature by Gillray.

against each other. Physical stress and intellectual demands were difficult to hold in balance, especially for women who tried to attain, as Mme Roland did, perfection in each domain. Historians who have pictured the Enlightenment rise of the warm, caring, nuclear, middle-class family, a 'haven in a heartless world', in this period have not measured the demands it made, especially of women. The roles of husbands and fathers in this new family were also contradictory. Men were supposed to participate at one and the same time in both this nurturing haven and also in the affairs of what the eighteenth century called 'the world', the absorbing domain of work, sociability and public life.

It is no accident that Mme Roland wrote to her husband while nursing her baby daughter. Breast-feeding was at the heart of contemporary controversy about the new family. The eighteenth century saw a new definition of middle-class childhood as dependent, innocent and in need of nurturing, and defined nurturing most insistently as 'natural' breast-feeding by the child's natural mother. This was a revolutionary proposal. Small babies were usually not nursed by their mothers at this period, but sent out to be nursed by village women with milk to spare. Well-to-do families would have the wet nurse living in their homes. This was such a deeply entrenched practice that historian Patrick Sussman has traced its survival down to the First World War. Often wet-nursed babies did not survive as a result of being looked after by women with more interest in being paid than in the welfare of the children. This was one ground of opposition to the practice mentioned by reformers such as Rousseau. It was also cited in many writings in the new science of pediatrics, a branch of medicine devoted entirely to the nutrition and ailments of children. This in turn was an important part of the construction of the new identity of the child as innocent and dependent, separated from adult life, and demanding a separate place in the middle-class family. The rise of the perception that women were 'naturally' fitted for breast-feeding was thus accompanied by the growth of the idea that children had a particular moral and physical constitution and were in need of particular emotional and physical experiences such as breast-feeding, and required the consequent formation of strong emotional bonds with their mothers. For the first time the family is presented as a pastoral, achievable utopia. Earlier books on child-rearing existed in large numbers, but they focused on manners and morals, rather than on warmth and nurturing, and took a child's participation in adult life as normal. They did not centre on the small details of a child's physical life, which were seen as confined to the mother's care; this was rather a world where boys could enter the navy in their early teens as midshipmen. Hence Enlightenment advice books, influenced by Rousseau, were often jeered at as being completely unrealistic. But what was at stake in them was an ideology of the relationship between mother and child.

Returning to Mme Roland, we see the relationship between her and her daughter mirroring not only the stress on mothers imposed by the ideal of companionate marriage but many other contemporary debates around children and the family. What psychologists would now call the making of 'drive and affect control', Mme Roland lived out as constant efforts to assert her authority over her small daughter. Mme Roland's relationship with Eudore was minutely chronicled in her correspondence with the often-absent Roland, in the autobiography she wrote while in prison and in her *Avis à ma fille*

MATERNAL LOVE

Eudore, the much-loved but unhappy daughter of Monsieur and Mme Roland, was the victim of her mother's determination to do the right thing. In this contemporary silhouette her marginalized position reflects all too accurately her place in the family. Against all the odds (not least her father's suicide and mother's execution) Eudore eventually married and lived a normal life with children of her own.

(*Advice to my Daughter*). In them she provides a detailed description of Eudore's birth, its impact on her health and physical self-confidence, and her behaviour during Eudore's infancy.

Mme Roland, as a convinced follower of Rousseau, decided to feed Eudore herself, and it was on this decision that most of her subsequent relationship with the child was to be based. Breast-feeding, however, turned out to be far from easy, and Mme Roland was forced to send Eudore out to a wet nurse. Undaunted, she made strenuous efforts to regain her supply of milk, hiring women to suck at her breasts to try to restart the flow. Having, against all expectation, succeeded in this, she continued to feed Eudore herself until the child was weaned at around two years old. However, in the period between losing and regaining her milk, she forbade Eudore to be fed on the normal pabulum. Not surprisingly, the child failed to thrive and seems to have been kept alive only by the secret actions of Mme Roland's servants, who risked dismissal to bring food to the baby.

Mme Roland's decision to breast-feed, however, was by no means a foregone conclusion even by the time of Eudore's birth in 1781, 20 years after the publication of *Emile*. This no doubt enabled Mme Roland to see herself as the heroine of a maternal drama in which her baby played only a very secondary role. When Eudore returned from the wet nurse, Mme Roland suffered agonies. She wrote to her husband about how Eudore would not accept her and sat crying on her lap, looking for the wet nurse, about how she thought that Eudore would never be hers again, but would always hanker after the woman who had been more of a mother to her than she had been. The wet nurse would receive Eudore's first smiles, and Mme Roland would not be compensated for the problems of birth and lactation by the caresses of her daughter. The people, she wrote, who tried to cheer her up by pointing to the fact that, in spite of everything, her baby was alive did not understand anything of her sufferings. This conclusion makes it very clear that for Mme Roland her baby's welfare was secondary to her own leading role as suffering mother in this drama. For her the issue was to obtain power over the infant through the special bond which was supposed to result from breast-feeding.

Mme Roland demonstrated this position even more fully in her *Advice to my Daughter*, a brief work written shortly after Eudore's birth but published only in 1799. Ostensibly a paean to the joy and glory of motherhood, it is in fact a minute description of the horrors of childbirth, with a full account of the breast-feeding epic, including Eudore's rejection of her mother in favour of the wet nurse. 'The beloved child who cost me so much pain' would surely have responded with guilt at the despair that her entry into the world had caused. Mme Roland details her post-partum experiences of mastitis, dysentery and broken sleep, before beginning on the struggle to regain her lost flow of milk. The *Advice* makes it clear that the struggle to breast-feed was a struggle not for Eudore's benefit, but for her own self-justification. The repeated personal pronoun in the following passage emphasizes the point: 'Even though my efforts had had to remain unsuccessful, I needed for myself to bear witness that I had tried everything I could for my child, that I had made it a duty to do so. If nature herself would not let me breast-feed, then the fault lay entirely with her.' As the last phrase implies, the breast-feeding saga functioned thereafter in Mme Roland's relationship with her daughter as a moral alibi. Since she had battled to feed the infant, it must and should remain forever attached to her, whatever her subsequent actions. By suffering as a mother, Mme Roland purchased moral immunity and emotional power. Motherhood became an arena of control, where 'a mother's eye places everything under surveillance'. By suffering, she had changed the balance of the family, creating, she hoped, a closer relationship between herself and Eudore than between herself and Roland.

Nothing therefore could have been more surprising or more reprehensible on the part of Eudore, or so Mme Roland felt, than the increasing difficulty of their relationship once early infancy had past. After an absence of three months in 1784, Mme Roland was amazed to find that her daughter rejected her on her return. Teaching Eudore to read the classic authors by the age of six was uphill work, enforced by Mme Roland as her moral due. By 1789, Eudore, mentioned continually in correspondence as an infant, fades out of her mother's communications and is scarcely noticed. When in March of that year the Roland family moved temporarily to Paris when Roland became a lobbyist for the city of Lyon to the National Assembly, Eudore was not even allowed to share her parents' flat but was put out to board. Mme Roland's attempts to act out the maternal role had clearly ended in failure, but through Eudore's fault rather than her own. (Eudore's story ends happily. After her father's suicide and her mother's execution, both in 1793, she became the ward of her mother's close friend the botanist Louis-Guillaume Bosc, creator of the Bosc pear. She married one of Bosc's friends, had several children and seems to have led an ordinary married life. She never liked to discuss her famous mother.)

The Comfortable Home

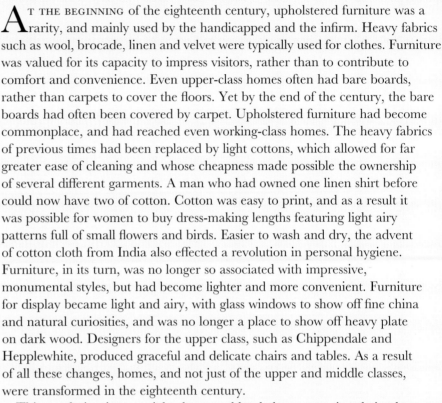

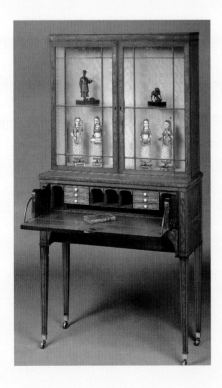

AT THE BEGINNING of the eighteenth century, upholstered furniture was a rarity, and mainly used by the handicapped and the infirm. Heavy fabrics such as wool, brocade, linen and velvet were typically used for clothes. Furniture was valued for its capacity to impress visitors, rather than to contribute to comfort and convenience. Even upper-class homes often had bare boards, rather than carpets to cover the floors. Yet by the end of the century, the bare boards had often been covered by carpet. Upholstered furniture had become commonplace, and had reached even working-class homes. The heavy fabrics of previous times had been replaced by light cottons, which allowed for far greater ease of cleaning and whose cheapness made possible the ownership of several different garments. A man who had owned one linen shirt before could now have two of cotton. Cotton was easy to print, and as a result it was possible for women to buy dress-making lengths featuring light airy patterns full of small flowers and birds. Easier to wash and dry, the advent of cotton cloth from India also effected a revolution in personal hygiene. Furniture, in its turn, was no longer so associated with impressive, monumental styles, but had become lighter and more convenient. Furniture for display became light and airy, with glass windows to show off fine china and natural curiosities, and was no longer a place to show off heavy plate on dark wood. Designers for the upper class, such as Chippendale and Hepplewhite, produced graceful and delicate chairs and tables. As a result of all these changes, homes, and not just of the upper and middle classes, were transformed in the eighteenth century.

This revolution in material culture could only have come into being because of the Industrial Revolution of the eighteenth century. Fundamental changes in production resulted in the substitution of large factories for small workshops in many trades. The 'division of labour' used in many such enterprises meant that instead of one craftsman making an object from beginning to end, the process was split into tiny actions, each the speciality of a particular workman. The economist Adam Smith gave the classic example of the division of labour in his 1776 *Inquiry into the Nature and Causes of the Wealth of Nations*: 'To take an example, therefore, from a very trifling manufacture, but one in which the division of labour has been very often taken notice of, the trade of the pin-maker; a workman not educated to this business (which the division of labour has made into a distinct trade), nor acquainted with the use of the machinery employed in it … could scarce, perhaps with the utmost industry, make one pin a day, and certainly could not make twenty. But in the way in which this business is now carried on, not only the whole work is a peculiar trade, but is divided into a number of branches, of which the greater part are likewise peculiar trades. One man draws out the wire, another straights it, a third cuts it, a fourth points it, a fifth grinds it at the top for receiving the head; to make the head requires two or three distinct operations; to put it on is a peculiar business, to whiten the pins is another; it is even a trade by itself to put them into the paper; and the important business of making a pin, is, in this manner, divided into about eighteen distinct operations.' Smith goes on to point out how many more pins may be made be made by this method than by the artisanal mode of production. He calculates that each worker, rather than making one pin a day, can now make 4,800 a day. As the number of pins increases, so the unit value falls in price. Pins – or any other commodity, such as textiles – become accessible to those to whom they were not accessible before. And more pins have to be sold before the pin-maker can make a profit. It was this increase in the number of objects made and sold which was the pre-condition for the emergence of comfortable things, to such an extent that Smith considered, if rather too optimistically, that a 'universal opulence … extends itself to the lowest ranks of the people'.

How did this concept of comfort come into being? As the American historian John E. Crowley has noted, until approximately the middle of the century the word 'comfort' in the modern sense rarely appears. Far more common was its use in the sense of spiritual support. Famous phrases in Handel's *Messiah* of 1742 enjoined the prophet to speak 'comfortably to my people'. It was only when mass-produced objects came into being that 'comfort' started to be used in the modern sense. However, this dramatic shift in meaning was accompanied by considerable debate. Eighteenth-century

French fashions conquered Europe. Ulla Tessin, of Stockholm, was the wife of Carl Gustav Tessin, an important official at the court of King Gustav III. He was the son of the architect Nicodemus Tessin the Younger and himself travelled abroad, especially in France and Italy. While he was away Ulla managed the household and not surprisingly her study reflects French taste in its desk, cabinet, wallpaper, etc (*opposite*).

The wide use of upholstered furniture made for greater comfort as well as aesthetic appeal. Its various forms – for chairs, drapery, mattresses, etc – are illustrated in a plate from the *Encyclopédie* (*below*).

Informality and comfort went together. When François Boucher painted his wife (*below*), he posed her in the relaxed attitude of a reclining odalisque, but he dressed her in the light, artfully artless style of the 1740s. She is not asserting a social position, but is shown as if caught unawares in an apparently casual costume that belies its sophistication. The purpose is not to impress but to seduce.

But comfort was not the only priority. Much Rococo furniture was distinctly *un*comfortable and not even functionally strong (*opposite*). In spite of upholstery, which softened the hard surfaces of earlier pieces, the desire for ornament and for thin serpentine shapes was sometimes paramount. *Below:* chaises longues and chairs illustrated in the *Encyclopédie*. It was another novel feature of the period that furniture was mostly not designed by the craftsmen who made it.

thinkers pondered the question of whether the increase in comfort could be counted as 'luxury', a useless and corrupting superfluity of goods which diverted men from their duties to others and to society at large. For Rousseau, the answer was clear. In his 1750 *Discourse on the Arts and Sciences*, he saw luxury as nothing more than corrupting for man. The more simply human beings lived, the more moral they would be. David Hume strongly disagreed. Less dogmatic than Rousseau, he pointed out only two years later, in his 1752 essay *Of Refinement in the Arts* (whose original title was *On Luxury*) that 'Luxury is a word of uncertain signification, and may be taken in a good as well as in a bad sense. In general, it means great refinement in the gratification of the senses; and any degree of it may be innocent or blameable, according to the age, or country, or condition of the person … indulgences are only vices when they are pursued at the expense of some virtue … when they entrench on no virtue, but leave ample subject whence to provide for friends, family, and every proper object of generosity or compassion, they are entirely innocent.' Hume also acknowledges the importance of luxuries in economic and social terms in a way that Rousseau does not: 'The increase and consumption of all the commodities which serve to the ornament and pleasure of life, are advantageous to society; because, at the same time that they multiply those innocent gratifications to individuals, they are a kind of storehouse of labour, which, in the exigencies of state, may be turned to the public service.' Consumption, comfort and the strength of the state all go together.

Hume grasped the connection between comfort, refinement and economic structures. More than any other development during the Enlightenment, the rise of comfort illustrates how objects embody ideas, and how those ideas depend on industry for their embodiment.

Mme d'Epinay (shown here in a portrait by Liotard) was another disciple of Rousseau who wanted to feed her own baby. But her husband dismissed the idea with derision and forbade her to think of it.

'Male' and 'female' defined

Mme Roland's devotion to *Emile* was by no means universal. Even by Rousseau's death, maternal breast-feeding was often still viewed as a dangerous experiment. Mme Roland had the mortification of seeing a near neighbour, a young and frivolous women, become a mother at the same time that she did, put her baby with a wet nurse, and immediately resume the life of parties, drives into the country and intermittently visiting beaux that had been hers before. Mme Roland on the other hand felt trapped by the demands of motherhood. The state of contemporary opinion was perhaps better represented by a lively conversation between Rousseau's patron and friend Mme d'Epinay and her husband when she asked for permission to feed her baby herself, so that she should become dearer to it. 'What a foolish idea is this?' responded her husband. 'Feed your baby yourself? I could die laughing. Even if you were strong enough, why should you want everyone to laugh at you? Of course not. Why should I give my consent to such ridiculous goings-on? So, my dear, in spite of anything the doctors may say, you can stop thinking about this, it's nonsensical. What satisfaction is there in nursing an infant? Who the devil gave you such an idea?' Many Enlightenment debates were fought out over the bodies of small babies, just as they were also over the bodies of exotic peoples.

The struggle over breast-feeding came to symbolize the Enlightenment chase after nature, and its concurrent struggle to define gender. Few children were actually brought up according to the rest of the precepts of *Emile*, and those parents, such as Thomas Day, the English educationalist, or Richard Lovell Edgeworth, the famous Anglo-Irish author of parental help books (and father of the novelist Maria), who did follow Rousseau's in fact highly artificial 'natural' regime, a sort of experiment with living children, almost all had cause to regret it. Wives who fed their own babies continued to be ridiculed. But the Rousseauist debate on education is significant because it stands at the junction between two important, and highly ambiguous, Enlightenment debates: over 'nature' and 'gender'. Women were supposed to be more natural than men, more defined by their bodily constitutions. Since natural also meant right and 'ineluctable', women had no way of escaping a destiny linked entirely to their reproductive identity.

As the century progressed, medical attention increasingly focused not just on the rearing of babies and small children, but also on the physical constitution of women. Doctors increasingly argued that the bodies of men and women showed absolute difference. In anatomy, structures that had once been thought of as homologies or versions of each other, like the skeleton and the nervous system, were now differentiated. Organs such as ovaries and testes which had once shared names were now relabelled to show gender difference. Anatomical studies of women's brains argued that they were of smaller size, and thus conclusively demonstrated women's unfitness for intellectual pursuits. Though women were educators of children in the family, they themselves were judged difficult to educate. Even women themselves seemed to have accepted some of these ideas. For example, the writer and poet Laetitia Hawkins wrote, in spite of her own intellectual pursuits, in her 1793 *Letters on the Female Mind*: 'It cannot, I think, be truly asserted, that the intellectual powers know no difference of sex. Nature certainly intended a distinction … In general and almost universally, the female intellect has less strength and more acuteness. Consequently in our exercise of it, we show less perseverance and more vivacity.'

At the same time, however, this complex definition of femininity as 'natural' or close to nature went hand in hand with the idea that woman was the unique carrier, within the family, of a new morality through which the unnaturalness of civilization could be transcended, and a society created which was yet natural. Society could be redeemed from the artificial and corrupt, that which Emile is brought to flee, by women. This sentiment was expressed by the popular writer Bernardin de St Pierre in his 1787 best-seller *Paul et Virginie*: 'Women lay down the first foundations of natural laws. The first founder of human society was a mother of a family. They are scattered among men to remind them that above all they are men, and to uphold, despite politics and laws, the fundamental law of nature. Not only do women bind men together by the bonds of nature, but also by those of society.'

Unlike Rousseau, Bernardin de St Pierre, the author of *Paul et Virginie* (1787), took an exalted view of women as the foundation of natural laws. *Paul et Virginie* is the story of the pure and innocent love of two children who grow up together on the tropical island of Mauritius. 'One day,' says the narrator, 'I saw Virginie running towards the house with her petticoat thrown over her head in order to protect herself from a shower of rain. At a distance I thought she was alone: but as I hastened towards her I perceived that she held Paul by the arm, almost entirely enveloped in the same canopy, and both were laughing heartily at their being sheltered together under an umbrella of their own invention.' Shown here are illustrations from the English edition of 1796.

'**The stream** on the banks of which Paul and Virginie were standing rolls foaming over a bed of rocks. The noise of the water frightened Virginie and she was afraid to wade through the current: Paul therefore took her up in his arms and went thus loaded over the slippery rocks which formed the bed of the river, careless of the tumultuous noise of its waters.' But Virginie is drowned in a shipwreck (typically because she refuses to be saved by a naked sailor) and Paul dies of a broken heart. Although incredibly sentimental – the dog dies of a broken heart too – the novel was immensely popular, and was fervently admired by Napoleon.

Das Hällische Wäysenhaus

1. Das vorder-Gebæude des Wæysenhauſes. 2. Die Apotheke.
3. Der Buchladen. 4. Die Claſſen der Lateiniſchen Schule und
Wohn-Stuben der Wæysen-Knaben. 5. Das Seiten-Gebæude
zur rechten Hand. 6. Der Singe-Saal. 7. Der Speiſe-Saal.

Schaut ihr dis Wæysenhaus und deſſen Umfang an
ſo lernt, daſs Gott uns aus Wenig machen kan,
Bemit ſeiner Almacht mehr als unſre Sinnen trauen;
So könt ihr eitel Luſt an ſeinen Wundern ſchauen.

8. Das Wohnhaus der Wæysen-Mægdlein. 9. Das Seiten-Gebæude,
zur lincken Hand. 10. Das Ober und Unter-Collegium darinnen Studioſi und Knaben wohnen. 11. Das neue Hauſs
zur Bibliothec. 12. Das Pædagogium Regium.

The German theorists took a path
completely different from that of Rousseau.
Far from keeping the child in a state of natural
ignorance, August Franke and Joachim
Heinrich Campe believed in a vigorous
programme of instruction through books, play
and social conditioning. There was a strong
moral and religious bias to these ideas. Franke's
school and orphanage at Halle catered for over
600 students housed in a vast complex of
buildings (*above*), a centre of the movement
known as Pietism. He died in 1727.

Two of Campe's books had wide influence
and were translated into other languages.
Opposite above: a page from his *New Method of
Teaching Children to Read* (1778): 'Hey, you bees,'
growls the Bear. 'Give me your honey right
now, or I shall smash you and your hive.'
'What if we defend ourselves?' says a small bee.
'Defend yourselves! You must be kidding.' The
title-page engraving by Chodowiecki of his
Young Robinson (*bottom*) shows him with his
abundant family.

The German experience

In the German Enlightenment, the making of society was seen as being as
much the work of the child as of its mother. In a degree unparalleled in other
regions the German-speaking lands were both preoccupied by education and
by the child, and actual institutions, often with the support of territorial princes,
were established to turn educational ideals into reality. In no other region did
large numbers of children actually go through programmes of instruction
inspired by educational theorists such as August Franke or Joachim Heinrich
Campe, or Count Nikolaus Ludwig von Zinzendorf, leader of the Moravian
Church. No satisfactory explanation has ever been given for the unique way
in which educational theory and practice came together in the German states
in this period. The many hundreds of young people in Germany who went
through similar educational programmes is proof that, far from being restricted
to the domain of theoreticians such as Rousseau, education was becoming
a practical programme to change the world. Here in Germany, more than
anywhere else, the eighteenth century truly was the era of the child.

Joachim Heinrich Campe, probably the major educational reformer of
the century, opened in 1779 the famous Philanthropins institution in the small
German princely town of Dessau, now an hour's ride south-east of Berlin.
Receiving support from Herzog Karl Wilhelm Ferdinand, the objective of the
institution was to turn its pupils into 'friends of humanity'. The educational
philosophy behind it was consciously linked to the Enlightenment, especially
its aim of disposing its pupils to religious tolerance. Religious teaching in the
Philanthropins was carried out in a non-confessional way. The goal was to turn
the (male) pupils first into men, friends of humanity, and thence into *Weltburger*,

or citizens of the world. It was an education concentrating not so much on the inner world as on the way in which the pupils would live in the world, without any confining allegiance to state, party or religion, and with a sense of fraternity with all men. Instead of the 'negative education' of Rousseau, the Dessau Philanthropins prepared its pupils squarely for the world. The teachers put play and the training of the senses at the centre of their pedagogy. The pupils put on plays, played games to stimulate memory and learning, and were kept active by physical training, gardening and handicrafts. The Philanthropins educators in fact were well aware of the consequences of the separation of hand and head. They also knew that games and toys train vital faculties such as attentiveness, alertness and the ability to distinguish between form, line and colour.

It is clear how deeply this educational practice was linked with the experience of the Enlightenment in the German-speaking lands. Religious toleration was a hard-won right (see Chapter 1). The cosmopolitanism of this programme was an obvious necessity in the face of the 300 or so states in which pupils might find themselves living and working even if they stayed within Germany. The feeling of fraternity with all mankind was also a strong part of Campe's programme. It fitted well both the situation of the German states of that time, forced to look beyond their own borders, and the Enlightenment interest in Freemasonry, a secret society which also had as its objective the increase of human fraternity. The Philanthropins, as its name suggests, was an institution based on the teaching of brotherly love. It was also one where equality among the students, whether noble or commoner, was insisted upon. Distinctions were founded on virtue and work, not birth.

In 1776 Herzog Karl Wilhelm Ferdinand had appointed Campe *Edukatsionsrat*, or controller of education, in the tiny principality of Anhalt-Dessau, a post which gave him control of its school system. Campe used this opportunity to set up a printing works devoted entirely to the production of books for children. This was the first such press, and it is to around this time that we can date the production of the first books written for child readers only. Nor were these books unduly solemn. Writers took to heart John Locke's hint in his *Thoughts Concerning Education* of 1693 to make reading seem a 'sport' rather than a 'task'. Campe's books followed this line, as can be seen from the title of his famous and much reprinted *Robinson der Jungere, zur angenehmen und nuztlichen Unterhaltung für Kinder* (*The Young Robinson, or, Pleasant and Useful Entertainment for Children*). History adapted for young children, such as *The Discovery of America*, was published by the Little Library. Educational reformers like Campe taught that children should not merely read books, but enter into an intimate relationship with them.

Campe's reputation was unique in the German states. His work, however, should be seen in the context of an Enlightenment Germany gripped by a wave of educational reform which achieved institutionalization far beyond anything in France or England. Tiny Anhalt-Dessau was far from the only state, of whatever size, which supported new educational thinking. In Württemberg, for example, the ruler himself set up the Karlsschule (named after himself), an academy whose pupils included the future poet and playwright Friedrich Schiller and the naturalist Georges Cuvier. Education at the Karlsschule, like the Philanthropins, was conducted along lines of religious tolerance and equality between pupils. Its curriculum, designed to train professional

Play for Campe was essential to the learning process. Education had to be as entertaining as a story, welcomed as a pleasure, not undertaken as a task. An 1806 ABC by him (*above*) reflects this happy situation.

The young reader painted by Greuze (*below*) fits ideally into the way enlightened educationalists saw the process of learning. Greuze was one of the artists who headed Diderot's plea that painting should inculcate serious moral lessons.

administrators, included courses in law, forestry, mining, history and natural history. New universities, such as that of Göttingen (1737), were also founded with similar objectives, as well as acting, as many said at the time, as finishing schools for young gentlemen. Technical schools such as the Freiburg Academy of Mines were also established. Industrial schools, including one established by Campe, also sprang up.

Why this wave of interest in practical education? Part of the answer comes from the devastation suffered by the German states in the Seven Years' War (1756–63). Reform and modernization, better exploitation of resources and, above all, better administration were vital to the German states. Education was thus an attractive investment for them.

The family, child-rearing, marriage and education formed a cluster of issues which drew the attention of thinkers in the Enlightenment in a degree unparalleled in previous eras. But this attention was far from producing any coherent synthesis. Educationalists in England, France and the German states faced very different social and political situations. Opinions differed dramatically. Some educational theorists, such as Rousseau, thought that human society was so terrifying and corrupting that their pupils should in the beginning be removed from it. Others, like Campe and the administrative schools, could not wait for their pupils to make their mark on that same world. Some iconic educational theorists, again such as Rousseau, loudly proclaimed woman's duty to fulfil the laws of nature and reproduce and breast-feed. The majority of society at most levels thought these injunctions foolish or ridiculous. At the heart of these debates is the meaning of 'nature'. This uniquely slippery word (scholars have found more than a hundred variant meanings in the works of Rousseau alone) had a particularly marked impact on thinking about the family. Both natural and social, the family stood at an intersection of meanings. To call something 'natural' was to imply that it was eternal and ineluctable. Nature could be a coercive word. The family was natural, and thus inevitable. Nature ordered society. Each family showed, however, that beyond the theories of the educationalists lay the irreducible and unique reality of each family, as it confronted the realities of child-rearing, marriage and schooling.

Books for children were an innovation of the Enlightenment. Two English examples (*opposite*) proclaim their messages on their title-pages. *The Young Gentleman and Lady's Golden Library* (1783) aimed to establish 'Plainness, Simplicity, Virtue and Wisdom'. *Little Goody Two-Shoes* (1777) included 'the Means by which she acquired her Learning and Wisdom'.

LEO the Great LION.

THE

LILLIPUTIAN MAGAZINE:

OR, THE

Young GENTLEMAN and LADY's

GOLDEN LIBRARY.

BEING

An Attempt to mend the World, to render the
Society of Man more amiable, and to eſtabliſh
the Plainneſs, Simplicity, Virtue, and Wiſdom

OF THE

GOLDEN AGE,

So much celebrated by the POETS and HISTORIANS.

Man in that Age no Rule but Reaſon knew,
And with a native Bent did Good purſue;
Unforc'd by Puniſhment, unaw'd by Fear,
His Words were ſimple, and his Soul ſincere.

LONDON:

Printed for T. CARNAN, Succeſſor to Mr.
J. NEWBERY, in St. Paul's Churchyard.
[Price One Shilling.]
MDCCLXXXIII.

Little
Goody Two-Shoes.

THE

HISTORY

OF

Little Goody Two-Shoes;

Otherwiſe called

Mrs. Margery Two-Shoes.

WITH

The Means by which ſhe acquired her Learning and Wiſdom, and in Conſequence
thereof her Eſtate.

Set forth at large for the Benefit of thoſe,
Who from a State of Rags and Care,
And having Shoes but half a Pair,
Their Fortune and their Fame would fix,
And gallop in their Coach and Six.

See the Original Manuſcript in the *Vatican* at
Rome, and the Cuts by *Michael Angelo;* il-
luſtrated with the Comments of our great
modern Critics.

LONDON:

Printed for T. CARNAN and F. NEWBERY,
jun. at No. 65, in St. Paul's Church-Yard.
MDCCLXXVII.
[Price SIX-PENCE, bound and gilt.]

4

The Global
Enlightenment

PREVIOUS PAGES
The death of Captain Cook. The world's horizons were rolling back at an unprecedented rate in the face of the great campaigns of exploration and discovery. By the end of the 17th century the outlines and extent of the earth's land masses and oceans had been roughly established and the world had been several times circumnavigated. But vast areas were still wrapped in mystery. The very existence of Australia, New Zealand and the Polynesian islands was little more than a vague rumour. During the 18th century, with the detailed surveying of the Pacific, a flood of information came to the West from there and elsewhere, upsetting many generalizations that had hitherto been taken for granted – about the nature and divisions of mankind, social organizations, languages, religious instinct and political structures. Repeatedly, it was a case of alien cultures coming into contact and attempts being made on both sides to comprehend the incomprehensible, not to mention the large and disconcerting expansion of knowledge about strange new animals and plants. James Cook made three voyages to the Pacific, adding more to the 18th-century world-picture than any other explorer. He was killed in a scuffle with islanders in Hawaii in February 1779. He was only 50.

The freezing coast of eastern Siberia was equally remote, inhabited by Aleutian islanders who had had no contact with Europe. Georg Steller, a German physician who accompanied Vitus Behring to the Behring Strait, published his account of Kamchatka in 1774 (*below*).

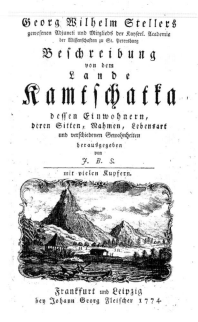

On 7 April 1773 the famous navigator James Cook stood on a beach at what is now Dusky Sound, South Island, New Zealand, rubbing noses with a Maori warrior. The Maori had never seen a European before, and James Cook had seen very few Maoris. To get the terrified Maori to come to the point of rubbing noses had been a complex process. Johann Reinhold Forster, a German naturalist travelling with Cook, remembered how 'Captain Cook went to the head of the boat, called to him in a friendly manner, and threw him his own and some other handkerchiefs, which he would not pick up. The Captain, then taking some sheets of white paper in his hand, landed on the rock unarmed, and held the paper out to the native. The man now trembled very visibly, and having exhibited strong marks of fear in his countenance, took the paper; upon which Captain Cook coming up to him, took hold of his hand, and embraced him, touching the man's nose with his own, which is their mode of salutation … A short conversation ensued, of which little was understood on both sides, for want of a complete knowledge of their language.' To seem less threatening Cook had left behind in the boat his men. Cook had invited the Maori forward with friendly gestures. He had flung on the ground his own handkerchief, and pieces of white paper, in the hope that the Maori would understand the thin white objects as overtures of friendship. Cook managed to coax the man onto the beach in the end, and then they began to rub noses. In a similar situation 30 years before, a young German physician, Georg Steller, travelling on the explorer Vitus Behring's last, chaotic, disastrous voyage in 1740 between Vladivostok and the coast of Alaska, swapped rags of Chinese silk and old kettles, feathers and nails, with hitherto unknown Aleutian islanders. This meeting of cultures is part of what is meant by the 'global Enlightenment'. On the neutral space of the beach at Dusky Sound, or between kayaks and a Russian navy ship, cultures did indeed meet. A wealth of similar stories could be told from the eighteenth century. They allow us to bask in a nostalgia for a time when there were still unknown peoples to be encountered, and unknown places to be seen.

But isolated tales of first contacts between different races and cultures tell us little about the real nature of the global Enlightenment: about how and why Cook came into the Pacific, for example, or what objectives had tempted Behring near the freezing Alaskan coast and the long archipelago of the Aleutian islands. They also tell us little about how a navigator on a beach with a Maori or a young physician trading silk and feathers with an unknown people could have anything to do with competitions about the meaning of 'Enlightenment', with the theories of Locke, Hume and Rousseau, or with struggles for religious tolerance and judicial reform.

In fact, the Enlightenment may equally be seen as a world drama of cross-cultural contact, a drama with enormous consequences for both Europeans and indigenous peoples. This new theatre of exploration and exchange in previously unknown worlds was a place where the Enlightenment was to work out its own meaning as much as it did in the Berlin competition. For indigenous peoples, contact with Europeans often destroyed their societies. For Europeans, such encounters often triggered anxieties about the nature of European society, and about the meaning of their identity as 'civilized'. At the same time, encounters with other cultures supplied data used in important debates about the nature of human variety and difference, and about the possibility of a common human

Cook's first voyage had a scientific purpose:
to observe the transit of Venus. But he had
secret instructions to explore the Pacific and
claim any previously unknown lands for the
crown of England. He was an expert
mathematician and a thoughtful man fully
aware of the cultural significance of his
discoveries. This posthumous portrait is by
Nathaniel Dance-Holland.

In India the clash of cultures brought new knowledge but at the price of war and exploitation. One of the Indian rulers at odds with the invaders was Tipu Sahib, sultan of Mysore. In 1795 he had this life-size toy showing a tiger savaging an English soldier made by a Dutch engineer (*right*). Inside, a mechanical organ imitates the growling of the tiger and the screams of the victim.

More sympathetic were those Englishmen who adopted Indian dress and to some extent an Indian way of life. Dr John Wombwell (*below*) is shown smoking his hookah attended by an Indian servant in Lucknow in 1785. *Below right:* a British officer rides on an elephant. The painting is by an Indian artist.

Another officer, Captain Foote of the East India Company (*opposite*), cuts an imposing figure in a turban and Indian clothing.

history. Disturbingly for eighteenth-century people, knowledge of other cultures also posed the problem of relativism. Were there absolute standards, or as many standards as there were human societies? These concerns are still with us in the shape of concerns over multiculturalism. Should European values be the universal standard, or should there be a plurality of value systems and meanings? These very current questions were first posed during the globalization of the Enlightenment world.

The Enlightenment was a time when the world became truly 'global'. This is a tricky word to define. As historian David Armstrong has noted, 'Globalisation was no more a unitary practice than was internationalism before it: multiple tracks towards globalisation can be discerned, just as there are multiple movements against it.' What is clear from this definition is that globalization was a process which overrode national borders in a way that internationalism, which depends precisely on the existence of borders, cannot. As the American historians Dror Wahrman and Jonathan Sheehan have pointed out, globalization and the global consciousness involve a thickening of contact between previously separated parts of the world, underpinned by a growing consciousness of the world as an interlocking system. This is the history of the factors which with accelerating speed since the Enlightenment have come together to make the world a single system. Such factors might include: the movement of peoples, especially through the organized slave trade; the formation of interconnected markets; the worldwide circulation of both ideas and microbes, of commodities such as tea, furs, cotton, whale oil and gold; the expansion of merchant fleets to transport these commodities, and an expansion of international law to try to shape this increasing intensity of interaction; the state financing of geographical exploration which demonstrated how oceans

Was truth absolute or relative? Could there be a plurality of value systems? The question would have made no sense to medieval or Renaissance Europe, but in the Enlightenment things were no longer so simple. Instead of the world being divided between Christians (who were right) and infidels (who were wrong), it was now apparent that the religion of the West was only one of many, each making its own claim. This panorama of world faiths (*opposite*) was published in Holland in 1727. The Christian Churches – Catholic and Protestant – occupy the middle ground. Judaism lies defeated at the feet of the pope. In the foreground are the Muslims with a table of Quranic law, while in the distance are the pagodas and altars of the Far East.

'How the Kamchatkans Made Fire' (*left*): another illustration from Georg Steller's book, with their houses in the background.

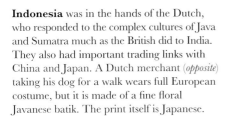

Indonesia was in the hands of the Dutch, who responded to the complex cultures of Java and Sumatra much as the British did to India. They also had important trading links with China and Japan. A Dutch merchant (*opposite*) taking his dog for a walk wears full European costume, but it is made of a fine floral Javanese batik. The print itself is Japanese.

How the Far East saw the Dutch. A Chinese pottery figure of a Dutch merchant (*above*) and a clay portrait of Undercargo Peter Mule made in Canton in 1731 (*above right*).

The Dutch East India Company was virtually an independent state governed by an administration housed in palatial premises in Amsterdam (*above far left and below*).

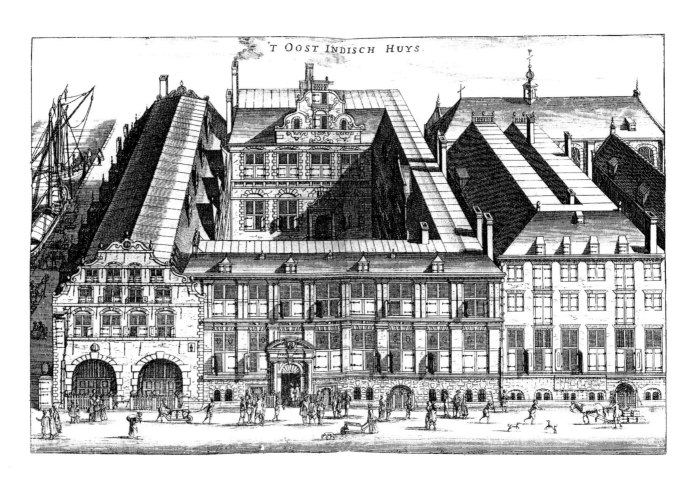

De groote party in de kamer van het opper Hoofd Zyn, op het Eyland.

The Dutch in Japan were kept at arm's length. They were confined to a small artificial island called Deshima, off the city of Nagasaki. This was the only place where people from the two countries could mix, and it enabled the Japanese to learn a good deal more about Europe than the Europeans learned about Japan. This view (*above*) shows a strictly controlled social occasion.

In China the city of Canton played a role similar to that of Nagasaki in Japan. This porcelain bowl (*right*), made in China for the export market, is decorated with views of several European 'factories' in Canton in 1775.

and continents are linked; the emergence of transcontinental empires very often administered on standardized bureaucratic models, and the increasing wealth of multinational trading companies such as the Hudson's Bay Company, the British East India Company and its Dutch equivalent, the Dutch East India Company. To this one could add a general perception of the world as being a whole. As Samuel Johnson wrote in his philosophical novella *Rasselas* (1759): 'You, Sir, whose curiosity is so extensive, will easily conceive with what pleasure a philosopher, furnished with wings, and hovering in the sky, would see the earth, and all its inhabitants, rolling beneath him and presenting to him successively, by its diurnal motion, all the countries within the same parallel.' Globalization was also domestic and personal. Tea, silk and fine china came to the European middle classes on ships from India and China. Cotton cloth made in India gave cheap, replaceable clothes for the first time to the working classes. Globes became part of the furnishings of houses, part of the instruction of small children, even erotic objects.

The dilemma of slavery

There was no lack of awareness in the Enlightenment that the discovery of the Americas had been crucial to the beginning of the process of globalization. The Scots economist Adam Smith said: '[the] discovery of America and that of a passage to the East Indies by the Cape of Good Hope are the two greatest and most important events in the history of mankind.' More dramatically the French writer the Abbé Raynal declared in his classic 1770 *Histoire philosophique et politique des établissements et du commerce des Européens dans les deux Indes* (*Philosophical and Political History of the European Establishments and Commerce in the Two Indies*) exclaimed: 'There has never been any event which has had more impact on the human race in general, and for Europeans in particular, as that of the discovery of the New World, and the passage to the Indies around the Cape of Good Hope. It was then that a commercial revolution began, a revolution in the balance of power, and in the customs, the industries and the government of every nation. It was through this event that men in the most distant lands were linked by new relationships and new needs … The produce of equatorial regions were consumed in polar climes … everywhere men mutually exchanged their opinions, their laws, their customs, their illnesses and their medicines, their virtues and their vices. Everything changed and will go on changing. But will the changes of the past and those that are to come, be useful to humanity? Will his condition be better or will it simply be one of constant change?' Raynal was right to point to constant change as a mark of globalization. It is only against this constant change that industrialization can be understood.

Raynal was also right to ask whether the unity of the globe increases human happiness. In the case of one commodity, that of human beings, the answer was in the negative. The eighteenth-century slave trade moved millions of people and their cultures from the west coast of Africa to the other side of the Atlantic. People sold as slaves on the coast of west Africa might work in the sugar plantations of the Caribbean islands, the dockyards of Cuba, the great estates of Brazil or the tobacco plantations of Virginia. Around this trade grew up a transatlantic financial system which accumulated capital and was part of the global circulation of gold. It is an inescapable truth that one of the most powerful globalizing forces of the Enlightenment was the slave trade.

The globe became a household object now that the dark areas of the earth's surface were being explored. The fact that it is so frequently represented in art, and in so many different contexts, is itself significant. Even the emperor of China, as imagined in a Beauvais tapestry of about 1700 (*centre*), could find his place on it; the bearded figure is the Jesuit Father Adam Scholl von Bell, who taught the emperor astronomy in the mid-17th century. Even the Freemasons – in this early Meissen group (*left*) wearing their aprons and insignia – drew a message from its universality. Pornographers, in a satirical print (*top*) of Voltaire relaxing from his literary labours, could even give it an erotic connotation ('Love Rules the World'?). The fine terrestrial globe (*above*) was made about 1728 for the Abbé Nollet, a noted scientist. *The Geography Lesson* by Pietro Longhi (*opposite*) was painted in Venice in about 1752.

The Four Continents

Throughout the Enlightenment, there they are – frescoes painted on ceiling after ceiling, wall after wall, images confined within glittering frames, the subject of poems and scientific debate. The Four Continents – Europe, Asia, Africa and America – are an eighteenth-century trope, one of the images one most expected to see in any picture gallery or on the walls of a grand house or palace. It was easy to identify them, though their precise configurations often differed. Africa was represented by a Negro, sometimes a Negro queen, as in the frescoes by Tiepolo which decorate the palace of the prince-bishop of Würzburg. Very often in the background there would be the typical animals of Africa, such as elephants, lions and cheetahs, dromedaries and a personification of the River Nile. Asia might be represented by the Pyramids (in a confusing overlap with the trope of Africa), elephants, slaves and bowing subjects, and tiger hunts. America (thought of as one undifferentiated continent in this period) was represented by a figure, usually female, wearing a feather head-dress and carrying a spear. In the background there might well be teepees, parrots and scenes of cannibalism, drawn from the writings by the Spanish and Portuguese about their colonies. Europe was often represented as a woman riding a white horse, or holding a globe to represent her mastery over the world. At her feet might be musical and mathematical instruments to show European civilization. Except for the feather head-dress of the New

Europe is represented in Tiepolo's Würzburg frescoes by the figure of Europa not exactly sitting on but leaning against the bull. Around her the arts, including music, bear witness to Würzburg's pre-eminence. Many of the portraits are of real people, including Tiepolo himself (leaning over the cartouche at bottom left) and the stuccoist Antonio Ricci (in the flowing cloak under the big pediment). The man sitting on a cannon, bottom right, is the architect of the palace, Balthasar Neumann, in the uniform of a colonel of the Franconian artillery. The point of all this is to stress the cultural superiority of Europe over the other continents. In the sky the prince-bishop is wafted upwards. To his left is Saturn, or Time, with a scythe and an hourglass, while other classical gods and goddesses join in the celebration.

America, wearing a feather head-dress, is sitting on a giant alligator while being served chocolate by a page. Hunters in the foreground have just killed a stag. An Indian is carrying a smaller alligator (upside down) over his shoulder. There are bleeding heads, indicating cannibalism. In the foreground a man in European costume seems to be secretly observing the scene.

World, the Negro for Africa, the globe for Europe, with musical and navigational instruments, and perhaps a magnificent ruler for Asia, artists varied the attributes of the Four Continents very widely, according to their fancies, the purses of their patrons and the dimensions of the areas they had been given to cover. In discussing the trope of the Four Continents, therefore, we are looking for a few particular symbols among a plethora of geographical symbols, rather than a consistent set of emblems such as those dedicated to Christian saints and martyrs.

This fluidity of attributes reflected the complex history and meaning of the trope of the Four Continents. For the eighteenth century, enthusiasm for representations of them could be seen as a reference to the global world that had recently emerged. Nonetheless, the Four Continents remained obstinately separate from each other. They did not flow together, as the global system did, but kept their own insistently visible symbolic character. All this complexity is reflected, for example, in their representation at Würzburg. Europe is represented by Fama (Fame) blowing a trumpet. On her right stands Diana, the moon goddess, on her left Saturn, the god of death and time. The latter's motto was 'time discovers truth'. In this picture Europe asserts her reign over, time, truth and the planets, which included the moon. Africa is represented by oriental merchants and wares. Enthroned is a Negro queen, and near her a dromedary, an elephant and a personification of the River Nile.

Just like the power of Apollo, the trope of the continents has its roots in the classical world. The three continents of the Roman world, before the discovery of the Americas, were represented by much the same attributes as in the

Enlightenment. They were somewhat more likely to be portrayed with appropriate rivers and their spirits, with the Nile close to Africa, and so on. The fourth continent, the Americas, was not added until the mid-sixteenth century, when it became clear for the first time that what the Spanish and Portuguese had conquered was actually a continent.

The Four Continents entered the vocabulary of painting as well as the verbal vocabulary in around the 1550s. We can date this by their appearance in Cesare Ripa's *Iconologia*, a sixteenth-century compendium of images and visual analogies widely used by artists for models and inspiration. By the early seventeenth century, the trope was well established in art, as we can see in Rubens' 1615 painting *Europa*.

Yet even here there is a complication. Sometimes Europe escaped from her three fellow continents and was painted alone, in a scene representing her on Crete. No such similar tropes were developed for the other three continents. It was difficult to find a stable place for the Americas. A late addition to the trope, it was unclear what was to be its relationship with the others. This of course mirrored the real-life problem of the integration of the Americas into the world's trading and intellectual systems.

One of the most famous signs of these problems of integration was the so-called 'debate of the Americas'. First traced by the Italian historian Antonello Gerbi, this consisted of allegations by the Europeans Buffon (see Chapter 7) and De Pauw, who maintained that American nature was weaker and frailer than that of the Old World, that it had fewer species, and that even man there was himself of smaller stature and mental abilities than in the Old World.

Asia rides on an elephant. Shackled slaves kiss the ground. To the left men are capturing a tiger, while on the right Cleopatra stands in front of a pyramid, with a block carved with signs that are meant to be hieroglyphs (did Tiepolo think that Egypt was in Asia?). In the foreground can be seen Calvary with two crosses.

Africa is a black princess seated between the humps of a camel. A kneeling man with a sunshade is offering incense, and a group of oriental merchants bring bales of goods and casks. In the foreground can be seen the river god of the Nile with a pelican, and an ostrich and dromedary covered with a carpet.

Such ideas directly reversed the wonder of the first explorers of the Americas at the variety and brilliant colours of the animals and birds which they saw. The birds of the Americas were indeed the first point of attack for Buffon and his followers, who asked whether the apparent inferiority of American nature as manifested in its birds was due to the climate, to the youthfulness of the continent or to the very constellations which shone in its sky. Nor was American culture, both north and south, civilized and savage, spared from this debate. Underlying these attacks was the unresolved question: could Europe maintain the superiority with which it was portrayed in art?

This was a new question. Previous accounts of the Americas had emphasized the continent's fertility, riches and geographical importance, and its status as a role model for utopian dreams such as Thomas More's *Utopia*. In the eighteenth century all this began to change. It started with one very definite question posed by Buffon: was the number of species greater or smaller in the Old World than in the New? Then came his question as to whether the species themselves were bigger or smaller. Buffon pointed out that there were no camels, elephants, giraffes or lions in the New World, and that the species there tended to be small. The sole exception was the tapir of Brazil, but even this would hardly come up to an elephant's knee. Perhaps this was due to the hostility of the climate in the New World. After Buffon's questions came the writings of the far more aggressive Dutchman Corneille de Pauw. In his *Recherches philosophiques sur les américains* (1768) he turned from Buffon's admission that not all species of the Americas were inferior to those of the New World to an attack on 'redskins' and the indigenous peoples of the Spanish and

Portuguese empires, whom he described as enfeebled by the influence of the climate and the hostility of nature which physical weakness rendered them unable to overcome. With de Pauw's work, the debate widened from the relatively precise questions, mostly on natural history, asked by Buffon into one characterized by fluidity, as the combatants tried to find a place in a global world for the Americas. The Abbé Pernty argued that Europeans had sought to compensate themselves for their own poverty by stealing the riches of the Americas. Pernty's involvement shows how this debate was often structured around truisms about which continent gave what to the other. Writers such as Raynal pointed out that the Europeans had brought only negative things to America, such as slaughter and syphilis, the forced expropriation of the population and the stealing of its mineral wealth. This was one of the themes not only of Raynal's work, but of William Robertson's *History of America* and Thomas Jefferson's prolonged polemic with Buffon.

Underneath this debate lay the problem of shoring up the superiority of Europe so strongly suggested in the trope of the Four Continents. Very little was really at stake concerning American nature. Many of those who intervened in the debate believed that American birds were mute, or that Patagonia was inhabited by giants, in spite of eyewitness evidence to the contrary from James Cook. But in the end this was not the point. Questions of whether American nature was better or worse than that of Europe or what one continent had given to the others aside, this was really a debate about the continuing superiority of one of the Four Continents over the others. It thus presupposed that the continents were by their very natures separate, at exactly the same time as America, Europe, Asia and Africa were in fact being pulled ever more tightly together. By the 1790s the debate had run out of steam. It was also in this decade that the young Alexander von Humboldt, far from distinguishing the nature of one continent from that of the others, was to make extensive visual and statistical comparisons which abolished the hard-and-fast differences between them. The trope of the Four Continents had reached its end.

The continents were equally popular in other media, but did not remain consistent in their iconography. This set of early Meissan figures is by Kändler.

comme les Negres
rament de bout

Commerce
des Esclaves

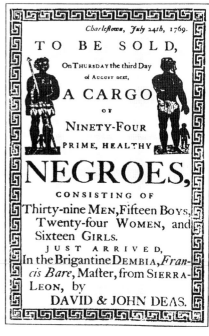

Charlestown, July 24th, 1769.

TO BE SOLD,

On THURSDAY the third Day
of AUGUST next,

A CARGO
OF
NINETY-FOUR
PRIME, HEALTHY

NEGROES,

CONSISTING OF
Thirty-nine MEN, Fifteen BOYS,
Twenty-four WOMEN, and
Sixteen GIRLS.
JUST ARRIVED,
In the Brigantine DEMBIA, *Francis Bare*, Master, from SIERRA-
LEON, by
DAVID & JOHN DEAS.

The slave trade – ignoring for the moment its moral issues – brought about the most spectacular example of 'globalization' that there has ever been. Millions of Africans were moved from one continent to another, permanently altering the racial balance of both North and South America. The commercial advantages that it brought to Europeans blinded them to its cruelty and injustice as well as to the long-term effects on their populations. It took a century of argument and protest to stop it. Before that there had been a few slave revolts but the only one to succeed had been in Haiti, where the heroic Toussaint L'Ouverture founded a republic in 1791. Three years later three deputies from St Dominique attended the Convention in Paris. One of them was Jean-Baptiste Bellay (*below*).

The bust behind him is of the Abbé Raynal, a vocal critic of the slave trade, though even he did not press for its immediate abolition.

The trade cycle began in west Africa, where local chiefs sold prisoners of war to European slave dealers (*opposite*). After crossing the Atlantic, a journey that many did not survive, they were auctioned in the British colonies of the Caribbean and the American east coast. The majority of slaves were actually sold in Brazil.

Once in America the slave was a mere item of merchandise. *Right*: slaves being sold in the French colony of Martinique. *Below right*: an incident related by Raynal – an Englishman of Barbados sells his black mistress.

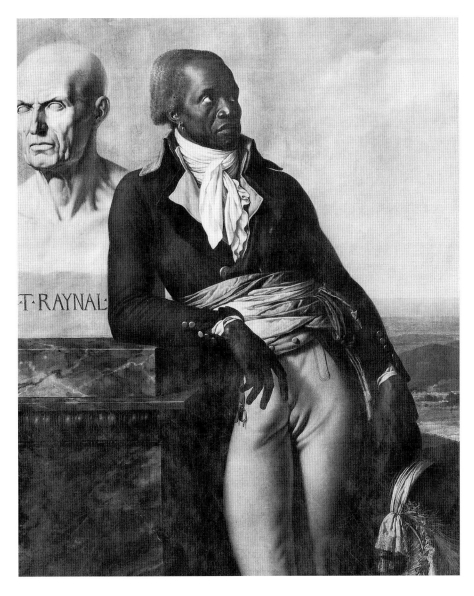

The Slave Emancipation Society was founded in 1787 in England, where the movement to abolish the trade gained strength throughout the late 18th century. The seal of the society (*above*) carried the image of a kneeling slave and the legend 'Am I not a man and a brother?'

The ruthless efficiency of the slave trade, depending on meticulous calculation and yielding huge profits for both the trader and the slave owner on his plantations, made it initially impossible to suppress. The iron laws of economics were impregnable to emotional or moral argument. A model prepared for presentation to the British parliament by one of the most zealous anti-slavery campaigners, William Wilberforce, makes the point in the most graphic way (*opposite*). It shows the inside of a slave ship in such a way as to demonstrate the living conditions of its black cargo. It was taken for granted that every voyage would result in the death of between 5 and 30 per cent of the slaves.

The most intensive regime of slavery, and that which attracted most attention from Enlightenment writers, was that of the sugar plantations of the Caribbean island of Jamaica. Luxuries consumed in Europe such as sugar and tobacco were produced by forced labour under harsh and cruel conditions. Plantation agriculture of this kind reaped enormous profits. There seemed no end to the European demand for these commodities, and slave labour cost little to maintain. As the century progressed the use of slavery in the Caribbean and the southern colonies of British North America, such as Virginia, steadily expanded.

Enlightenment reformers never tired of pointing out that the sugar spooned into tea was bought at the cost of human blood. Agitated depictions of the lot of the slave were common. Raynal at one point asks his readers to imagine the calculations which pass through the head of the captain of a slaving vessel, 'who considers at leisure, what number of firelocks he shall want to obtain one Negro, what fetters will be necessary to keep him chained on board his ship, what whips will be required to make him work, who calculates with coolness every drop of blood which the slave must necessarily expend in labour for him, and how much it will produce; who considers whether a Negro woman will be of more advantage to him by her feeble labours, or by going through the dangers of child-birth.'

Powerful passages such as these recur throughout Raynal's famous book on European colonialism. This particular one, however, is powerful in another sense: it emphasizes the sheer element of calculation which went into the practices of slaving and slave-holding. In the same way, the specially constructed ships which brought the slaves to the Americas had calculated down to the last inch the minimum number of cubic feet of space a slave needed to survive. Calculation and profit were at the heart of plantation slavery. Its enormous profits and careful calculations show that in the eighteenth century slavery was far from being a failing institution.

At the same time, slavery and the system of profits on which it rested were an affront to many Enlightenment ideas. Rousseau, in his *Discourse on the Origins of Human Inequality* of 1754, pointed out how colonialism and slavery were mechanisms for the perpetuation of inequality, and thus constituted a perpetual barrier to the realization of Enlightenment ideals. Yet few Enlightened thinkers wholeheartedly demanded the abolition of slavery. That would have been to demand the overthrow of a powerful economic structure, and to confront the chaos which all Enlightenment thinkers identified as the cost of emancipation. Even Raynal fell short of demanding the immediate abolition of slavery, urging that slaves would not know what to do with their freedom and that the collapse of the plantation economies would unleash violence and disorder. It was not to be until the end of the century that critics of the Enlightenment were to try to dismantle these ambivalent positions.

It was at this time that practical measures against slavery began to be taken. Typically, the lead was given by small Protestant sects, rather than the major Churches. John Wesley. for the newly founded Methodists, preached vigorously against slavery, both in England and in the American colonies. Quakers in Pennsylvania and Massachusetts refused to have slaves. In Pennsylvania, gradual emancipation began in 1780, and in Rhode Island and Connecticut in 1784. There were bans on the slave trade, though not on actual slave-holding,

DESCRIPTION OF A SLAVE SHIP.

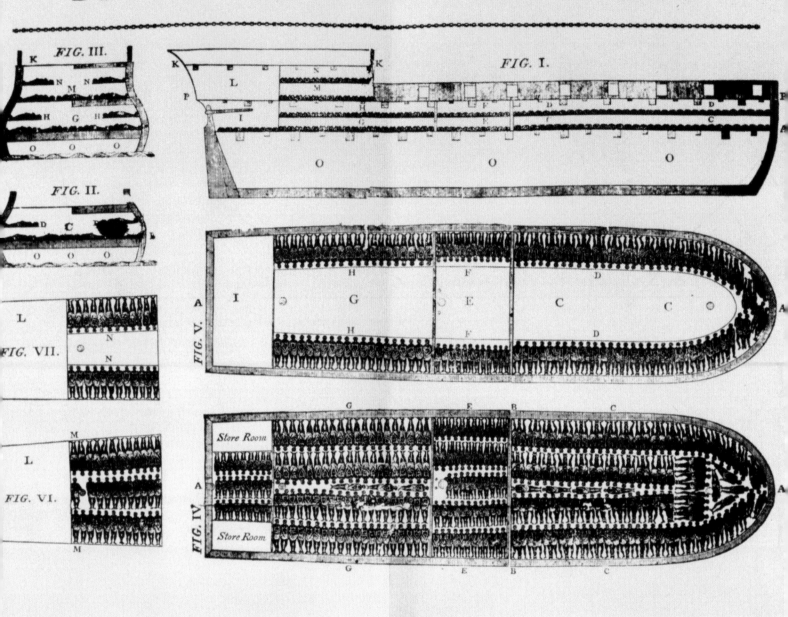

FIG. III.   FIG. I.

FIG. II.

FIG. VII.

FIG. VI.

FIG. V.   Store Room   Store Room   FIG. IV.

The PLAN and SECTIONS annexed exhibit a slave ship with the slaves stowed. In order to give a representation of the trade against which no complaint of exaggeration could be brought by those concerned in it, the vessel here described, a ship well known in the trade, and the first mentioned in the report delivered to the House of Commons last year by Captain Parrey, who was sent to Liverpool by Government to take the dimensions of the ships employed in the African slave trade from that port. These plans and sections are on a scale of the 8th of an inch to a foot.

DIMENSIONS OF THE SHIP.

	Feet	Inches
Length of the Lower Deck, gratings and bulk-heads included at AA	100	0
Breadth of Beam on the Lower Deck inside, BB	25	4
Depth of Hold, OOO from ceiling to ceiling	10	0
Height between decks from deck to deck	5	8
Length of the Mens Room, CC on the lower deck	46	0
Breadth of the Mens Room, CC on the lower deck	25	4
Length of the Platforms, DD in the mens room	46	0
Breadth of the Platforms in mens rooms on each side	6	0
Length of the Boys Room, EE	13	9
Breadth of the Boys Room, EE	25	0
Length of Platform, FF in boys room	13	9
Breadth of Womens Room, GG	28	6
Length of Womens Room, GG	16	6
Breadth of Platforms, HH in womens room	28	6
Breadth of Platforms in womens room	6	0
Length of the Gun Room, II on the lower deck	10	6
Breadth of the Gun Room on the lower deck	12	0
Length of the Quarter Deck, KK	33	6
Breadth of the Quarter Deck	19	6
Length of the Cabin, LL	14	0
Height of the Cabin	6	2
Length of the Half Deck, MM	16	6
Height of the Half Deck	6	2
Length of the Platforms, NN on the half deck	16	6
Breadth of the Platforms on the half deck	6	0
Upper deck, PP		

Nominal tonnage — 297
Supposed tonnage by measurement — 309
Number of seamen — 45

The number of slaves which this vessel actually carried appears from the accounts given to Captain Parrey by the slave-merchants themselves as follows:

Men	—	351	
Women	—	127	Total 609
Boys	—	90	
Girls	—	41	

The room allowed to each description of slaves in this plan is
To the Men 6 feet by 1 foot 4 inches.
Women 5 feet 10 in. by 1 foot 4 in.
Boys 5 feet by 1 foot 2 in.
Girls 4 feet 6 in. by 1 foot.

With this allowance of room the utmost number that can be stowed in a vessel of the dimension of the Brooks, is as follows, (being the number exhibited in the plan) and is 1½ to a ton, viz. †

	On the Plan	Actually carried
Men—on the lower deck, at CC	124	
Ditto on the platform of ditto, CC DD	66	
Boys—lower deck EE	58	
Ditto—platform FF	24	
Women—lower deck, GG	83	
Ditto—platform, HH	40	
Women Half deck, MM	36	
Platform ditto, NN	24	
Girls Gun room, II	27	41
General total	**482**	**609**

The principal difference is in the men. It must be observed, that the men, from whom only insurrections are to be feared, are kept continually in irons, and must be stowed in the room allotted for them, which is of a more secure construction than the rest.

In this ship the number of men actually carried was — 351
The number of men stated in the plan at 1 foot 4 inches each — 190
Difference — 161

LONDON: PRINTED BY JAMES PHILLIPS, GEORGE-YARD, LOMBARD-STREET.

'**Phillis Wheatley**, Negro Servant to Mr John Wheatley of Boston', had risen above her degraded condition to show that she was as intelligent and sensitive as her white owner. Her *Poems on Various Subjects, Religious and Moral* was published in 1773.

in Connecticut, Massachusetts, New York and Pennsylvania in 1788, and in Delaware in 1789. Mass agitation against slavery began in Britain, after prolonged struggle saw the slave trade banned in 1807. This was an equivocal victory. It was not until 1834 that slavery itself was outlawed in British possessions in the Caribbean. Slave-holding did not become illegal in the United States until the adoption of the Thirteenth Amendment to the Constitution in 1865. Slavery did not end in Brazil until 1888.

Slavery, which has been known in practically every time and culture, was thus a tenacious and highly profitable institution. It was one of the strongest underpinnings of the globalization process, part of an integrated world economy. It was also attacked in the Enlightenment far more strongly and effectively than before. Thinking about slavery brought many Enlightenment issues to the surface. One of the most important concerned the authority of the Bible. Small Protestant Churches such as Quakers, Methodists or Moravians were the first to attack the institution of slavery. But on what basis? They were all tied to a notion of biblical authority, yet there was no biblical support for abolitionism. Numerous Old Testament passages revealed the patriarchs holding slaves. The was no divine pronouncement against it. In the New Testament there is no discussion of the issue, and abolitionists had to fall back for legitimation on allegorical interpretations of the 'freedom' which comes to us from Christ. Pro-slavery opinion certainly did better here than did abolitionist groups. Struggles over the authority of the Bible also showed the difficulty of using it as an authoritative document. How much authority did the new Enlightenment ideals of benevolence and universal charity have measured against the Bible?

The search for appropriate authority in the conflict between pro- and anti-abolitionists ended in the law courts. Probably the most famous case of the century involving slavery concerned James Somerset, a slave held by a Boston trader called Charles Stuart. When Stuart came to England, he brought Somerset with him. When in October 1771 their return to Virginia drew near, Somerset deserted his master. Stuart recaptured him and imprisoned him in a ship waiting at anchor in the port of London and making ready for the voyage to Jamaica, where Somerset was to be sold. Stuart was using his power to dispose absolutely of Somerset as his property. Anti-slavery activists such as Granville Sharpe organized lawyers to act on Somerset's behalf, and the case opened before Lord Justice Mansfield in 1772. Stuart's lawyers argued that Somerset had to obey Stuart and return to Virginia, because he was, according to the laws of that state, Stuart's property. Somerset's lawyers argued that, by condemning the return, 'the revival of domestic slavery will be rendered as impracticable by introduction from our colonies and from other countries as it is by commencement here'. Mansfield ruled, with reluctance, that Somerset could not be forced to return to Virginia against his will. He remarked: 'The state of slavery is of such a nature that it is incapable of being introduced on any reasons, moral or political; but only by positive law, which preserves its force long after the reason, occasion and time itself from whence it was created, is erased from memory: it's so odious that nothing can be suffered to support it, but positive law … therefore the black must be discharged.' Somerset was discharged in order to avoid setting a precedent which would be tantamount to introducing slavery into England. Mansfield was also arguing that slavery could only be upheld by positive law, and could receive no support from natural law or from custom. However reluctant he had been to sanction disobedience in an inferior, his judgement implied that Somerset was no longer to be treated like a piece of inanimate property, but as a person entitled to his own will.

Anti-slavery activists hailed the Somerset case as a great victory. But it did not make statute law. It only resolved a particular issue between one slave and his master. The case did not abolish either slavery or the slave trade. But the Somerset case was undoubtedly a publicity success for the anti-slavery movement, and thus contributed to the mass petitioning against slavery which was gaining momentum in the 1770s. It captured the attention of the Methodist leader John Wesley and opened his mind to the evils of slavery, with dramatic consequences when Wesley preached in the British North American colonies. But it did not end slavery.

In spite of such dramas as the Somerset case, we know little about the millions of people displaced in what has been called the largest migration in history. Autobiographies by slaves have come down to us. By their very nature, these autobiographies do not chronicle the lives of ordinary slaves. Historians have often decried the authenticity of these texts, and pointed out their use as abolitionist propaganda. The autobiographies have been subject to literary analysis which shows that were almost all 'ghost-written' for their pretended authors. The autobiography of Olaudah Equiano, who sometimes called himself, or was called, Gustavus Vassa, a treasure trove for abolitionists, was an exception. Historians agree that Equiano, who could read and write, and spoke English well, almost certainly himself composed at least large sections of his autobiography, the *Interesting Narrative of the Life of Olaudah Equiano, or Gustavus Vassa, the African*. Equiano was probably born in around 1745. At the age probably of 12, he and his sister were kidnapped by slavers. He escaped plantation slavery, and was sold to a naval officer, Michael Pascal, who renamed him Gustavus Vassa. After being sold again in 1762, Equiano returned to the Caribbean. After extraordinary efforts, he finally managed to put together enough money to purchase his freedom. Equiano's life as a free man was even more marked by movement than it had been as a slave. From 1767 to 1773, Equiano was based in London, but worked on ships going into the Mediterranean and to the West Indies. He took part in the geographical exploration which was such an essential part of globalization when he joined an expedition to the Arctic in 1773. For years spiritually unsatisfied, Equiano became a Methodist and began to work with abolitionist activists in London in the years following the Somerset case. He published his *Narrative* in 1789 and married an Englishwoman in 1792. He died in 1797.

This extraordinary life story has three major threads: slavery and abolitionism, religious yearning, and travel. There are obvious reasons why Equiano should have been so concerned with slavery, so much so that his autobiography, wrongly, has often been seen as a largely abolitionist tract. Once settled in London, he joined the circle around Granville Sharpe, the abolitionist lawyer. In the wake of the Somerset case, he also tried to rescue John Annis, another slave caught up as Somerset had been with a master who wished forcibly to return him to the Americas. 'I proved the only friend he had, who attempted to regain him his liberty, if possible, having known the want of liberty myself.' Equiano obtained a writ of *habeas corpus* against Annis's master.

The fullest account of a slave's life is that given in the autobiography of Olaudah Equiano, who escaped several times and eventually bought his freedom, became a sailor, joined an expedition to the Arctic and married an Englishwoman. In London he took part in campaigns for the abolition of slavery. He published his life story in 1789 and died in 1797.

Mythical China: Chinoiserie, Mandarins and Markets

The European taste for things oriental – Chinoiserie – was nourished by very large-scale imports from China and Japan. This bureau for filing papers (*above*) was made in Paris in about 1740. The general shape and decoration are fairly mainstream Rococo, but there are numberless touches that betray Eastern influence: the black and gold in imitation of oriental lacquer, the two birds and the Chinese figures with pigtails who sit on either side of the clock.

Vast quantities of Chinese and Japanese ceramics are known to have been brought to Europe in the 17th and 18th centuries, a trade vividly highlighted in recent years when a wreck was discovered at the bottom of the sea off Vung Tau, the southern tip of Vietnam, in 1990. There were over 48,000 pieces of Chinese porcelain, of which these dishes and bowls are just a tiny sample (*opposite*). The ship was probably bound for Batavia in Java, where the cargo would have been sold to the Dutch East India Company for export to Europe. It must have sunk in about 1690.

With globalization came not only the exchange of goods, people and microbes, but also the exchange of images and styles. Of the latter, Chinoiserie must be the most important. Its emergence would have been impossible had it not been for the major European trading contacts with China and India. Without continuous links, such as the Dutch East India Company's presence in Canton or that of the English in India, the craze for Chinoiserie, so often associated entirely with the eighteenth century and with the light, sinuous style of the Rococo, could hardly have lasted as long as it did. It continued through the Victorian era and, in different ways, well into the twentieth century. In the mid-seventeenth century, it was common for ships arriving from the Dutch East Indies to be carrying several thousand pieces of export pottery made in China by Chinese craftsmen, but geared to the stylistic demands of European markets. In February 1661, for example, a Dutch East India Company ship arrived with 1,100 pieces of Japanese porcelain, 900 pieces of Chinese porcelain, 125 small parasols and 200 large parasols. On 12 February two more ships brought a further 5,990 Japanese cups, 400 large porcelain vases, 1,062 plates and 500 jugs. The demand was for brighter colours and more complex designs than those used on classical Chinese ware.

In the 1680s, a new stimulus was given to the craze for Chinoiserie by a series of events. In 1684 and 1686, two embassies from the king of Siam to the French court allowed artists and designers to have contact with Franciscan friars. In 1697, 45 volumes of Chinese paintings were presented to King Louis XIV. After the Siamese embassies, the French court also took up Chinoiserie, a powerful incentive for its adoption throughout Europe. By the 1730s Antoine Watteau had begun to paint scenes which were to become the models for Chinoiserie in France and Europe.

All this was given powerful impetus by the fact that China was probably the only oriental state respected by the European Enlightenment. Europeans commended what they thought was a society governed by wise mandarins. Deists saw the teachings of Confucius as parallel with their own. Voltaire's play *L'Orphelin de la Chine* (*The Orphan of China*) was decribed by him as 'a dramatization of the morals of Confucius'. Chinese 'visitors' were routinely used as satirical commentators in the pamphlets of the time. The philosopher Leibniz wrote an entire work on China. Jesuits revered China and at one time tried to syncretize Buddhism and Catholicism. Both Friedrich Schiller and the Italian playwright Carlo Gozzi wrote plays entitled *Turandot* (the origin of the later opera by Puccini, based on Chinese legend).

All these facts constitute a difficult problem in the history of Chinoiserie. To what extent was Chinoiserie modelled on real Chinese or oriental models, and to what extent was it a European creation? Art historians such as Hugh Honour tend to argue that Chinoiserie had very little to do with genuine Chinese styles, textiles and china, but instead reflected a European dream of 'Cathay' founded upon the travels of Marco Polo, the mythical travels of Sir

Import and imitation: the figurines with rockwork, globes and dragons are Chinese, probably brought to Europe in the 18th century (*left*). But the 'Japanese' lady holding an umbrella over a gentleman (*below*) was made in Meissen in about 1743 after a model by J.J. Kändler.

Among the tapestries commissioned from the Beauvais workshop about 1700 by the comte de Toulouse, already illustrated on p. 140, is this scene of the harvesting of pineapples (*opposite*). Together the set formed *L'Histoire de l'empereur de la Chine*, made under the direction of Philippe Béhagle. Dress, fruit, flowers and buildings all betray a close study of Chinese originals.

OVERLEAF
A French artist imagines what a Chinese emporium would look like. Everything that had ever come to Europe from China is included in this scene: screens, lacquered cabinets, vases, pots of all shapes and sizes, paintings, fans, textiles, porcelain animals and (least convincing) Chinese customers themselves.

John Mandeville and the thirteenth-century accounts of missionary journeys to the Mongol court by two Franciscan friars. Very little in fact was known about this distant kingdom by ordinary people. The same went for India, Siam and Japan. It is not surprising that different Chinese, Japanese and Indian styles were very often fused together. Similarly, the often accurate versions of Chinese products held by professional Sinologues such as Du Halde were sometimes confused with the delightful fantasies of artists and interior decorators. But we may in fact underestimate the extent of the overlap between these fantasies and the real China such as that presented by Du Halde or the volumes of pictures of China drawn from life by Jesuit missionaries presented to Louis XIV in 1697. The question of the realism of the Chinoiserie style must therefore remain open. It is far less straightforward than art historians have often proclaimed.

The elements of Chinoiserie are essentially those of pastoral. Apart from the portrayals of gods and goddesses based on Watteau's famous image which stands at the head of the Chinoiserie style, the basic elements consist of laughing children, fishing parties, dancing, young ladies idly swinging, solemn priests, pagodas, elegant young mothers with pigtails, lovers dallying in bamboo arbours, parasols, canopies suspended in mid-air, temples open to the sky, and a general air of gaiety and playfulness. Some of these motifs were also to be found in eighteenth-century French paintings, which set the tone for the rest of Europe. It was no accident that Boucher, who specialized in scenes of sensuous love-making, should also be the director of the Gobelins royal tapestry works, where so many tapestries were turned out to support the vogue for Chinoiserie.

If we examine the Chinoiserie style as a whole, however, we notice many factors which make it very different from much of the art of this period. First, in no sense could Chinoiserie ever be used as a style to glorify a ruler. Versailles could not have been built in the Chinoiserie style. It is also significant that buildings in the Chinoiserie style for royalty tended to be exactly places where they rested from the cares of state: for instance, the Chinese pavilion called

For the artists of the Rococo Chinese subjects were merely picturesque and exotic. Any deeper meanings that such images might have had at home were lost. Even the archetypally French François Boucher could not resist the temptation to try his hand at Chinoiserie. His *Chinaman Fishing* (*below*) was painted in 1742. *Opposite: The Empress's Tea.* *Above*: from *The Astronomers*. Both of the latter are details of the Beauvais tapestry set.

'Kina' which was built for the Swedish royal family at Haga, six miles from the main royal palace. Another still surviving example is in the grounds of the palace at Drottningholm or Frederick II's 'Chinese' (often called 'Japanese') tea house in the royal park at Potsdam near Berlin. A second feature of Chinoiserie is the abandonment, in most drawings at least, of both background and perspective. Perspective especially had been one of the features of European art since the fifteenth century. Its abandonment had the effect of making possible the playful effects of which Chinoiserie is full and which arise from its two-dimensional character. It also separated it from both the representative buildings of the Baroque and Rococo styles and the imagery drawn from classical mythology which dominated painting and architecture. Contemporaries were not slow to notice this. As the bluestocking Lady Mary Wortley Montagu wrote of Chinoiserie in a 1749 letter: 'Apollo and Venus must give way to a fat idol with a sconce on his head.'

The abandonment of symbolism was even more serious. The figures in Chinoiserie hardly ever have any symbolic meaning in the Western tradition. This is another reason why Chinoiserie cannot be a representative style. It also accounts for its feeling of playfulness. There simply is no space for the laborious interpretations of symbolic meanings which exist in mainstream Western art. There is no way that Chinoiserie features could have been used to ornament either the inside or outside of large-scale buildings, the style's application being confined instead to often temporary buildings, china, wallpaper, garden ornaments and textiles. Indeed, unintentionally, it offered one of the first successful challenges to the Enlightenment conventions of art.

He 'then proceeded immediately to that well-known philanthropist, Granville Sharpe Esq. who received me with the utmost kindness, and gave me every instruction that was needful on the occasion. I left him in full hopes that I should gain the unhappy man his liberty, with the warmest sense of gratitude towards Mr. Sharpe for his kindness. But alas! my attorney proved unfaithful… and when the poor man arrived at St. Kitts he was, according to custom, staked to the ground with four pins through a cord, two on his wrists and two on his ankles, was cut and flogged most unmercifully, and afterwards loaded cruelly with irons around his neck. I had two very moving letters from him while he was in this situation: and I made attempts to go after him at great hazard, but was sadly disappointed.'

After his failure to rescue John Annis, Equiano fell into a spiritual crisis. His is a spiritual autobiography, just as much as and even more than it is a simple story of his life in slavery and freedom. The spiritual autobiography was a genre which detailed its subject's struggle for belief in salvation and which already had a long history behind it in the eighteenth century. As Equiano describes his spiritual crisis: 'I was under strong convictions of sin, and thought that my state was worse than any man's, and viewed all things around me as emptiness and vanity, which could give no satisfaction for a troubled conscience.'

Equiano's spiritual odyssey happened at the same time as his physical odyssey. As already noted, he travelled no less when he was free than when he had been a slave. He confessed to a 'roving disposition' and a desire to see 'as

'Bahama Banks, 1767': an illustration from Equiano's autobiography describing the storms encountered by his ship, the *Nancy*.

many different parts of the world as I could'. His travels, sometimes as an ordinary seaman, sometimes as ship's barber, took him from Turkey to the Arctic, from Naples to the Americas. His was a global life, showing him a prodigy of adaptation. Continually moving from one culture into another, from one language into another, from one religion into another, Equiano's life shows how much globalization depended upon an almost infinite human capacity to adapt.

Around slavery was also built a supportive edifice of racial thinking. One of the consequences of the different peoples of the earth coming more into contact with each other was the urge – in Europe at least – to find a theory of race. By the end of the century assertions were commonplace that black Africans formed a race uniquely fitted for slavery, even that it was 'natural' to them. Satires on this point of view had not been wanting. The French thinker Montesquieu remarked ironically in his *De l'esprit des lois* that he could defend slavery by pointing out that 'Those concerned are black from head to toe. And they have such flat noses that it is impossible to feel sorry for them. One cannot get it into one's mind that God, who is a very wise being, should have put a soul, above all a good soul, into a body that was entirely black. It is impossible for us to assume that these people are men because if we assumed they were men one would begin to believe that we ourselves are not Christians.'

In spite of protests such as these, however, it was easy for Europeans to make a connection between race and slavery. Indentured labour by Europeans died out by the mid-century. From the end of the seventeenth century the slaves who reached North America, Brazil and the Caribbean were almost all black Africans. This allowed debates on slavery to become connected with debates about race. It is in this century that man becomes an 'object of natural history', as Thomas Jefferson wrote in his 1781–82 *Notes on the State of Virginia*, an object to be subjected to scientific scrutiny, with the Negro as the test case. Both the philosopher Montesquieu and the French naturalist Buffon argued that appearance, disposition and temperament were not innate, but shaped by climate and geography. The dark skin of the Negro was thus an acquired characteristic. The hot sun of Africa had given him his dark skin. If he were to move to more temperate regions, the skin colour of his race would gradually become lighter.

By the end of the century, things had begun to change. Anatomists Petrus Camper and the Göttingen professor Johann Friedrich Blumenbach began to work on a racial theory not so much concerned with skin colour as with 'deeper' differences such as skeletal structure and cranium size. This was a very new way of thinking about race. The two anatomists argued from skeletal structure that the difference between races seemed to go well beyond what could be accounted for by climate and environment. Racial difference started to sound both inevitable and ineluctable. Such studies had ambiguous effects. Both Blumenbach and Camper appeal to the universal human bond. But their work legitimated the idea of a hierarchy of races, and indirectly aided the pro-slavery cause. Thomas Jefferson, later third president of the United States, suspected that 'the blacks, whether originally a distinct race, or made distinct by time and circumstances, are inferior to the whites in the endowments both of body and mind. It is not against experience to suppose that different species of the same genus, or variations of the same species, may possess different qualifications ... This unfortunate difference of colour and perhaps of faculty,

The analysis of racial differences became a typical subject of enlightened scientific study. One of its pioneers was the German anatomist Johann Friedrich Blumenbach, whose work comparing the skulls of diverse races was published in 1740.

Blumenbach's comparisons between the skulls of various races did not necessarily help the abolitionist cause, since his findings could be used to support theories of the superiority of the Europeans. Men such as Thomas Jefferson were horrified at the thought of compromising racial purity by mixing peoples.

is a powerful obstacle to the emancipation of these people.' In fact, Jefferson displays an exaggerated concern for the purity of race. In his *Notes on the State of Virginia*, he uses the language of natural history to argue that if they were freed, emancipation should be immediately followed by the deportation of all former slaves. He exclaims: 'Will not a lover of natural history then, one who views the gradations in all the races of animals with the eye of philosophy, excuse an effort to keep those in the department of man as distinct as nature has formed them? ... Among the Romans, emancipation required but one effort. The slave, when made free, might mix with, without staining, the blood of his master. But with us a second is necessary, unknown to history. When freed, he is to be removed beyond the reach of mixing.' The emancipated slave is to be immediately deported, before sexual relations with white people can occur. Jefferson here both acknowledges and denies that African slaves are of the same race as whites. He thought slaves were human, but did not want to face the consequences of seeing them as so human that they could form sexual relationships with whites. Jefferson's thinking on slavery was fragile and conflicted. In that he was hardly unique. Like many others who detested slavery, he continued to hold slaves, and like many others who detested racial mixture, he had a long relationship with a slave woman. Such contradictions made themselves felt at the political as well as the personal level. In a letter of June 1786, very shortly after the foundation of the American republic, he bemoaned the state of Virginia's failure to legislate for slave emancipation, thus inflicting on slaves 'bondage more dreadful than that which they had risen against from England'. The new state, whose founders claimed liberty for themselves as an inalienable right but simultaneously denied it to their slaves, was left with the serious problem identified by Jefferson. But neither his presidency, nor any subsequent one managed to resolve this contradiction, which was only finally to be resolved by civil war more than 70 years later.

The politics of globalization

The globalizing world of the Enlightenment was not founded solely on the forced links between peoples represented by slavery. The building of a global consciousness also depended largely on the enormous expansion of knowledge of the globe that is an outstanding feature of this time. There has probably never been a time in history, apart from the turn of the fifteenth and sixteenth centuries, which saw the discovery of so many hitherto unknown lands and peoples. In the eighteenth century, Europe explored a second 'New World', as the Australian historian Alan Frost has called it. The greatest of the navigators who went into the Pacific was James Cook, who was killed on the newly discovered island of Hawaii in 1779. Cook was to make three voyages into the Pacific, in 1768–71, 1772–75 and 1776–78, and the result was a substantial proportion of all our current knowledge of the ocean.

Of the vastness of the Pacific, which covers one-third of the earth's surface and contains more, probably, than 25,000 islands, it is even now difficult to conceive. Cook sailed into it at a time when most of it was uncharted, and when only a few European ships entered it each year. On his first voyage, Cook sailed into the Pacific with a single ship, the *Endeavour*. He mapped the east coast of Australia and claimed it for King George III, established that New Zealand is composed of two islands, and discovered more than 100 islands.

Z

1

C.F.S.Reuſs. del:

Cook's voyages were the first to be deliberately organized for the acquisition of new knowledge. His death at the hands of Hawaiian islanders has been variously depicted. In the more familiar picture, reproduced on pp. 128–29, he is shown trying to pacify the two sides and being struck down from behind. A recently rediscovered watercolour (*right*) is probably more accurate. Cook, in white, is taking an active part in the melee.

Plants, animals and human artifacts totally new to the West excited enormous interest when Cook brought his collection home. That interest was not confined to his own country. Johann Reinhold Forster sailed with Cook on his second voyage and published his own account of it in 1778 (*opposite*), with illustrations of Barringtonia's fruit and leaves and personal ornaments from the Marquesas Islands. The engraving of the kangaroo is taken from Stubbs' reconstruction based on a kangaroo skin.

Behind exploration often lay geopolitical motives. There were massive shifts in the balance of power among the European states after the end of the Seven Years' War in 1763. Britain replaced France as the major European power both in India and in what is now Canada, becoming for the first time a global power, owner of an empire so vast and so scattered that it could only be defended and administered by control of the seas. It was no wonder that Cook was sent to explore the Pacific. The search to establish spheres of influence in hitherto unknown and unexplored territories revealed by exploration was the objective of each of the major colonial powers – Britain, France, Spain and the Netherlands. The extent of their global competition made it a rational goal to try to establish both presence and possession in these wide expanses of the ocean.

Yet the motives of exploration could also be broader than those of geopolitical advantage. Cook's instructions from the Admiralty enjoined him to gather information about animals, peoples and geography. The voyages of exploration of the eighteenth century were the first to be centrally concerned with the gathering of such information. A circumnavigation such as that of the English freebooter William Dampier, who died in 1715, had resulted in the first contact with Australian aboriginal peoples, and the mapping of part of the coastline of western Australia. But these had been the accidental benefits of a voyage whose objectives were loot and plunder. The deliberate search for new knowledge of lands, peoples, plants and animals by Cook and other explorers was thus new.

James Cook undertook his first voyage as part of an international effort to observe the transit of the planet Venus, which thus, rather than geopolitical motives, determined the whole timing of his travels. For Cook and his contemporaries, deliberate gathering of knowledge about new cultures and

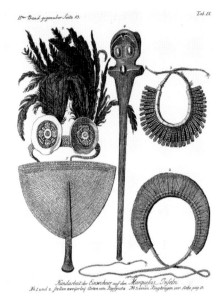

The new world discovered by Cook was revealed to the reading public at second-hand. Cook gave his notes to a professional writer, John Hawkesworth, who in important respects misrepresented what Cook wanted to say. This applied particularly to the expedition's stay in Tahiti (*right, below and opposite top*), which Hawkesworth represented as an island paradise of sublime mountains and lush scenery inhabited by endless numbers of beautiful, permanently available girls – an idea which took over a century to fade.

AN
ACCOUNT
OF THE
VOYAGES
UNDERTAKEN BY THE
ORDER OF HIS PRESENT MAJESTY
FOR MAKING
Discoveries in the Southern Hemisphere,
And successively performed by
COMMODORE BYRON, CAPTAIN CARTERET,
CAPTAIN WALLIS, And CAPTAIN COOK,
In the DOLPHIN, the SWALLOW, and the ENDEAVOUR:
DRAWN UP
From the JOURNALS which were kept by the several COMMANDERS,
And from the Papers of JOSEPH BANKS, Esq;
By JOHN HAWKESWORTH, LL.D.
IN THREE VOLUMES.
Illustrated with CUTS, and a great Variety of CHARTS and MAPS relative to
Countries now first discovered, or hitherto but imperfectly known.
VOL. I.

LONDON:
Printed for W. STRAHAN; and T. CADELL in the Strand.
MDCCLXXIII.

The Romantic image of the South Sea Islands was consolidated by Sir Joshua Reynolds's portrait of Omai (*below*), who returned with Cook from Tahiti in his second voyage in 1773. Omai seems indeed to have been a pleasant and intelligent (not to mention courageous) young man, but Reynolds, by dressing him in a turban and flowing robe and giving him a classical pose, makes him a type of the 'noble savage'. After two years Cook took him back to Tahiti and he died before 1785.

new areas of the natural world was high on the agenda. Exploration in the Enlightenment was reconfigured into an information-gathering activity. Nor was the knowledge recovered by Cook and other explorers simply an addition to scientific knowledge. It also became key to several Enlightenment debates on the nature of man.

However, when Cook returned to London after his first voyage, he found that the new information which he had gathered had already become enmeshed in some very different concerns from the information-gathering which had been his objective while at sea. He entrusted, with considerable later regret, his notes on the voyage to a professional popularizer and ghost-writer named John Hawkesworth. From them Hawkesworth produced a European best-seller by focusing on Cook's stay in Tahiti, which, over Cook's protests, he represented as an island paradise, full of sexual freedom. According to Hawkesworth, the climate removed any need for labour and care, and produced an egalitarian society watched over by 'kings' and 'queens'. That this was a misrepresentation of Tahitian society goes without saying. But it was a misrepresentation which Europeans wanted and needed to believe. Tahiti was a projection screen for European desires. The vision of Tahiti emerged in a Europe increasingly concerned with issues of individual liberty and equality, power, corruption and justice. There could have been no better timing for the appearance of such a fantasy. Hawkesworth's vision of Tahiti purported to show that utopias, far from being literary confections, could really exist in an actual location where the people really were natural, simple and free. This vision of Tahiti as a real-life utopia was only further enhanced by visits to London and Paris by the natives of Tahiti Omai and Atourou, and was prolonged by the appearance of poems and plays about Tahiti which were performed to full houses.

No century before the Enlightenment had ever witnessed the publication of so many accounts of newly discovered places and cultures. The first edition of Hawkesworth's account of Cook's voyage, and that of the contemporary

French explorer Louis-Antoine de Bougainville, sold out in a few days. There were also new sources of information. For the first time, naval expeditions of discovery carried professional artists, whose images of hitherto unknown plants, peoples and animals could be cheaply reproduced by means of engravings. As the Australian historian Bernard Smith has demonstrated, these images gave a new and highly charged aesthetic dimension to exploration. Without them it is impossible to understand the impact of cross-cultural encounters on Enlightenment Europe. The printed accounts and images of the new and the exotic became an important part of the European repertoire of ideas, hopes and feelings. This flow of information and imagery was eagerly taken up by a reading public defining itself as enlightened precisely in virtue of its encounter with the printed word, theatrical performance and the pictures given wide currency by engraving. It was this expansion of the culture of print and reading that allowed cross-cultural encounters beyond the edges of the known world to become the imaginative property of ordinary Europeans who never ventured far from home.

Can cultures meet?

Thus the information – or quasi-information – provided by Hawkesworth really did have an impact which can be measured up and down the social scale. Its insertion into more specific debates on the nature of man and society was also important. There were, however, problems. In April 1776, Cook himself had confessed to James Boswell, the biographer of Dr Johnson, that 'he and his companions who visited the South Seas could not be certain of any information they got, except as to objects falling under the observation of the senses, and anything which they learnt about religion, government, or traditions might be quite erroneous'. Cook's confession pointed to an important problem for Enlightenment thinkers. Was it possible to transmit knowledge between incommensurable cultures? If so, then was it likely or possible that human beings from different cultures were more like each other than unlike, and might well share a similar rationality? And if so, why were there such differences between cultures? Would it ever be possible, especially on basis of information provided by Cook and other explorers, to construct a universal human subject for the new global world?

The question of the commensurability of cultures was also important for those who were involved in the construction of what contemporaries called the 'science of man', which would integrate knowledge into a law-based, scientific explanation for the diversity of cultures and human beings.

Explorers were the vital information-gatherers for this enterprise. The German scholar Johann Reinhold Forster, who sailed on Cook's second voyage, remarked, in a way which captures the initial excitement of the new, in his essay 'Cook the Discoverer': 'Let us look, however, as the most important object of our researches, at our own species; at just how many races, with whose very name we were formerly unacquainted, have been described down to their smallest characteristics, through the memorable efforts of this great man! Their physical diversity, their temperament, their customs, their modes of life and dress, their form of government, their religion, their ideas of science and works of art, in short everything was collected by Cook for his contemporaries and for posterity with fidelity and tireless diligence.'

Yet such information-gathering was beset with problems. Cook's scrupulous avowal to James Boswell should be remembered. The incident with which we began this chapter shows Cook's difficulty in making any contact with the Maoris he encountered. In the absence of a common language, Cook made contact by using small and (to him) unthreatening objects – his handkerchief, some pieces of paper. Objects could hardly be more important in these encounters. Cook rubs noses with the Maori and at the same time makes the transition from boat to shore. He moves out of his own world and into the Maori's. In the island world of the Pacific, the defining place of contact is the beach. Cook himself was to die on Kealaekua Beach in Hawaii in February 1779. The ever-present fear was that, in the absence of a common language, and in ignorance of the meaning of body language in each culture, every encounter could easily turn into violence. These are not promising conditions for the gathering of information.

Another obstacle to information-gathering came from the Europeans. They idealized Tahiti and other Pacific islands, but they also saw the islanders in terms of their own societies. They made faction leaders into kings and queens and gave names from the *Odyssey* and *Iliad* to islanders they encountered. It was probably the ordinary seamen, who entered into sexual and formal friendship relations with islanders, who got to know most about the real nature of island societies. A mixture of idealization and realism was otherwise present in almost

The 'Tahitian girl' whom Louis-Antoine de Bougainville claimed to have seen on his voyage of 1768–69 was surely not drawn by an artist on the spot. The illustration is included in his account of 1771, but owes more to the popular genre of travellers' tales and vaudeville.

The landscape at least can be trusted. William Hodges was Cook's official artist on his second voyage and this view of Tahiti was painted from sketches made at the time. Note, for instance, the anthropomorphic carving of a deified ancestor on the right. Even so, Hodges could not entirely escape the conventions of his time. The mountains are even more romantic, the idyllic atmosphere more Arcadian and the figures in the foreground and in the water more European than Polynesian, in spite of the anthropologically authentic tattoos of the nearest woman.

A serious approach on the part of European philosophers and churchmen to the moral problems of the clash of cultures produced thinkers such as Count Nikolaus Ludwig von Zinzendorf, who refounded the Moravian Church as a missionary body in the 1730s. Moravian missionaries were established in South Africa, Jamaica, North America and Siberia. Unlike the Jesuits, who had taken their sophisticated theology to China and Japan, the Moravians relied on an essentially simple doctrine of salvation.

every encounter between Europeans and indigenous peoples. A world away from the Pacific, a stereotype developed for example of the American Indian, through writings such of those of the French adventurer Lafiteau, Baron de Lahontan, and Voltaire himself, who, in his short story 'L'Ingénu' ('The Innocent'), created the character of a Huron Indian who wanders through French society with a critical eye. However, the questions of the incommensurability of cultures which bedevilled the science of man became insoluble due to this mixture of literary idealization of and projection onto indigenous societies.

Missionary work was also highly important in the making of a global experience of encounter. Missionary activity outside Europe had begun at the inception of white settlement in the Americas, and had been extended into China and Japan by the Jesuit order by the sixteenth century. In the eighteenth century, Quakers sought for converts among the Indians of Pennsylvania and Delaware, and Jesuits had substantial missions in what are now Venezuela, California, Texas and Mexico. The list could be extended. The Enlightenment also saw the emergence of a new Church whose missions would have been incomprehensible outside a globalizing age. The Moravian Church, founded in the sixteenth century as a radical offshoot of Lutheranism, was refounded as a missionary Church by Count Nikolaus Ludwig von Zinzendorf in the 1730s. Missions were established on the Cape of Good Hope, in Jamaica for the slaves, in Labrador and Greenland among the Inuit, in Pennsylvania among the Indians, in Siberia, in the Russian Arctic and Archangel, even in London.

A Church wholly devoted to the mission field could never have emerged before this age of cross-cultural contact. Zinzendorf described his Church as 'the salt of the earth' to be scattered by God on earth wherever it could most usefully fall. The Moravian Church differed substantially from its parent Lutheran Church in its Christ-centred theology and its emotional appeal. Cutting through generations of complex theology, Moravians believed that the assurance of salvation lay in a child-like surrender to Christ, through and in the heart. This was an experience potentially available to all men, not just Europeans. Theology, instead of being an abstract matter, reached out to the potential convert. This was a Church, tiny in itself, whose organization and theology equipped it for a worldwide mission

Paradoxes of Enlightenment

Enough has been said by now to show the complexity of Enlightenment experiences and responses to a globalizing world. By the last decades of the eighteenth century, as Cook was making his way across the Pacific, a critique of the colonialism which was an essential part the making of the global world had also begun in earnest. Rousseau's *Discourse on Inequality* (1750) had already pointed out that colonialism and the relationships of gross inequality which it fostered constituted a perpetual barrier to the realization of Enlightenment. The existence of slavery in particular contradicted the increasingly important idea that human beings had rights at least partly in virtue of their common humanity. James Cook, whose navigations had done so much to pull together people previously unknown to each other, also clearly saw that indigenous peoples had made only questionable gains by being discovered and colonized. He wrote in his journal: 'What is still more to our shame as civilised Christians,

HISTOIRE
PHILOSOPHIQUE
ET
POLITIQUE

Des Etablissemens et du Commerce des Européens dans les deux Indes.

LIVRE QUATORZIEME.

Établissemens des Anglois dans les isles de l'Amérique.

Un nouvel ordre de choses va se présenter à nos regards. L'Angleterre est, dans l'histoire moderne, la contrée des grands phénomènes politiques. C'est-là qu'on a vu la liberté le plus violemment aux prises avec le despotisme, tantôt foulée sous ses pieds, & tantôt par l'écrasant à son tour. C'est-là qu'elle a fini par triompher, & que, jusqu'au fanatisme de religion, tout a concouru à son triomphe. C'est-là qu'un roi, traîné juridiquement sur l'échafaud, & qu'un autre, déposé avec toute sa race par un arrêt de la nation, ont donné une grande leçon à la terre. C'est-là qu'au milieu des convulsions civiles, & dans les intervalles d'un calme momentané, on a vu les sciences exactes & profondes

For the Abbé Raynal, whose *Histoire philosophique* (*left*) we have met in connection with the slavery issue, that subject was only one aspect of the whole problem of justifying colonialism, which he attempted to do on the grounds that it made a more efficient use of natural resources. This table (*below*) lists the value of goods which Great Britain received annually from the West Indies.

É T A T

Des Productions que la Grande-Bretagne reçoit annuellement de ses Isles des Indes occidentales.

DENRÉES.	QUANTITÉS.	PRIX.			MONTANT.
		liv.	sols		liv.
Sucre	1,600,000 quintaux	à 40		le quintal	64,000,000
Rum de première force	1,200,000 galons	à 3		le galon	3,600,000
Rum plus foible	6,300,000 galons	à 1	10	le galon	9,450,000
Café	73,000 quintaux	à 50		le quintal	2,250,000
Cacao	5,000 quintaux	à 50		le quintal	250,000
Coton	85,000 quintaux	à 150		le quintal	12,750,000
Piment	10,500 quintaux	à 42		le quintal	441,000
Gingembre	3,700 quintaux	à 70		le quintal	259,000
Indigo	40 milliers	à 8		la livre	320,000
Bois de teinture & de marqueterie					500,000
				TOTAL	93,820,000

A British mission arrived in Beijing in 1793 led by Lord Macartney. Its purpose was to negotiate trading terms but the emperor, Ch'ien-lung, could conceive of it only as an offering of tribute by the king of England, whose 'respectful submission' he commended. Macartney tried to impress the imperial court by his train of 90 wagons, 200 horses and 3,000 coolies carrying expensive presents, and clearly to some extent he succeeded, judging by this tapestry depicting 'The Arrival of the Ambassador Ma-Kha-Erh-Ni Bringing Tribute from the King of the Red-Haired People of England'. It is doubtful, however, whether the artist actually witnessed the scene. His Englishmen were copied from earlier pictures of Elizabethans and his globe and armillary sphere from Dutch instruments – made far too big.

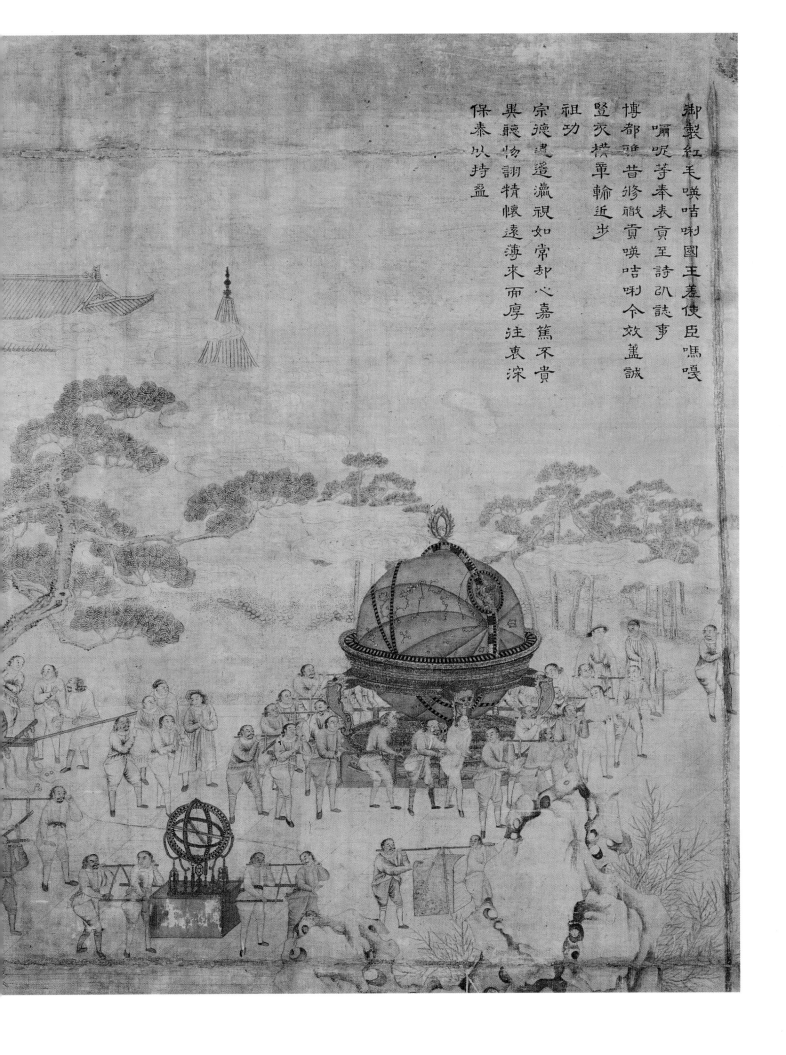

御製紅毛嘆咭唎國王差使臣嗎嘎

嘅呢茇奉表貢至詩以誌事

博都雅昔修職貢嘆咭唎今效藎誠

豎亥横軍輸近步

祖功

宗德逮遙瀛視如常却心嘉篤不貴

異聽物詢精懷遠薄來而厚注衷深

保泰以持盈

we debauch their morals already too prone to vice, and we introduce among them wants and perhaps disease which they never before knew, and to disturb that happy tranquillity which they and their forefathers enjoyed. If anyone denies the truth of this assertion let him tell me what the natives of the whole extent of America have gained by the commerce they have had with Europeans.' On the other side, many Enlightenment people still accepted that it was the duty of man to exploit the earth's resources (by forced labour if necessary), and viewed commerce itself, including the growing colonial trade partly supported by slavery, as a positive ethical value. Unanswerable problems abounded. What would be the cost of ending slavery, or of ending colonialism?

Raynal's massive work is valuable to us as a compendium of all the Enlightenment knew of this topic of the history of colonialism. It is also a compendium of the ambivalent attitudes which underpinned the Enlightenment's relationship with colonialism. Raynal admits that in principle reason and equity do not provide any justification for slavery or colonialism. But he then argues that in practice the latter can be justified because it aids the spread of 'civilization', or permits the better exploitation of natural resources. Raynal admits that slavery is unjustifiable. Nevertheless, he falls short of demanding its immediate abolition: slaves would not know what to with their freedom, and the collapse of plantation economies would unleash disorder and violence.

By the end of the century, considerably more direct criticism was being levelled at the European colonialism which was one of the mainstays of the making of a global world. By the time of the French Revolution, unresolved political and economic problems could no longer be projected onto the peoples of the Pacific or the American Indian. Ideas that exotic peoples were somehow happy and natural were superseded by a new vision – that of corrupted indigenous peoples, perhaps facing extinction. Probably the most powerful critic of colonialism was the German thinker Johann Gottfried Herder, who began to explore the European impact on exotic societies as a way into a critique of the Enlightenment. Herder challenged the optimistic view of human history held by many Enlightenment thinkers. It was argued by the French thinkers Condorcet and Turgot, who were among the first to work on a theory of globalization, that human beings by virtue of their common humanity would possess reason and would gradually discard superstition, and bring human affairs into harmony with the universal natural order. The progress of history would therefore result in an increasing harmonization of cultures into a world culture, so that mankind would become a cosmopolitan whole.

Herder strongly rejected these ideas, which gave all too much justification for colonialism as a way of forcing European ideas of 'progress' onto indigenous peoples. The high-minded men of the Enlightenment had in this way justified the dominance of European cultures over others by positing a universal human nature somehow independent of history, culture or climate.

He quarrelled with the 'general philosophical philanthropic tone of our century which wishes to extend our own ideal or virtue and happiness to each distant nation … it has taken words for works, Enlightenment for happiness, greater sophistication for virtue, and in this way invented the fiction of the general amelioration of the world.'

It is difficult to quarrel with Herder's views. The enormous progress towards a global world witnessed by the Enlightenment was bought at a high cost. The global world of the Enlightenment set the agendas which still concern us, and have turned into real-life problems of cultural conflict, relativism and the fate of indigenous peoples under globalization, to name only a few.

In 1793 Lord George Macartney landed in China at the head of a diplomatic mission to the emperor of China. He brought with him numerous gifts including astronomical models, reflecting telescopes, chandeliers, air pumps and electrical machines. Arriving in the Celestial Empire, Macartney reached the recently constructed Summer Palace in Beijing. He found, however, that the Chinese were resolutely unimpressed by his gifts. They pointed out how many Western toys they had already received, so many in fact that a special Palace of the Western Ocean had been opened to accommodate them all. They grumbled that Macartney's gifts had little about them that was specific to his country, that they were common to many other countries. The Chinese caught the way in which globalization meant a growing uniformity of technology between Western countries, and showed how Western goods had encircled the globe in order finally to arrive at the Summer Palace, only to meet their counterparts in the Palace of the Western Ocean.

Lord Macartney, depicted here more realistically by the English artist William Alexander, was dismissed rather scathingly by the Chinese emperor with the statement that 'our celestial empire already possesses all things in prolific abundance'.

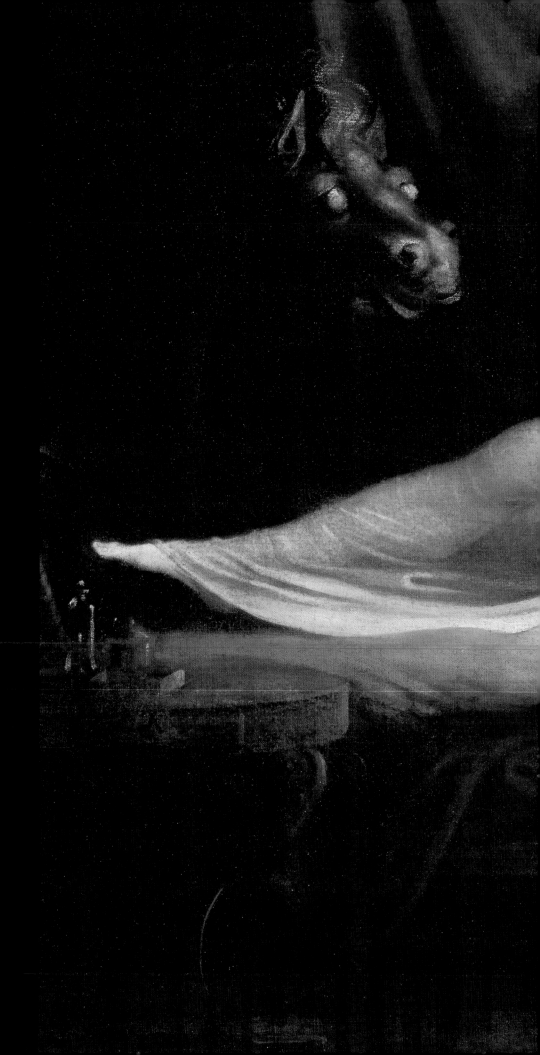

5

Exploring
the Self

One of the paradoxes of the age of light was its fascination with darkness, for bringing reason to bear upon the human psyche meant uncovering a world of unreason – a hidden world of unconscious desires and irrational fears, fully accessible only in dreams, which were systematically recorded and studied as never before. Henry Fuseli's extraordinary painting *The Nightmare* still speaks powerfully to us today even after the revelations of Freud and the discoveries of psychology. It was to be an age of courageous self-examination, of intimate diary-keeping and the probing of character and the emotions in the realistic novel.

'I have entered upon an undertaking which is without example and which, when it is done, will have no imitator. I mean to present my fellow mortals with a man in the complete truthfulness of nature; and this man shall be myself.' So begins Rousseau's *Confessions*, and to a considerable degree he succeeded, revealing intimate details of his life and psychology that most people would prefer to keep secret. It was published after his death with this slightly absurd frontispiece by Claude-Nicolas Cochin, depicting 'Rousseau unveiling his inner self' (*opposite*). One of the most innovatory books ever written, the *Confessions* was a genuine attempt to explore the self. But Rousseau was wrong in thinking that it would have no imitators.

MORE THAN A MILLENNIUM before the Enlightenment, the Greek philosopher Aristotle had taught that to search for self-knowledge was a duty and would help to avoid the sometimes disastrous effects of self-deception. Self-deception meant that one did not stand aright to truth about oneself, and hence one did not stand aright either to oneself or to the surrounding society. Self-deception, lack of knowledge about the reality of oneself, could thus weaken the strength of the entire community. Self-knowledge was an inherently civic, even political duty.

The hard work involved in 'knowing thyself' depended on a sustained attentiveness, a trained awareness of the inner world. Other consequences also followed. Without self-knowledge real love was not possible since the self could never achieve completion in another person. Without self-knowledge, the incomplete self, still searching for completion, was not able to resist conformity to its age. Religious conversion, which was essentially irrational, was almost a parody of Enlightenment. Conversion tested the demand for rationality to the hilt. All these topics – love, conversion and the organized search for the self – are part of this chapter. They are part of the enlightened life, and how they were interpreted not only shaped the values and characters of individuals, but also of whole social groups.

The philosophers

In 1741, Eliza Lucas, a bright, self-educated and independent-minded adolescent girl, born into the planter society of South Carolina, became concerned at her rapid mood swings. By writing her fears into her diary, she tried to regain stability and wholeness, to gain self-knowledge, and thus to have a sense of her self as stable in spite of the bewildering volatility of her emotional life. She was following the ancient injunction 'know thyself' (*nosce te ipsum*). Her diary entries also demonstrate how widely concerns about possessing a coherent self had entered European and American thinking, even so far away from European centres like Paris and London. Eliza also knew where to go to find discussion of her problem: 'I was forced to consult Mr. Locke over and over, to see wherein personal Identity consisted, and if I was the very same Self.'

It was not by chance that Eliza Lucas decided to direct her search for stability, and a secure idea of what it was to be a self, in the direction of the English philosopher and political theorist John Locke. In a famous passage in his 1690 *Essay Concerning Human Understanding*, Locke announced his idea of the way the self is brought into being and begins to experience itself. According to Locke, at the beginning of life, infants come into the world without any innate ideas. They have no experience of themselves, and when newly born may be compared to a blank sheet of paper, awaiting the pen. Locke explains: 'Let us then suppose the mind to be as we say, composed of white paper, void of all characters, without any ideas; how comes it to be furnished? Whence comes it by that vast store which the busy and boundless mind of man hath painted on it with an almost endless variety? Whence has it all the material of reason and knowledge? To this I answer in one word, from EXPERIENCE. In that, all our knowledge is founded, and from that it ultimately derives itself. Our observation employed either about external, sensible objects, or about the internal operations of our minds perceived and reflected upon by ourselves, is that which supplies our understandings with all the material of thinking. These

John Locke, the father of modern empirical philosophy (*right*), traced all knowledge, including self-knowledge, to the impressions of the senses. His *Essay Concerning Human Understanding* (1690) went further than Descartes in arguing that there were no 'innate ideas', and that even abstract thought was based on experience. In England he paved the way for Berkeley and Hume, in France for Diderot and the *Encyclopédie*. A French translation was published in 1751 (*below*).

ABBRÉGÉ
DE
L'ESSAY
DE MONSIEUR
LOCKE,
SUR
L'ENTENDEMENT
HUMAIN,
Traduit de l'Anglois
Par Mr. BOSSET,
NOUVELLE EDITION.

A LONDRES,
Chez JEAN NOURSE.

M. DCC LI.

two are the foundations of knowledge, from whence all the ideas we have, or can naturally have, do spring.'

For Locke, people come to know that they are – or have – individual selves by a twofold activity involving the processing of sense impressions from the outer world, and the practice of introspection into the inner world of the self. His formulation makes it clear that, in describing introspection, Locke understood how reflexive is this practice of the self talking to the self; *nosce te ipsum* enjoined just such an inner conversation.

Locke and others who emphasized introspection were describing Enlightenment as the product of a conversation of the self with the self, not as a gift of light originating from outside themselves. This is very different from the way the gaining of Enlightenment is normally represented as a gift of light without connection to an inner state.

Locke's work stood at the head of a debate which would rage throughout the century. Thinkers became fascinated by the problem of how people came to know themselves as different and distinct from all other people, whether through sense impressions or through introspection. Locke knew that both the individual's sense of his separateness and his capacity to introspect rested on the possession of memory, to the extent that the self was not conceivable except as an entity able to retrieve its specific memories and conscious of its own movement through time. Locke answered the question of what makes a person continue as the same person over time by stressing the importance of the continuity of association of the self with its own memories. Prolonged loss of memory, which often accompanies, for example, concussion, breaks down that continuity on which the self depends. Paradoxically, basing the self on memory and consciousness on sense impressions was to do a great deal to undermine belief in the self as stable and bounded. Both memory and sensory experience are dependent on the outside world and may easily be disrupted.

For Locke, the self and the soul are two distinct entities. The self depends on introspection, on memory and on a consciousness of the passage of time. The soul is eternal, a gift from God, not a product of personal introspection or the processing of sense impressions. It is independent of personal memory and its being can never be interrupted. Separating the soul from the self in this way was a revolutionary idea. A fully secular idea of the self had never before existed. The Churches taught that each human being was given an immortal soul by God, that this soul was a source of eternal yearning for contact with God, that ideas of God were innate in each infant, and permanently present. The last decades of the seventeenth century saw this position begin to break down. Interest began to shift from the soul, an unchanging object given by a power external to each person, to the self, something interior, and constantly in movement to shape and reshape itself. The self was a self-generating system. It did not depend on the gift of the soul, a gift coming from outside the self, from a power infinitely superior to it.

The separation of the soul from the self must rank as one of the most important ways in which the Enlightenment contributed to the making of the modern concept of a person. Basing his ideas once more on theories about newborn infants, Locke argued in the fourth chapter of the *Essay Concerning Human Understanding*: 'If we will attentively consider new born children, we shall have little reason to think that they bring many ideas into the world with them … there is not the least appearance of any settled ideas at all in them, especially of ideas answering the terms which make up those universal propositions which are esteemed innate principles. One may perceive how, by degrees, afterwards, ideas come into their minds and that they get no more, nor no other, than what experience, and the observation of things that come in their way, furnish them with; which might be enough to satisfy us that they are not original characters stamped on the mind.' (The childless philosopher seems to have made little first-hand study of infants.) 'If any idea can be imagined innate, the idea of God may of all others, for many reasons, be thought so, since it is hard to conceive how there should be innate moral principles, without an innate idea of a Deity.' If the idea of a deity were innate, surely we would find it stamped on his creation? 'But how late is it before any such notion is discoverable in children? … it is easy to take notice how their thoughts enlarge themselves only as they come to be acquainted with a greater variety of sensible objects, to retain the ideas of them in their memories and to get the skill to compound and enlarge them and several ways put them together.' Nonetheless, Locke still argues that a god must exist. 'We are capable of knowing certainly that there is a God. Though God has given us no innate ideas of himself, though he has stamped no original characters on our minds, wherein we may read his being; yet having furnished us with those faculties our minds are endowed with, he hath not left himself without witness.'

Even Locke was unable to remove the difficulties caused by reliance on sense impressions as the basis of the self. Was there even any guarantee that each person would experience sense impressions in an orderly enough manner to

The Abbé Condillac (*above*) developed Locke's ideas. For him introspection could only happen through the mediation of language, which thus assumed a more crucial role than Locke had given it. His degree in theology from the Sorbonne and his status as a priest seem not to have had much effect on his religious views. Indeed, he made it more than ever difficult to define the soul as a distinct and enduring entity.

Baron d'Holbach (*below*) worked on, and helped to finance, Diderot's *Encyclopédie*, writing articles on a whole range of subjects from chemistry to Christianity. Among the mechanistic thinkers, he was the most uncompromising atheist, believing that any religion stood in the way of progress. For him only science would solve the problems to which religion claimed to provide answers. The portrait is by Carmontelle.

undergo that reflective processing that Locke described? The Scots philosopher David Hume, in his 1739 *Treatise of Human Nature*, described his own experience of sense impressions: 'I may venture to affirm of mankind, that they are nothing but a bundle or collection of different perceptions, which succeed each other with an inconceivable rapidity, in a perpetual flux and movement.' If selfhood depends on the processing of sense impressions, what happens if people experience themselves as a continuous, rapid flux of impressions rather than a stable, continuous consciousness?

Self and sensation

Hume questioned whether there could be an epistemological unity of consciousness. The French philosopher Condillac in his *Traité des sensations* of 1754 pursued the same theme. While Locke distinguishes two sources of ideas, that is, sensation and reflection, Condillac recognizes but one, and makes reflection and introspection a product of the senses. He wants to solve the problem of the uniqueness of 'me' without having to deal with the soul and self-consciousness. To explain his argument, Condillac dispenses with any hint of the introspection so vital to Locke, and uses only the heuristic device of a living statue which is capable of seeing, hearing, smelling and touching, but can only slowly come to life as parts of its marble covering are endowed with sensation. First, the marble of its nose is made alive. Now the statue has only the sense of smell, but no sense of extension, form, sound or colour. Its consciousness, its 'me', is nothing but the smell of a rose. Since this sensation is the only thing that the statue has experienced, that single sensation becomes its idea of its self. If we take the rose away from the statue, it retains a trace of the scent, and this trace is memory. If a flower with a disagreeable scent – say, of asafoetida – is put before the statue, it compares the scent of the rose against that of the plant

'Man the Machine.' Partly because of his medical training, Julien Offroy de La Mettrie took the mechanistic theory further than even Locke or Condillac and did not shrink from the conclusion that he had eliminated God altogether. This was a step that even the most radical of the *philosophes* were reluctant to take. His book *L'homme machine* (1748) was translated into several languages (*right*) but aroused such hostility that he was obliged to leave France and even the more tolerant Netherlands. He ended his life (relatively early, in 1751, at the age of 42) under the protection of Frederick the Great, who pronounced a eulogy in which he said that La Mettrie was 'born with a fund of natural and inexhaustible gaiety', a judgment that both this portrait (*opposite*) and its inscription confirm.

Sous ces traits vifs, tu vois le Maître
Des jeux, des Ris et des bons mots;
Trop hardi d'avoir de son être,
Osé d'ébrouiller le Cahos,
Sans un sage il étoit la victime des Sots.

Musis Amicus DD de Marschall
Musis amicum sacravit

Fortgesetzte Magie,
oder, die
Zauberkräfte der Natur,
so auf den Nutzen und die Belustigung
angewandt worden,
von
Johann Samuel Halle,
Professoren des Königlich-Preußischen Corps des Cadets
zu Berlin.

Mit 6 Kupfertafeln.

Dritter Band.

Berlin, 1790.
Bey Joachim Pauli, Buchhändler.

with the disagreeable scent. Now the statue has a source of comparison between the scent of asafoetida (unpleasant) and that of the rose (pleasant). The statue compares memory images. It begins to want the one and hate the other. Here arise passions and desires, and the will. The will is not a new faculty added to sensibility; it is a transformation of sensation. For Condillac, the will has nothing to do with the conversation of the self with the self associated with introspection. All qualities, for him, arise from the state of the senses. The statue even produces ideas out of the comparison of copies of the direct sensations of pleasant and unpleasant odours. It directs its attention to two different ideas and compares them. By now it is also capable of abstraction. In this system, abstraction is a modification of sensation, which therefore embraces all the faculties of the soul. The inner perception, or the 'me', is merely the sum of the sensations we now have, but the 'me' so far exists entirely in the world of smells.

Condillac now adds the other senses. Touch reveals to us the objective world by giving us the ideas of extension, form, solidity and body. Even sight cannot suggest them. Echoing the famous 'Cheseldon experiment', Condillac writes that persons born blind cannot, upon receiving their sight, distinguish between a ball and a block, a cube and a sphere, until they touch these objects.

As it comes into full consciousness, the statue utters the painful words: 'I know that that the parts of my body belong to me, but I am unable to understand how. I see myself, I touch myself, in one word, I experience myself, but I do not know what I am. Once I believed that I was sound, taste, colour, smell, but now I know no longer what I should believe that I am.' The statue's words vividly describe the difficulty of founding the concept of the self on sense impressions. Such problems in the definition of the self were insoluble. Strict

La Mettrie's mechanistic explanation of the self encouraged the invention of real machines that could 'think'. It was the beginning of the rage for automata, the most sophisticated of which (illustrated by Carol Gottlieb Windisch, 1783) could actually play chess (*right*) – prefiguring the modern fascination with chess-playing computers which similarly raise the problem of 'artificial minds'. For the 18th century it was almost magic (*above*).

Other automata were constructed to play musical instruments – one (*opposite above*) by Jacques de Vaucanson of 1738 was so convincing that Voltaire called its creator 'a rival to Prometheus, who seemed to steal the heavenly fire in his search to give life'. Another (*opposite below*), by Pierre Jaquet-Droz and his son Henri-Louis in 1774, could even write.

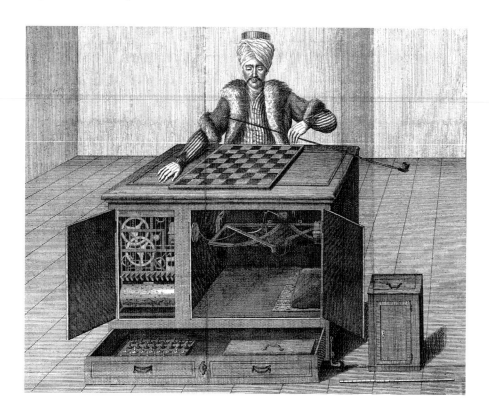

sensationalism such as that of Condillac left so many questions unanswered about the relation between man's physical constitution and his sense of himself as a unique 'I' that it never commanded general assent.

Another attempt to solve this conundrum involved denying the presence both of the soul and of the self, and instead likening man to a machine. This viewpoint was argued among others by Julien Offroy de La Mettrie and Baron Paul d'Holbach, who denied the existence of the soul and made man little more than a living machine. It is easy to see that the views of such philosophers would be anathema to the Christian Churches. La Mettrie's idea in his book *L'Homme machine* that man was a sort of automaton caused a scandal in Paris and in much of western Europe, while his *Histoire naturelle de l'âme* (1745), in which he defended his materialist theses, lost him his post as doctor to the famous regiment of the Gardes Françaises. He spent the rest of his life in Berlin where, quite contrary to his reception in France, Frederick II made him a member of his newly formed Academy of Science, and wrote a eulogy on him upon his death. D'Holbach's immense wealth saved him from the persecution faced by La Mettrie, but his book the *Système de la nature* was nonetheless violently criticized and eventually condemned to be burnt by the public hangman in Paris. D'Holbach describes man's body as made up purely of matter. There is no room for the soul in this thesis.

Masks and Masked Balls: Disguising the Self

FEAR AND WONDER cluster around masks. Central to the ritual life of every known human society, they are worn by men when they need to evoke the powers of nature and come into contact with the spirits of dead. Masks are vital to ceremonies of initiation and of the rituals which mark the passage of the seasons and the stages of life. Masks remind us of powers we might prefer to forget, and of terrors we pretend, as modern people, that we no longer experience. Yet even in this modern age, something of this ritual power, which makes masks into catalytic objects, still survives in the ceremonies and rituals that take place in the Balkans, in Switzerland and south Germany, and all over Italy and Spain. Now, as in the Enlightenment, terrifying whole-body masks portraying giants, or wolves, or shaggy forms with wild and furious faces accompany the celebration of seasonal ritual. These rural masks are quite different from the masks used in urban and courtly masked balls. The full-body masks of the villages had a magical significance which transcended rather than obliterated the identities of those who wore them. The masks of the rural traditions were the mustering places for natural and supernatural powers of which the urban or courtly masquerade had long been oblivious. The games with individual identity which the urban and courtly mask so easily facilitated and focused in the Enlightenment were thus a deviation from the millennial history of the mask.

Enlightenment people were more familiar with the experience of wearing masks, and of establishing relations with other people who were masked, than we can easily imagine today. Masks allowed games with presence and absence to become part of social life. They also allowed mask-wearers to live out the problems debated by philosophers such as Locke and Hume over the nature of human identity. To Locke's dogged struggles to give a new identity to the self, the masquerades opposed a delighted refusal of a unitary self.

In the masked balls, commonly worn costumes allowed everyone to appear that which they were not. Costumes included some which mimicked physical hermaphrodites, and costumes of which one side was male and the other

Pietro Longhi's picture (*above*) is a reminder of the sinister side of the masked ball. A young woman, holding an unopened fan, averts her face from another masked and heavily cloaked figure who clutches at her dress. In the background masked women turn round to stare, and card-players have to abandon their game when their cards drift onto the floor, perhaps symbolizing the instability of fortune. The opportunities which the masked balls provided for intrigues and seduction were stressed by contemporary moralists.

Empress Maria Theresa is portrayed by Liotard in 'Turkish' costume, holding a double mask – a mask painted on to another mask (*left*). The black part of the mask looks like the small ones worn by revellers in the Venetian carnival, which could hide no one's identity, but conventionally discouraged recognition. Masked balls were an important part of the ceremonial life of the court at Vienna.

Such was the fame of the Venetian carnival that in order to take part in it Gustavus Hamilton (*opposite*) travelled from England three times in the 1730s. Hamilton wears the lace veil, the *battuta*, characteristic of carnival costume. Under his tricorne hat is tucked a mask. His face and the mask touch each other. The picture, by Rosalba Carriera, plays with the question: which is his real face?

female, one side soldier and one side demure miss. Other costumes were split down the middle between black and white, or between miller and chimney sweep. This reconciliation of opposites in some costumes was paralleled by those which contained simple reversals. Masqueraders delighted in wearing costumes of the opposite gender; women would arrive at balls dressed as soldiers, priests, cardinals, pirates or grand viziers, while men might appear as nuns or witches. Enlightenment curiosity about the world outside Europe caused costumes of Turkish ladies, Chinamen and American Indians to become even banal. The barriers of class went down, and upper-class men and women appeared dressed as street sellers or servants, peasants or milkmaids. Others appeared as gods and goddesses, mythological heroes, or plants and animals, echoing the themes of Ovid's *Metamorphoses*. Those who could not afford to rent or make such elaborate character costumes could still wear a 'domino', or dark-coloured cloak, reaching from head to toe. Its deep hood hid the wearer as effectively if not more than a mask, and the domino was regarded as the costume which above all facilitated amorous liaisons of all kinds. The masked balls facilitated disguise. They were therefore connected with all that was forbidden socially and sexually: adulterous liaisons, seduction plots, meetings of young lovers without the sanction of marriage or parental approval, transvestism and homosexual affairs for both sexes caused continuous criticism from the guardians of public morals, which as usual failed to deter the public from the much-loved excitement and opportunities of the masquerade.

Many of those attending a ball would wear more than one costume, thus making recognition even more difficult. Thomas Steavens wrote to his friend Sir Charles Hanbury Williams from Vienna on 4 January 1748 about a masquerade early in the carnival season: 'I went first in a woman's dress, and had the finest fun imaginable, several Ladys took me for a whore, and abused me terribly; at last my voice discovered me, and I was obliged to go out for another dress which I had ready, to which I made on purpose. This was that of a madman which was the best and compleatest [*sic*] mask I ever saw, among many other ridiculous things I had a gingerbread Order about my neck. My mask pleased me so extremely that I had a crowd at my heels till the masquerade was over.'

Such delighted responses to the experience of the masquerade could be multiplied a hundredfold. Yet the Enlightenment also heard strong voices raised against masks and masquerades, on deeper grounds than the repression of sexual immorality. Social commentators were concerned with the more general issues of hypocrisy, deceit and insincerity to an extent unparalleled since the Reformation. It was no wonder that the novelist and journalist Daniel Defoe exclaimed in a letter written in 1709: 'This, Sir, is an

A hermaphrodite figure, half soldier and half young lady, takes cherries from a basket (*above*). The scene is doubly erotic because the gender of the figure cannot be known and nor can that of his/her companions. One of a series of frescoes, brilliant *trompe-l'oeil* representations of a masked ball, painted in 1748 for the Schwarzenburg family by the Austrian fresco painter Joseph Lederer in their Bohemian castle of Cesky Krumlov.

Costumes from the *commedia dell'arte* were among the most popular at the masquerade balls. Their use of masks in stage performances made the costumes easy to adapt. This fresco (*opposite*) by G.B. Tiepolo shows Pulchinella, one of the *zanni*, or servant characters, with typical hunchback and tall white cap.

The demand for masks was met by specialized artisans. They made them from materials as diverse as cardboard, velvet, leather or waxed cloth. Here (*left*), in a painting by Giovanni Grevemboch, we can see masks of all kinds, ranging from the standard white Venetian three-quarter mask held by the artisan and the black oval masks fashionable for women to the 'character' masks such as the bearded mask and the mustachiod masks hanging on the wall.

A masked young woman is surrounded by threatening figures in carnival dress (*above*). The caption reads 'No one knows themselves' – an allusion to the old injunction *nosce te ipsum*, or 'know thyself'. In Goya's engraving, from *Los Caprichos*, the mask and the maxim *nosce te ipsum* are incompatible.

Many disapproved of masked balls on moral grounds and Hogarth's engraving (*above*) expresses their views forcefully. Introduced to London by the German entrepreneur Heidegger, these were very different from court and aristocratic masquerades, or the genteel private masked balls of the middle class. Heidegger's entertainments were open to all who could pay, and it was feared that this heterogeneity would enhance the opportunities for immorality already present in the masquerade.

Faces wearing different kinds of mask look down at the rhinocerous during its exhibition in Venice in about 1751 (*opposite*). In Pietro Longhi's painting the three figures cloaked in black wear the conventional white Venetian carnival mask made of plaster on a linen backing. A young mother wears the black oval face mask fashionable for women in this period, and her servant holds another in her hand. Seated nearest the rhinoceros, a woman wears the long lace veil characteristic of the carnival. Her face is so composed that it is difficult to know whether we are seeing her real face or a mask. Only the small child and the rhinoceros' keeper show their natural faces.

age of Plot and Deceit, of Contradiction and Paradox … it is very hard, under all these Masks, to see the true Countenance of any Man.' Defoe's outburst reflects beliefs widely held in the Enlightenment about the persuasiveness and pervasiveness of disguise, the variability of appearance, and its implications for the possibility of a stable, singular human identity. How far is the real person a prisoner of the empire of appearances? Educational thinkers from John Locke in the early eighteenth century onwards argued that practices involving masks and disguises were harmful for children's moral and intellectual training, because they substituted appearance for reality, and paradox for simple truth.

The association of the mask with deceit and hypocrisy, with paradox, and with confusing and frightening games with identity and appearance was thus very present to the eighteenth century. Paradoxically, the wearing of masks was also a widespread practice in the Enlightenment. Even if most regions did not come near the Venetian level of mask-wearing, in all European societies and social classes mask- and masked costume-wearing clearly gave pleasure, caused excitement, and allowed many, even without moral transgression, to experiment with switches in gender and social class, to act out, as with the black/white costumes, the reconciliation of opposites, or, as yew trees and tigers, to personify metamorphosis.

El sueño de la razon produce monstruos.

Dreams and dream research

None of the numerous philosophical systems created to deal with the problems of the formation of a conscious identity had commanded universal assent. It was not only philosophers like Locke who had been puzzled by how the self could remain the self in the face of everyday experiences such as sleep, fainting, dizziness, concussion, intoxication, orgasm, daydreaming or any other form of loss of the self's awareness of itself. The seeming impossibility of answering this question led to the emergence of other programmes concerned with the project of the making of the self. By the 1770s organized dream research had emerged, with its own scientific journals and community of scholars. Dream research became co-opted into broader, ultimately political agendas of the making of middle-class identity, particularly in the German states.

Many older forms of dream interpretation of course persisted vigorously throughout the eighteenth century. Indeed, the most famous writer on dreams, the Greek Artemidorus of the second century AD, was repeatedly reprinted or excerpted in widely available handbooks on dream interpretation. Dreams had been interpreted since classical times as providing answers to problems in daily life, to moral problems facing the dreamer or, alternatively, as offering prognostications about the weather or political events. In some ways, dreams took on the functions of astrology. Orientated primarily to the present and the future, older traditions of dream interpretation by and large did not parallel the widespread assumption today that dreams are very often traces of traumatic events in the past of the dreamer. Artemidorus, for example, explained sexual acts in dreams as a picture of the future economic condition of the dreamer. Our present culture would more or less automatically interpret a sexual dream as a trace of a past event, or as an attempt to work out problems of sexual identity, and would find no connection with economic problems.

None of these older uses of dreams was wholly abandoned in the eighteenth century. Very often, people interpreted dreams, just as the Romans would have done, to discover what their 'fate' was to be, to find out how their life would turn out, and in particular to find out about its end. Such an approach to dreams implied a self which was not so much passive, as caught up in larger forces like fate, the Fortuna who appeared in so many sculptures of this period. But such interpretations certainly became increasingly rare.

What was new was the Enlightenment's insistence on the connection between dreams and sustained introspection. Such was the resonance of this topic that many people throughout the Enlightenment world began to keep their own private dream diaries. The English poet William Cowper, for example, kept a journal of his dreams in the 1790s, as did the prominent Virginia gentleman William Byrd.

Organized research into dreams began in enlightened circles in Germany. Significantly enough, the first journal in this field, published from 1783 and edited by Karl Philipp Moritz, was called *Gnothi Sauton, oder Magazin zur Erfahrungsseelenkunde als ein Lesebuch für Gelehrte und Ungelehrte*. The first phrase in the title is the Greek version of *nosce te ipsum*, 'know thyself'. The second – 'Magazine for Empirical Psychology as a Reader for the Educated and the Uneducated' – allies the journal with the agenda of Moses Mendelssohn who wished to make the Enlightenment open to ordinary people, the unlearned as well as the learned. The attitude of the journal was that self-knowledge

The darker side of dreams – unconscious, irrational, shameful – in many respects contradicted all that the Enlightenment stood for. Perhaps for this reason it became a key element of the movement that came next: Romanticism. Certain artists and writers seem to stand midway between the two, at home in the sunlight but aware of the shadow. One of these was Henry Fuseli, whose *Nightmare* has been illustrated earlier. Another was Goya, whose extraordinary drawing *The Sleep of Reason Brings Forth Monsters* (*opposite*) exactly depicts the wild hallucinatory world of horrors that comes when the conscious mind is not in control.

The first 'dream book' was by the Greek writer Artemidorus in the 2nd century AD. It was translated into English in 1786 (*below*) as 'a treatise of great value and esteem, and very useful and entertaining for all sorts of people'. It offered a bizarre mixture of interpretations of dreams as solutions to moral problems and predictions of the future.

THE

INTERPRETATION

OF

DREAMS,

By that most celebrated Philosopher

ARTIMEDORUS.

First written in GREEK, and afterwards translated into divers foreign Languages, and now made into ENGLISH.

BEING

A Treatise of great Value and Esteem, and very useful and entertaining for all sorts of People.

A NEW EDITION.

LONDON:
Printed for J. BEW, No. 28, Paternoster-Row,
1786.

The _Dream Book_ of Hieronymus Birck-Mayer (_far right_) was one of many founded upon Artemidorus.

Novelist, philosopher, traveller and friend of Goethe, Karl Philipp Moritz (_below_) was a typical Enlightenment figure. Among his interests was dream research and he edited a periodical called _Gnothi Sauton_ (the Greek form of _nosce te ipsum_) (_right_). His thesis was that self-knowledge could be obtained through dreams, and he wished this knowledge to be available to all, 'the learned and the unlearned'. His novel _Anton Reiser_ is still read and he also left records of his travels in England and Italy.

The comedy of dreaming is one of the themes of Francis Coventry's novel _Pompey the Little: The Life and Adventures of a Lap-dog_ (1751), a satire featuring a number of identifiable contemporaries and much admired by Samuel Richardson and Lady Mary Wortley Montague. In 1782 it was translated into German under the amended title of _Der Kleine Cäsar_ and illustrated by Daniel Chodowiecki (_opposite_). The heroine, Charlotte, is dreaming of her lover. 'Sighs of longing came from her lips. In her sleep she put out her arms and cried "Yes, my love". Pompey [or Caesar], thought the words were meant for him and woke her up with his barking.'

could be obtained through the analysis of dreams. Such analysis, in turn, was seen as a particular form of _Aufmerksamkeit_, or attentiveness to the inner world. It suffuses the new ways current in the last third of the century of finding and constructing the self.

It was characteristic of this time to focus on personal introspection in all its forms. To be sure, the results of that introspection were to be used to produce general information; but it began with inexorably personal observations. For dream research, this change of viewpoint meant that sleep was no longer a blank space defined as it had been for centuries as a place where the continuities of self-consciousness were interrupted. On the contrary, sleep became a place which was fully continuous with the conscious self, a place where a new form of exploration, the dialogue of the self with the self, became possible. This was a place where self-knowledge could be produced. Memory, just as Locke had argued, was a constituent of the self. But when that memory began to include the contents of dreams, as well as the external events which had been the subject of memory for Locke, then a far more dynamic view of the self could emerge, one not just engaged in processing sensory impressions coming from the outside, but talking to itself on the inside. The poet Novalis was to call this area the 'inner Africa', the dark and undiscovered continent of the self. Many saw it as the 'key' to the whole problem of human personality.

When we compare the thinking of Locke, Condillac and even Hume on the making of the self with the projects of the end of the century, we seem to be in different worlds. That introspection and dreams suddenly mattered so much was connected with the revolt against the Enlightenment which quickened in pace in the last quarter of the century. In 1778, the theologian and philosopher Johann Gottfried Herder, in his essay 'Vom Erkennen und Empfinden der Menschlichen Seele: Bermerkungen und Traume', used the major visual metaphor of the Enlightenment to discuss contemporary philosophy ironically, calling it 'light and sunny' – too light and sunny, in fact, to be able to cope with the 'dark discoveries, forces and temptations' revealed by dreams. Dream

To the philosopher Johann Gottfried Herder dreams posed a more intellectual problem, since they led the mind not towards light and truth but towards darkness and delusion. This was symptomatic of the way philosophy would develop in the coming century (Herder died in 1803), when reason would no longer occupy its throne unchallenged. As he is portrayed in this silhouette with his wife Caroline in 1785, no one could seem more enlightened. But Caroline herself eagerly recorded and collected her own dreams.

research also broke with the assumptions of the Enlightenment that dreams, just like visions, angels, apparitions, devils, magic or spirits, were the result of superstition, and had no real existence. The setting of dreams centre stage as a way to self-knowledge was itself a symptom of the slow dissolution of the classical theory of the mind from around the 1770s onwards, as was the admission of other new areas of experience as legitimate objects of study – dreams, 'superstition', belief in the invisible, faith and revelation.

Dream research and introspection also fitted into the typically late Enlightenment agenda of the creation of a 'science of man', the bringing together of all knowledge about man, whether medical, historical, geographical or emotional. The project had been given a powerful impetus by the information about the newly discovered island people of the Pacific brought back by explorers such as Cook and Bougainville in the late 1760s and early 1770s. How alike were human beings and how different? How did they respond to different climates, and why did they have different histories? These were all questions for the science of man. Dream research was a part of this, bound up in a maxim (*nosce te ipsum*) applying to the whole of mankind.

Another major context for the interest in dreams was the shift in thinking about the soul and the self. Locke's influential arguments allowed dreams to be seen as the actions not of the soul but of the self. It was this that gave dreaming its seriousness, and went to prove that sleep involved no loss of continuity in the life of the self.

It would be a mistake to see dream research as the first step towards Freud's theory of dreams. Rather it was both an aspect of the turning of individuals to a different idea of self-consciousness (i.e., a part of the 'science of man'), and a way in which the bourgeoisie of later eighteenth-century Germany created a common language and common agendas and attitudes out of their individual struggles with dreams. Many private dream diaries were written at this period; some were published in dream journals. The line between private and public in accounts of dreams was very fine. Dreaming was never a totally private activity. The study of dreams, far from being the ultimate in narcissism, stood at a crossroads between the inner and the outer world. It stood also between reason and irrationality, between light and dark, unsuspected parts of the irrational self.

Dream research had many enemies, and not just the typical enemies of the Enlightenment. The great German poet and playwright Goethe, for example, dismissed the importance of dreams because they were unreal. He referred to Kant's arguments on the limitations on our possible knowledge. He distrusted anything that seemed to distract the mind from everyday experience to the unseeable and unknown. Caroline Herder, the wife of Goethe's near neighbour in Weimar Johann Gottfried Herder, became fascinated by her own dreams and eagerly collected them. Goethe's response was to argue that over-concern with dreams at the expense of waking life could turn one into a dream. What is real, the dream or the rest of life? What concept of reality could one use in this context? asked Goethe.

The Gothic imagination as it blossomed in the late 18th and early 19th centuries was blatantly anti-Enlightenment, valuing emotion above reason and revelling in the mysterious, the horrific and the unexplained. Another of Fuseli's watercolours illustrating the medieval *Niebelungenlied* shows Kriemhild (Wagner's Brünnhilde) seeing the dead Siegfried in a dream.

The Island of Love

OVERLEAF
The Pilgrimage to the Isle of Cythera by
Antoine Watteau is among the most evocative
expressions of an important aspect of the
Enlightenment that contrasts sharply with
the intellectual vigour, realism and cynicism
that have been prominent in the preceding
chapters: sentiment. In literature one looks to
Rousseau, Sterne or Bernardin de St Pierre;
in painting above all to Watteau. Cythera was
sacred to Aphrodite, and the *Pilgrimage* is clearly
a picture dedicated to love, but a harmonious,
happy and fulfilled love rather than sensual
passion. Indeed, the atmosphere of calm, with
even a touch of wistful melancholy, has led to
divergent interpretations. Is this party of young
men and women setting off for Cythera, have
they just landed or are they about to depart
from it?

A different sort of love was celebrated by
François Boucher. His *Dressing Room of Venus*
(*opposite*) perhaps confirms Diderot's contention
that concealing part of the goddess's body
made it salacious and indecent.

CYTHERA, A SMALL ISLAND in the Aegean, was sacred to the Greek goddess
of love, Aphrodite. Classical poetry was full of references to the island,
and in the Enlightenment it remained a byword for sensual passionate love.
So much so that Fénelon's best-selling novel *Télémaque* (1698), which recounted
the life and adventures of Odysseus' son Telemachus, contained a warning
against the allure of Cythera.

Watteau painted this picture (*overleaf*) somewhere between 1710 and 1717,
and it gained him admission to the Academy of Painting. By then, new visual
genres had emerged. Pictures of pleasure parties (*fêtes galantes*) in the open air,
skating, picnics and games such as blind man's buff became commonplace in
the work of painters such as Nicolas Lancret, and popular with the picture-
buying public. They both represented and fed into the elite cult of love, play
and amusement, and the general search for refinement and 'good taste',
especially strong in the first half of the century. Though the ancestry of the
Pilgrimage may be traced to Rubens' painting *The Garden of Love*, which Watteau
certainly could have seen in Paris, the picture itself was fully the production of
the Regency, that period in French history in which the tight cultural controls
which had obtained under Louis XIV relaxed after the king's death in 1715,
to allow the painting of apparently frivolous subjects, such as *fêtes galantes*.
Watteau himself was to paint other pictures which placed themselves fully
into the tradition of the *fête galante*, such as his *Fête vénitienne*.

The audience for which such pictures were intended was an elite one.
The values implied in them seem the direct opposite of those of the middle
classes, and we can gauge from this the very different ideas the social classes
had concerning the meaning of love. This large picture (about 6 feet long) is
surrounded by ambiguities. It is not even clear what its real title is. Modern
scholars cannot decide whether it should be called *Embarkation for Cythera*, or
by the title which it was given by the Academy of Painting, *The Pilgrimage to the
Isle of Cythera*. This is an important point for the interpretation of the picture.
The former title implies that the painting represents merely a party of pleasure-
seekers going to the island of love. The latter title indicates something far
more interesting. In the painting, many of the lovers do in fact carry staffs
representing the traditional palm fronds carried by real-life pilgrims. On the
right, a small page in pilgrim costume plucks at the dress of one of the lovers,
as though to urge the members of the pilgrimage party to get started.
A pilgrimage of love to the island of Cythera, sacred to a goddess of pagan,
sensual love, reworks – in fact inverts – the Christian notion of pilgrimage,
as well as the much more aesthetic Christian idea of love.

Whichever title Watteau might have wanted his picture to have, the painting
surprises us by how small the human figures are in the composition. In spite
of their intense interest in each other, they are dwarfed by sky, forest and
the opening vista of the strait up which they will sail. As many critics have
suggested, there is also something very theatrical in the composition of the
painting, perhaps due to Watteau's early training as a theatre-scenery painter.
The picture itself has its ambiguities. The late-afternoon light indicates that the
pleasure party will soon break up, and in the left-hand corner a dead tree trunk

counterbalances the gaiety of the 'pilgrims'. The statue of Aphrodite is hung with garlands of roses, but it is also mutilated. Yet overall, as has often been remarked, the picture looks like a utopia, a place and a gathering where nothing discordant will ever appear. It seems like a utopia of love where each pair of lovers behaves in an absolutely characteristic way. Few if any other painters of this period were capable of conceiving the detail of the young lady being pulled to her feet by her lover.

There is also nothing in this picture which implies that love could have anything to do with marriage, or virtue with love. The concerns of the middle class find no echo in this picture, and few among it would have been sympathetic to the picture's equation of love with sensuality. There were many different sorts of love in eighteenth-century France.

The *philosophe* Diderot remarked in his 1767 *Salon* that it is not a woman in the nude that is indecent, it is a woman whose skirts are tucked up. He

continues: Adorn the Medici Venus with rose-coloured garters and tightly pulled white stockings, and you will strongly feel the difference between decent and indecent. That Diderot used the example of Venus, the goddess of love, to demonstrate the nature of obscenity shows how the image of that goddess was changing in the Enlightenment. Far from the self-contained, inward-looking statues of Venus that have come down to us from Greece and Rome, with few exceptions, Enlightenment depictions of the goddess show her as engaged with the picture's audience. She retains her typical iconography from the classical world: of doves, of her son Amor or

Diderot's accusation that partial clothing was more provocative than nudity may be true of Boucher's *Venus and Amor* (*above*) but can hardly be held against his portrait of Louise O'Murphy (*opposite*), the mistress of Louis XV. She must surely represent the most straight-forward image in all art of unembarrassed sensuality.

Cupid, of the giant shell in which she rose from the sea-foam when she first appeared on earth and, lastly, of roses. All these iconographical symbols are present in François Boucher's *Venus and Amor* of 1742. But while the goddess is clearly identified, her 'meaning' has changed. Here, she fulfils some of Diderot's definitions of obscenity, an impression that is heightened by the painter's interest in her skin tone and texture. Boucher's technical skill also lets us see through the glowing and rosy skin to the flesh beneath. Much the same could be said of Boucher's *The Dressing Room of Venus* of 1751. Painted nearly a decade apart, these pictures could have been created in the same year, so consistent is their view of Venus. In each, the obscene, by Diderot's definition, or the erotic, by Boucher's probable intention, dominates the picture. In each, the goddess looks away, which allows the spectator to inspect undisturbed both the goddess herself and the surrounding objects. The spectator becomes a voyeur. It is easy to see the slide between pictures of Venus and pictures that were simply meant to be erotic. Perhaps the most famous example of the century was Boucher's 1751 picture of Louise O'Murphy, King Louis XV's current mistress. A rose on the floor beside the couch preserves a tenuous link with the mythology of Venus, but the intention of the picture is hardly mythological. There is some evidence that these pictures of Venus were seen much further down the social ladder than the aristocratic patrons who commissioned them. The autobiography of the French master-glazier Jacques Menetra mentions seeing a noblewoman in her charms just about the way Venus looks in paintings. But these Venuses had been for the most part divorced from Venus mythology: her marriage with Vulcan and affair with Mars, for example, rarely appear in this century. This process is part of the Enlightenment transformation of the classical image which is one of the themes of this book.

6

Authority and
Architecture

To separate the symbolism of authority
from the authority of symbolism today
requires an effort of the imagination. It
is hard to realize how powerful courtly
symbolism was, at least as long as it
commanded unquestioning belief. (Something
of its power can still be glimpsed, for instance,
in the rituals of totalitarian regimes or in
ceremonies associated with the Church.)
During the 18th century, kings, queens and
princes, including prince-bishops, expressed
their authority largely through the
performance of symbolic actions.

To celebrate a victory in the War of Austrian
Succession, which challenged Maria Theresa's
rights as heiress to the Hapsburg empire, she
held a so-called *Damenkarusell* (literally 'ladies
merry-go-round') in Fischer von Erlach's
Vienna Riding School on 2 January 1743.
Frederick II and his French allies had taken
Prague in November 1741. In December of
the following year Maria Theresa recaptured
it – hence the celebration – and was crowned
queen of Bohemia in May 1743. In this painting
by Martin van Meytens she is pictured on
horseback in the foreground, with other ladies
circulating around her in carriages, replete
with the trappings of royalty. It is a sort
of 'ritual journey', one of the ways in which
monarchs could assert their unique status,
their remoteness from their subjects.
To renounce these trappings would be
to diminish the monarch.

The park of Wörlitz castle near Halle
in Germany was conceived by its owner,
Prince Franz of Anhalt-Dessau, as a kind
of ideological landscape, bringing together
a whole collection of enlightened ideas in an
atmosphere of universal toleration. Features
include a church (*right*) and a synagogue,
classical and Gothic buildings and an island
monument imitating Rousseau's tomb at
Ermenonville (*opposite*). It was one of the earliest
examples of an English landscape garden
outside England.

From the oligarchial republics of Venice, Genoa and the Netherlands
to the great national monarchies of England and France; from the vast
multinational empires such as Austria and Russia to tiny German states ruled
by prince-bishops and grand dukes; from the states ruled by the pope and the
kingdom of Naples to the European colonies, the Enlightenment saw a huge
variety of forms of government. Each of these states struggled for power and,
in that struggle for power, it was important to mobilize symbols and symbolic
sites. It is thus no wonder that this age was not only one of intensified warfare
and competition between states, but also a time as never before when rulers
built ceremonial buildings. Some of them are encountered elsewhere in this
book. This chapter concentrates on two pivotal buildings: the palace of Sans
Souci built near Berlin by Frederick II of Prussia, and the royal salt works at
Arc-et-Senans, or Chaux.

To grasp the full significance of these buildings, it is necessary to understand
something of the world in which eighteenth-century states lived during the
Enlightenment. The first fact of life was warfare. There was only one decade –
the 1720s – which was relatively peaceful. Sometimes war was due to succession
crises, like the War of the Spanish Succession which concluded in 1714, or the
War of the Austrian Succession which began in 1740, or of the Polish Succession
which began in 1733, or of the Bavarian Succession which began in 1778. Wars
of succession were common because of the dynastic nature of the majority of
European governments. Peace or war depended on the health and fertility of
the monarch and his family. Succession wars were always accompanied by
seizures of territory. The classic example is the war which began in 1740,
ostensibly over the succession to the throne of Austria, but which was initiated
by Frederick II of Prussia's grab for the rich Austrian province of Silesia. The
wars of succession illustrate how unstable was the structure of international
relations within which the European states existed. They were caused by the
deaths of kings and princes. Royal mortality ensured permanent instability to
the states system. Such was its importance that ambassadors were constantly in
touch with their masters concerning the illnesses of the monarch and other

members of the royal family to whom they were accredited. The fertility of young brides and the likelihood of the production of an heir was another leading topic. Everything depended on the bodily history of the monarch and his family. The risks taken in battle by Frederick II of Prussia were enormous. Had a bullet ricocheted right or left, the whole history of the eighteenth century would have been quite different. A death without heirs, or leaving only a female heir, could lead – as Empress Maria Theresa of Austria discovered to her cost in 1740 – to a free-for-all territorial grab. This was particularly the fate of Poland in this period. This unhappy nation was partitioned between Austria, Russia and Prussia three times, in 1775, 1792 and 1795.

War also enhanced instability by producing rapid shifts in the balance of power. After the end of the Seven Years' War (1756–63), almost all of France's colonial possessions were transferred to England. The whole of what is now Canada, all of France's territories in India and some of its Caribbean islands abruptly fell under British rule. The stage was set for the making of the British empire. Imperial states such as Britain and France, with possessions flung over several continents, had come into being since the end of the seventeenth century. In the Seven Years' War, France and England had fought each other not just in Europe but in their colonies in India and the Americas as well. Such wars led to overwhelming, and overwhelmingly expensive, logistical problems. State finances were stretched to breaking point and massive state debt accumulated. War costs money. Without it, men, materials, ships and horses, gunpowder and uniforms, tents and weapons cannot be procured.

To obtain that money, governments might engage themselves in loans at ruinous rates of interest. Or they could raise taxes, or collect existing taxes more effectively. Most monarchies encountered serious difficulties in the second and third activities. Few disposed of a large disposable income under their own control. In France, for example, the *Ferme Générale*, a body independent of the government, collected taxes on the king's behalf, if necessary by using its private army. Tax farmers were not running a charitable institution. Their right to collect taxes was profitable because they were allowed to take the revenue collected and invest it for a period of time. This effectively deprived the monarchy of this interest, and made forward planning impossible. At the same time, the French monarchy found it difficult to extract taxation income through the representative bodies of the kingdom. In many areas, provincial assemblies, or Estates, controlled some taxes. They, like the Estates of the aristocracy, proved highly reluctant to disburse these monies. The Austrian monarchy had similar problems. The exercise of monarchical power in the eighteenth century was not smoothly effective. On the contrary, it required endless negotiations with other well-entrenched bodies. In this situation, the prestige of monarchs fluctuated according to their success in war or their strength in the negotiations necessary to extract taxes. The prestige of the French monarchy declined catastrophically after the Seven Years' War had caused the loss of the majority of its colonies, to such an extent that some historians have seen the war as one of the factors opening the way to the French Revolution.

If monarchies were troubled by warfare and its consequences, so they were also by religious issues. Catholic entities such as France, Austria and the Italian states had struggled since the Middle Ages for jurisdictional control over a Church which loudly asserted its rights as a universal monarchy and

Problems of succession were responsible for eventually wiping out Poland as an independent nation. It was partitioned three times in the 18th century. An engraving of 1775 (*above*) shows it being divided between Catherine II of Russia, Joseph II of Austria and Frederick II of Prussia, leaving the rump to the Polish Stanislaus II.

Maria Theresa (*opposite*) inspects her troops near Heidelberg during the War of Austrian Succession. This was an era of almost constant warfare, largely due to the intricacies of dynastic inheritance.

The Salines de Chaux

Ledoux created a new style for the salt works, one which combined the vocabulary of Neoclassicism with a startling originality expressive of primitive strength. The director's house (*opposite*) has a portico with giant Doric columns in which cylindrical sections alternate with square blocks.

IT WOULD BE HARD TO THINK of any building, apart from royal palaces, so intimately connected with royal power as were the *salines* (salt works) of Chaux in the eastern French province of the Franche-Comté. Designed by the architect Claude-Nicolas Ledoux, the commission for the *salines*, begun in 1775, had come about through his extensive network of patronage at the royal court. Ledoux was well known as the favourite architect of Mme du Barry, the mistress of King Louis XV. He was also strongly linked to men who became government ministers, enlightened bureaucrats such as Trudaine de Montigny, well known as an agricultural reformer, and Anne-Marie Turgot, who was minister of finance from 1772 to 1774. Ledoux was interested in social and economic reform (which does not make him into an early twenty-first-century liberal). He had strong links to the economic reformers known as the Physiocrats, who included Turgot. The Physiocrats believed that the source of wealth was natural products (including the heavily processed salt). They also believed that the market should set prices, a practice which, when Turgot deregulated the grain trade in his brief tenure of office, was enough to cause shortages and rioting. Another Physiocrat belief was the need for a strong monarchy to hold the ring between the competing economic interests brought into being by the deregulation of markets.

The salt works themselves were part of the intricate system of royal finance. Salt was vital for the preservation of food to be eaten during the long winter months. It was important for cooking and as a condiment. It was also an important ingredient in many industrial processes. In addition, it was heavily taxed. The salt works designed by Ledoux were owned by the *Ferme Générale*, the major tax-collecting body of eighteenth-century France. Not surprisingly, it was one of the most hated bodies in France. To confuse matters further, the salt works of Chaux were actually administered not only by the inspectorate of salt works, but also by a new body of industrial inspectors and commercial policy-makers, the Bureau du Commerce.

Such complexity was characteristic of pre-revolutionary France. Far removed from administrative actions, interactions and down-right quarrels, the king had little real control of the bureaucracy which ruled in his name. The *Ferme* itself, though intervening in production as well as taxation, was ruled by a group of private financiers, who bought from the king the right to collect certain taxes. This only semi-governmental body was thus crucial for the collection of many taxes throughout the kingdom, using its private army if necessary. On the other hand, workers at Chaux and other salt works joined with salt smugglers in order to augment the low wages offered by the Bureau. All this meant that considerably less than the total of all the tax due or collected ever reached the royal treasury. The salt works of Chaux, therefore, exemplified the administrative confusion of old-regime France. Ledoux glided over all these

The extraction of the salt took place in two identical buildings round the circumference of a half-circle (*below*). The salt water was first partially evaporated and then boiled to leave the salt as a deposit.

After 1789, when Ledoux no longer had a job, he went on playing with the idea of the salt works, turning it into a fully realized vision of an ideal city – which, however, he never imagined could actually be built (*right*). The original half-circle was expanded into a complete circle, with many more extra buildings (some purely symbolic) around and outside it, which he illustrated in drawings published shortly before his death.

The administrative office for clerks uses Ledoux's favourite device of banded rustication carried to a typical extreme (*below*). The salt works' employees were generously treated but their lives were strictly controlled. It was as much an experiment in social engineering as an industrial enterprise.

Entrance to the whole complex, which was surrounded by a high wall to prevent theft, was through a stark Doric portico leading into an artificial grotto (*above*).

problems when he wrote that 'the artist [has] the means to join the interests of art with those of government'.

Nonetheless, whatever Ledoux may have thought, the question of tax collection, crucial to any government, was too important to be left to architects, especially in late eighteenth-century France. A series of disastrous wars had left the monarchy bankrupt, a financial crisis that deepened further after France's involvement in the American War of Independence. In spite of determined efforts by the monarchy, the bankruptcy seemed uncontrollable. It was certainly one of the main causes of the outbreak of the French Revolution in 1789. It was in this context that a new salt works, producing a taxable product, was ordered to be built.

There was, however, more to Ledoux than royal favour and a commission which reflected the complex administration of salt taxation and the just as complex methods of its production. Acutely aware of the link between successful architecture and industrial production, he wrote: 'It is up to the architect to oversee the principle; he can activate the resources of industry, husband its products and avoid costly maintenance; he can augment the treasury by means of the prodigal compositions of his art.' Not only did he view architecture as encouraging productive efficiency, important though that was both to the *Ferme* and to a declining monarchy: he also saw it as a way of expressing a symbolic universe.

Urns embedded in the peripheral wall gush stone 'water', alluding to the source from which the salt was extracted – a bold invention typical of Ledoux's extraordinary imagination.

The director's stable has the same palatial dignity as his house.

Ledoux's building may be seen in the light of many different beliefs. He saw the building complex as contained within an arc, itself recalling the cosmic travels of the sun, and hence of the monarch (see Chapter 1). Later, when working on plans to make Chaux into an ideal city, he wrote that it was to be 'an immense circle, with a form as pure as that described by the sun'. In typical Enlightenment fashion, Ledoux went on to underline the importance of the circular form by pointing to nature: 'Everything is circular in nature. The stone that falls into the water propagates infinite circles; centripetal force is incessantly countered by a rotary motion; the air and the seas move in perpetual circles.' In these plans for the new city, Ledoux, also typically for the Enlightenment, wanted not only to turn Chaux into a major commercial centre, but also to 'naturalize' it, to justify its existence by making parallels between it and nature. The semi-circular shape of the original salt works was to be closed to form a circle, thus also reflecting even more clearly the orbit of the sun referred to by Ledoux.

It has also been argued that Ledoux's circular plan was influenced by those projects favoured by contemporary medical reformers, many of them known to Ledoux, for hospital buildings. A central viewpoint would enable control and inspection to be exercised over patients in the axes between the central point and the outside circle. As Ledoux wrote in reference to the salt works at Chaux: 'One of the great moving forces linking governments to the profitable outcome of every instant is the general disposition of a plan that gathers to a common centre all the parts of which it is composed.'

In designing the salt works at Chaux, therefore, Ledoux set himself in the middle of a complex bureaucratic order, which in turn ruled over one of the most highly processed of natural products. In this context, Ledoux certainly increased productivity by his understanding of the 24-hour process needed to make edible salt from sea-water salt. But he also saw his building complex at Chaux as illuminated by the exhibition of a symbolic order, as well as by a humanitarian ethos, the demands of royal finance and the needs of industrial production. The salt works were complex indeed.

Joseph II, Maria Theresa's son and successor, was in many ways the ideal enlightened despot. His policies were governed by rational, humanitarian principles, though he was only partially successful in putting them into practice. The military hospital in Vienna (*right*) of 1785 was a typical initiative. His freedom from religious dogma and belief in toleration brought him into conflict with the Church. Personally, he was drawn to Freemasonry (he is thought to be the original of Sarastro in Mozart's *Magic Flute*) and his reforms included the emancipation of the serfs, the dissolution of some of the monastic orders and the transfer of their property to the state. This allegory (*below*), commemorating the Edict of Toleration of 1781, alludes to Freemasonry (the eye in the triangle) and the confiscation of the Church's wealth in the large net at the bottom. Joseph stands on another Mount Sinai.

proclaimed its consequent rights to tax the laity and to hold its own courts in the midst of the monarchal state. The monarchies struggled with the Church over jurisdiction and the much-needed tax resources which could be extracted from their subjects. In most countries, the Church was the largest landholder, and yet did not pay taxes, again reducing tax revenue. The Church held down huge resources in land which the states involved in the increasing international competition of the eighteenth century were eager to divert to themselves. The Church's lands were also inalienable, which meant that they reduced the supply of land entering the market. Prices were high, meaning that few peasants could afford to buy land, and that agriculture – and the taxes to be gained from it – were depressed. Lastly, an even wider question of allegiance soured the relationship between Church and state. The universal claims of the Catholic Church cut clean across the monarchy's demands for allegiance. Rulers responded to these problems with considerable vigour. In Austria, recruitment by contemplative religious orders was stopped in order to provide a greater pool of subjects for the army and for agricultural labour. The number of saints' feast days and holidays was reduced in order (theoretically) to do away with the scenes of wild disorder which often accompanied battles between rival villages and their saints. Celebrations of Mass were accompanied by far less splendour. Above all, the reforms were aimed at schools. Dominated by the religious orders, these, in the emperor's view, taught nothing but credulity, and their religious allegiance was to the pope rather than to him as secular ruler. As far as possible lay teachers replaced monks. Their curriculum had the objective of teaching a rational attachment to the emperor.

Monarchy and its myths: ritual travel

The stresses and strains of monarchy also led to a remodelling of monarchy itself. Monarchs in this period were caught between the old ceremonial forms, the etiquette that expressed their distance from other men, and their new role in the new world where they thought of themselves as bureaucrats rather than as the lieutenants of God. Royal travel is one example of this transition. From the fourteenth to the mid-eighteenth century, kings moved about in a highly ritualized way, progressing through their territories accompanied by a considerable retinue and punctuating their travels with stops at major cities. The symbolism emphasized their closeness to God. At the entrance to each city, delegations would appear to welcome the monarch with both panegyric and petitions. Temporary arches would be erected, decorated with figures drawn from mythology, such as Hercules or Apollo, whose exploits would be reinterpreted in relation to the heroic history of the monarch and his dynasty. After this formal welcome, the monarch would be handed the city keys and allowed to enter. Such travels allowed the monarch to demonstrate his mastery of his territories. But what really stood out was the ritualized character of these visits, which legitimated the monarch's claims to supremacy by tracing his ancestry to the ancient heroes of Greek and Roman mythology. The central image of the ceremonies that marked the halts in the king's progress was that of the monarch as Apollo: the god tirelessly travelled the skies just as the king tirelessly travelled his dominions.

Yet in the Enlightenment we find some of the most important monarchs of the time, such as Joseph II and Frederick II, giving up the practice and imagery of ritual travel. The French monarchy became largely sedentary after Louis XIV moved his court and bureaucracy to the palace of Versailles. Louis XV hardly left Versailles and the region around it, except to travel briefly to the battlefields of Flanders during the Seven Years' War. No British monarch in the eighteenth century held progresses and none set foot in Ireland, Scotland or Wales, let alone the American colonies. George III hardly left the area around London. A progress planned by George II's ministers in 1725 had to be scrapped in the face of the monarch's marked lack of enthusiasm. These are the years when the word 'progress' began to change from meaning a formal journey by a monarch to its modern sense: 'a state of steady improvement.' Movement over territory changed into improvement through time.

In the Austrian monarchy, the decline of ritual in general, and ritual travel in particular, can be traced with great precision. Throughout the period of sole rule by the empress Maria Theresa, ritual travel continued as before. Trouble began during the period from 1769, when she reigned jointly with her son the emperor Joseph II. Joseph increasingly questioned the practice. After heated exchanges with his mother, he absolutely refused to travel ritually, or to make formal entrances into cities. The dispute between Maria Theresa and Joseph indicates that by the 1760s not only the practice of ritual travel but the whole ritual of monarchy was under threat.

The evidence preserved in the lengthy exchanges between the co-rulers of Austria-Hungary gives us a clear insight into the issues at stake. Angry notes were taken back and forth by pages walking the entire length of the palace of Schönbrunn. For the empress, ritual travel mattered because it was intrinsic to what she called 'the ineffable character of princes', which differentiated them from the common man to the extent that the difference was literally unspeakable, ineffable.

Such travel, the empress argued, was also the way in which the prince made himself visible to his subjects. The phrasing is important. Maria Theresa was perfectly clear that the point of the ritual journey was not that the prince

Triumphal arches designed by Fischer von Erlach were erected for the wedding procession of Joseph I in 1699. These temporary but expensive structures were important elements in the symbolism of power.

OVERLEAF
Ritual travel, involving pageant architecture, large retinues, receptions and loyal addresses, were part of the royal image, putting the monarch symbolically on a level with Apollo. A contemporary painting shows Maria Theresa's arrival in Pressburg (now Bratislava) on 25 August 1741.

The formality of court life was designed to keep the monarch at a distance from the people. Maria Theresa believed strongly in 'the ineffable character of princes' but Joseph II took a different view. He opened the Augarten (*above*) to the public, so that the Viennese people could identify more closely with their ruler. He gave up 'ritual travel' and even, as we have seen (p. 19), had himself represented behind a plough. *Right:* the pavilion, or Lusthaus, in the Prater of Vienna, another popular meeting place.

should see his subjects but that he be seen by them. His presence restored the rightful focus of their vision. In this way, his travelling demonstrated the reality of his sovereignty. Joseph, however, rejected both the ritual element in royal travel in general and this idea of royal travel as a means of attracting the gaze of the subject onto the monarch. He described himself in a note to his mother as 'an enemy of all formality'. It was the formality of royal travel that he detested, not the travel itself. Of that, he was not shy. Joseph's biographers have taken pleasure in calculating the thousands of miles he covered throughout his reign over the roads of his vast dominions. He travelled tirelessly, inspecting, noting down, questioning, planning, involving himself in everything from large-scale strategies to minor local issues. Joseph himself defined his philosophy of travel. During a long tour of northern Italy in the summer of 1777, he wrote in his diary, with apparent simplicity: 'My occupations don't in reality resemble those of Hercules, either in crushing monsters, or spinning for Omphale. I go about, I learn, I see, I inform myself, and I make notes. That's more like being a student than a conqueror.'

Travelling as a student: what did that mean for the eighteenth century? It meant that the king put himself on a level with all those other studious travellers who moved about the inner spaces of Europe as naturalists, as fact-gatherers for bureaucracies, as political or economic experts, just as at the same time James Cook moved painfully over the unknown vastnesses of the Pacific Ocean. To travel as a student meant to travel, like an explorer in a distant land, with focused attention, watching for the emergence of patterns in what initially appears strange. It meant to travel as a person who is in the process of learning. It meant that one was in process, was not perfected, that one was doing, not being. Such travel also reversed the direction of the gaze between ruler and subject. Formerly, the subject looked at the ruler, Now, the ruler, a student, looked at the subject. It meant that the prince is not ineffable.

Joseph was not unique in this. The hatred he showed for court formality of all kinds, not just ritual travel, was paralleled by his rival and model, Frederick

The luxury of the Viennese imperial coach, far surpassing any vehicle that a subject could own, further distanced the monarch from the people. It epitomizes Rococo taste: a precious casket on wheels, in which the sovereign was enclosed like a gem. The design for Frederick the Great's coach (*above*) is by Johann Michael Hoppenkaupt the Elder: there are eagles under the corners of the roof and a crown between the rear wheels.

The urge to escape from the stifling atmosphere of the court led some members of royal families to construct an artificially simple life. In this portrait by Antoine Vestier (*above*) the Queen of France, Marie Antoinette, pretends to be a country woman on her farm in the grounds of Versailles. A portrait of 1741 by Joseph Hikel (*opposite*) shows the emperor Joseph II wearing the uniform of a mere dragoon in his own army.

II of Prussia. As Goethe observed in 1810, in notes for a continuation of his autobiography *Dichtung und Wahrheit* (*Poetry and Truth*): 'Frederick separated himself from his court. His bedroom contained a state bed, he slept in a camp bed beside it; Joseph too dispensed with the outward forms. When travelling, instead of sleeping in the state beds, he slept beside them on a mattress placed on the ground; the Queen of France dispensed with etiquette. This point of view spread continually.'

Shifts in the monarchs' relations with the traditional ritual of their dynasties were accompanied by profound changes in the imagery of their reigns. The image of the monarch as Apollo began to fall into disuse. No one described the meaning and origin of that image better than Louis XIV of France, who explained in his autobiography the reason he had chosen Apollo as his emblem: to be perceived as the sun was to be perceived as ineluctable light, as ceaselessly in motion and yet always at the centre, penetrating the world with fructifying warmth, and nourishing a world made transparent to an all-seeing eye. Implicit in this imagery was the claim to universal monarchy: as Apollo passed over the whole world, so did the king. Nor was this homology of Apollo with the king emphasized simply at a verbal level. The very layout of Louis XIV's palace at Versailles was arranged so that the rays of the rising sun entered the king's bedchamber at dawn in keeping with the Roman trope of the *oriens Augusti*, that is, of the emperor rising like the sun. The king's great chamber was known as the *chambre d'Apollon*, the room of Apollo. Nor was solar monarchy confined to France. One could turn one's gaze across half of Europe and see how, at the same time that Louis was building Versailles, on the plains of Brandenburg the city of Berlin was being laid out on an east–west axis that later generations came to know as Unter den Linden.

We have seen the extent of the opposition to ritual, Apollonian travel in the later eighteenth century by the emperor Joseph. In France, Louis XVI hardly travelled outside the region around Paris, except for a 1786 trip to inspect some new harbours and fortifications at Cherbourg on the Breton coast. One of the most poignant comments in French history must be that uttered by Louis XVI on his return from that journey: 'I wish I had done this sort of travelling before.' It was a comment which had been wrested from the king by the experience of the long journey from Versailles into Brittany. This was his most extended passage through his dominions. Loyal subjects had lined the streets and had insisted on building old-style ceremonial arches at city gates. Louis was welcomed with formal speeches and panegyrics as he passed through the towns. When he arrived at Rouen, to dine at the archiepiscopal palace, townspeople insisted on the doors and windows of the palace being flung open, so that they could crowd in and watch the king at his evening meal. It had not been planned this way. It was his subjects who wanted it, wanted the old ways more than the king. Louis's forlorn comment reveals a sudden *prise de conscience* of a country unvisited, of a people whom he had never seen and who had never seen him, of a territory for too long unmarked by his passage. In the eighteenth century monarchs no longer insisted that their travels brought them near to the god Apollo and the movements of the sun. Louis XVI in his leisure time made clocks. He no longer likened himself to the cosmic system which caused time itself.

It remains to discuss the meaning and causes of the collapse of ritual travel during the Enlightenment. It is not enough to say that the diminution

Two royal lifestyles: Marie Antoinette's *hameau* – a simple country settlement – in the gardens of Versailles (*below*) contrasts with Fischer von Erlach's original plan for Schönbrunn Palace (*bottom*), which would have outshone Versailles itself.

of discontent on the part of aristocratic elites, and the increasing size of bureaucracies, between the Baroque and the Enlightenment stabilized government, rendered it less personal, and thus rendered ritual royal travel otiose. This is too simple an explanation. For rulers like Joseph II and Frederick II continued to travel extensively and carried out the supervisory functions of monarchy by that travelling. What disappears is the ritual element.

Ritual in the Enlightenment had a very bad press. It was often seen, along with other forms of performance, as being little more than a deceptive way to drape the realities of oppression. Against ritual was pitched a new ideology proclaimed by Rousseau and others, which privileged 'things as they really are', whose cognates were objectivity, reality, authenticity, purity. This was the ideology of the emperor Joseph. Things must only be themselves and so the monarch cannot be Apollo. Monarchy as bureaucracy for the good of the state becomes the dominant ideology.

It was in this century that royal families all over Europe began to build. There is no lack of evidence of a construction craze from Buckingham House (later Palace) in London and Sans Souci and the Neues Palais built by Frederick II of Prussia, to the Nymphenburg of the king of Bavaria and the vast palace of Schönbrunn, along whose corridors Joseph and Maria Theresa had sent pageboys carrying their letters to each other; and from the royal palace in Madrid, to the royal palace in Berlin. Even older buildings often underwent substantial renovation: for example, the Residenz in Munich.

Many historians have assumed that the existence and plan of these often huge new or renovated buildings depended on the structure and ceremonial of their owners' court life. This is undoubtedly true in the case of the kings of Bavaria, whose royal residence in Munich had a longer array of anterooms leading up to the throne room than any in Versailles, because the fine distinctions between different ranks of nobility were even greater in Bavaria than in France. The great occupied an anteroom close to the throne room, and so on backwards. However, we also find that huge new palaces are built by monarchs who are known to have downplayed court ceremonial – Joseph II, Frederick II and even Charles III of Spain. So we are left with the explanation that these new buildings were undertaken largely with the purpose of impressing friend and foe alike with the resources they displayed. A bankrupt Frederick II built the Neues Palais in the middle of the Seven Years' War for this very reason.

Monarchy under question

While monarchy deconstructed itself, outside forces were also pushing it in the same direction. Enlightenment political theory, and some political action, turned around the question of sovereignty. Monarchy as a form of government was no longer taken for granted. In the mid-seventeenth century the English political thinker Thomas Hobbes, who died in 1679, argued, in the aftermath of the English civil wars, for the importance of a strong version of sovereignty. In his most famous work, *Leviathan* (1651), which remained influential into the eighteenth century, he observed that man's life was, in the famous phrase, 'nasty, brutish and short', and that man was engaged, in a similarly famous phrase, in the 'war of all against all'. To avoid this situation, Hobbes argued in favour of a form of sovereignty unmediated by other bodies: men gathered together to avoid disorder and bloodshed to make a covenant to accept a common sovereign ruler. Equally, the group of French economic thinkers

Every ruler was obliged to build a grandiose palace simply to maintain his status. Frederick the Great had his intimate Sans Souci at Potsdam, but in 1755, when he could barely afford it, he embarked on the much larger Neues Palais (*above*) by Carl von Gontard.

Mars and Minerva (*below*) stand in the grounds of Schönbrunn. The god of war makes to draw his sword, but the goddess of wisdom lays a restraining hand on his arm.

Sans Souci: Frederick II of Prussia, Palaces and a Chinese Pavilion

IN 1744, AT THE HEIGHT OF THE SILESIAN WAR called into being by Frederick II of Prussia, the king decided to build a new palace. To commit such extravagance in the midst of conflict could be seen as a gesture of defiance towards his enemies. The palace, however, had a second meaning for Frederick. It was to be a retreat from the gloomy royal palace in Berlin. This is why he called it Sans Souci, 'Without Care'. For Frederick it seems to have been a place where he hoped to replicate the palace at Rheinsburg which he had occupied as crown prince, to which he had given the name of the 'Brandenburg Arcadia'. This had been a 'play court', a court without the responsibilities of government, with space for masques and dances, and time for reading his favourite author, Ovid, and for writing and playing music, poetry, history and drama. Frederick often showed in Sans Souci that he wished to be free there of the cares of government, and to be able to carry on characteristically Enlightenment activities. So important was the palace to Frederick that he personally chose the interior decorative style in the so-called 'Frederician Rococo', characterized by naturalistic garlands of flowers and wide expanses of pastel colours. It was not for nothing that he often called himself by the title not of monarch, but of '*philosophe* of Sans Souci'. His last will and testament was signed by him not as king, but in the latter style.

The palace of Sans Souci, whose actual construction began in 1747, was built outside the small town of Potsdam, then, as now, on the periphery of Berlin. In this choice Frederick was emulating some other classic absolutist palaces of the time. The French monarchy, for example, rarely used its palaces in Paris, but lived, with the majority of its bureaucracy, in the palace of Versailles, an afternoon's ride from the capital. The Spanish monarchy had the Buen Retiro, which served similar functions as Sans Souci. Most of the German princes had residences of the same type. In building Sans Souci as a secondary residence to the royal palace in Berlin, therefore, Frederick was aligning himself with a tendency common to all princely governments in western and central Europe. In beginning its building in the middle of a war, however, he showed unusual bravado.

The single-storey palace was sited on a former vineyard, which was built into the final plans of the palace as terraces of vines lining the long staircase up to the central block of the new palaces. Such staircases are characteristic of absolutist architecture. They make the subject toil painfully up towards the monarch who occupies the position of dominance at the top of the steps. On arriving there, the subject would see a central block of one-storey buildings, illustrated, in order to prolong the theme of the vineyard, with stucco depictions on the walls of Bacchus-like figures. The building was symmetrical, another characteristic of absolutist architecture, and its central block was flanked by an orangery and a picture gallery. The central block boasted 25 enormous windows, reaching from floor to ceiling, to allow Frederick to survey the gardens below. Symmetry was preserved in the formal plan of the gardens, which were organized around what Germans would call *Blickpunckten*, points marked by obelisks, statues or, in Berlin itself, very often by churches. Alleys in

Sans Souci was designed by Frederick's court architect Georg Wenzeslaus von Knobelsdorf in the royal park at Potsdam. It faces south on rising ground which is terraced for the cultivation of vines (*opposite*). At its foot is an ornamental pond decorated with mythological sculpture (*above*). The palace is the epitome of Rococo elegance, almost of frivolity – a side of Frederick's character that contrasts with the stern seriousness of his political and military life but that is in keeping with his expertise as a flute-player.

Meandering trails, vegetal motifs, golden asymmetrical lines curling and curving across precious surfaces, all proclaim the interiors of Sans Souci to be among the masterpieces of Rococo art. *Opposite:* a detail of Frederick's library. *Above:* the library ceiling.

Emerging Neoclassicism replaces Rococo in the king's workroom and bedroom (*right*), remodelled by his nephew and successor Friedrich Wilhelm II after 1786. The designer was Friedrich Wilhelm von Erdmannsdorff. (The portrait of Frederick II over the sofa is that reproduced on p.33.)

the garden were organized so that the spectator's eye would be inexorably drawn towards the most distant point. In this way, the design of the gardens of the sovereign seized control of the eye of the subject. It is because of this that in studying Sans Souci we are faced with a paradox, which is that the palace that Frederick II built as a place of retreat displays all the features of formal absolutist architecture.

Sans Souci, however, was not static. It rapidly became a name not for one but for a complex of palaces. This trend continued into the nineteenth century, so that the park of Sans Souci which we see today contains not only the first palace that Frederick II built, but rather a complex of palaces, gardens in various styles, and ornamental buildings like the Chinese pavilion built by Frederick II. Sans Souci was not a single, stable building. Even in Frederick's time the palace had begun to change. In 1755, for example, the orangery was turned into guest rooms for members of the royal family, foreign ambassadors and leading members of the aristocracy. It was only in the same year that construction started on the picture gallery.

By 1755 plans were already in existence for the Neues Palais, situated at the west end of the Allee in the grounds of Sans Souci, a much larger building than the first palace at Sans Souci, but construction did not begin, significantly enough, until 1763, the last year of the Seven Years' War. Many have seen Frederick's actions as instrumental in the outbreak of the war. Be that as it may, it is certain that he was bankrupt by its end. To begin a major new palace far larger than the first palace in the old vineyard at this time, and with building plans which dated from 1755, has often been interpreted as Frederick's desire to show the rest of the world that the reports of the death of the Prussian state had been much exaggerated. For example, the palace, originally planned with a brick construction, was in fact built in the more quickly worked but more perishable sandstone, so that the ruler would more rapidly have something with which to impress the outside world. Frederick only slept there a few times during his reign. This fact above all demonstrates that Frederick

thought the Neues Palais was out of tune with the objectives of the rest of the park of Sans Souci.

Far more in tune was the small engaging building situated in the park and variously called the Chinese house, pavilion, palace or temple, or the Japanese tea house. All these names have one thing in common – their oriental reference points. The style of the pavilion, with its Chinese figures and golden palm trees supporting the columns on the outside gallery of the pavilion, put it squarely in the tradition of Chinoiserie. Growing from the late seventeenth century, oriental styles and images became well known to Europeans through objects, paintings and decorated manuscripts brought back through the Dutch trade with the East Indies. Increasingly, oriental motifs became mixed with Baroque decorative styles, usually of a playful nature. The Chinese Pavilion is one of the most important examples of this style. It was started in 1757, at the height of the Seven Years' War, when Prussia faced bankruptcy and was about to be invaded by Russian troops. Though its small size makes it impossible to regard it as a prestige project like the Neues Palais, the Chinese Pavilion still showed Frederick's will to proceed with the elaboration of the park at Sans Souci, rather than calling a halt in the name of war economy. The building of the pavilion, finally completed on 30 April 1764, lasted the whole length of the war, which involved most of Europe between 1756 and 1763.

The original form of the pavilion was sketched by Frederick himself, possibly from the plan of a similar pavilion in Luneville, the city given to Stanislaus Leszynski, deposed king of Poland. The pavilion was built to a clover-like ground plan, not in the slightest influenced by Chinese architecture. Outside, almost flush to the building wall, are gilded sculptures of Chinese figures playing a whole orchestra of musical instruments, such as violins, horns, cymbals, guitars, castanets, harps, triangles and clarinets. Under sheltered arches, gilded figures with Chinese features function as an audience for the musicians as they drink tea and coffee, and eat melons and pineapples. The pavilion at first offers a welcomely frivolous aspect. In that it redeems the solemnity of the Neues Palais, and takes the first palace at Sans Souci to a logical conclusion of playfulness.

How Chinese is Frederick's Chinese Pavilion? The answer seems to be: not very. But it can reasonably count as a wonderful piece of Chinoiserie. Designed by J. Gottfried Buerin, it was built between 1754 and 1757. The gilded sandstone figures are by Johann Peter Benkert and Johann Matthias Gottlieb Heymüller. Frederick used to take tea here, using a service of Chinese porcelain.

known as the Physiocrats also believed in a sovereign strong enough to be able to hold the ring between different economic forces. There were, however, differing views. John Locke, to cite one of the most influential thinkers, emphasized an idea of kingship as a contract between monarch and people: the latter, in his view, contracted freely, whereas in Hobbe's account populations did so because there was no other way to avoid violence and anarchy. This idea of a free contract was again part of the message of Jean-Jacques Rousseau's famous *Contrat social* (*Social Contract*) of 1762. Contract becomes the essence of attempts by political theorists to define the nature of sovereignty. This represents a dramatic change from older definitions of sovereignty, which did indeed emphasize the 'ineffable character of princes', and saw them as God's appointed lieutenants on earth. This view would have been (for different reasons) as reprehensible to Rousseau as it was to Frederick II, who described himself as 'the first servant of the state'.

By the end of the century, outright attacks on monarchy by radical thinkers were not uncommon. One example is provided by the German writer and traveller Johann Gottfried Seume. As he was about to become a theology student, Seume was pressed into the Hessian army in 1781. Hessian regiments were 'leased' as mercenary troops to the English government who used them to fight against American colonists in the War of Independence. Back in Germany in 1783, Seume deserted as a rumour spread that the troops were to be leased again, this time to Prussia. Recognized and returned to his regiment, Seume passed another four years in service, before being released and starting to make a living by teaching, translating and reviewing in 1787. In 1801 he set off on a journey to Syracuse which was to make him famous. His account of his travels appeared in 1803 and, along with *My Summer: 1805*, the record of another journey, offers such sharp criticism of aristocracy and monarchy that it was banned in several countries. 'Equality is the hallmark of justice' was one of his most famous aphorisms.

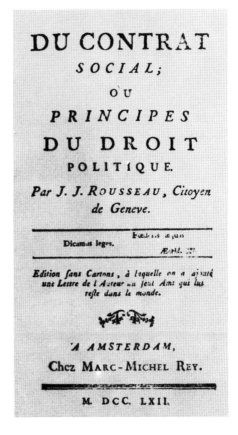

An alternative theory to that of absolutism slowly gained ground throughout the 18th century, originating from Rousseau's hugely influential *Social Contract* (*above*), according to which rulers derived their authority only from the consent of their subjects. This view, which culminated in the French Revolution, seeped through into every stratum of popular culture, even that of playing cards (*opposite*).

7

Science and Medicine

In 1752, the Swedish naturalist Carl Linnaeus gave a lecture about his experiences as a scientist to a popular audience. Not in the least impressed by his eminence as a botanist, the crowd reacted with loud laughter and ugly jeers. The very purpose of science was questioned. 'One question,' he wrote afterwards, 'is always asked, one objection always made, to those who are curious about nature, when ill-educated people see natural philosophers examining the products of nature. They ask, often with mocking laughter, "What's the use of it?" … Such people think that natural philosophy is only about the gratification of curiosity, only an amusement to pass the time for lazy and thoughtless people.'

Such an encounter reflects the contempt in which science was often held in the early Enlightenment. The satirist Jonathan Swift had taken this attitude to extremes in his famous 1726 novel *Gulliver's Travels*. His hero visits the kingdom of Laputa where scientists are engaged in a number of ridiculous pursuits. The first one Gulliver encounters 'had been eight years upon a project for extracting sunbeams out of cucumbers, which were to be put into vials hermetically sealed, and let out to warm the air in raw inclement summers'. The scientist – perhaps we have here one of the prototypes for the figure of the 'mad scientist' – was of a 'meagre aspect, with sooty hands and face, his hair and beard long, ragged and singed in several places. His clothes, shirt and skin were all of the same colour.'

Science in the Enlightenment was far from having the status which it enjoys today. Its intellectual justification was doubted, its institutions thin on the ground. Educational institutions in most countries paid little attention to disseminating scientific knowledge. Only a few men could support themselves by full-time scientific work. Indeed, the word scientist had yet to be invented. It appeared in English only in the 1830s, and any uses of the words science and scientist in this essay are to be taken simply as useful anachronisms.

This low status of science arose partly from its uncertain status as a form of knowledge. For us today, this may seem a surprising state of affairs. We are

'What's the use of it?' For a long time the early scientists met with nothing but derision. In literature one thinks of Swift's mad 'projectors' on Laputa; in art such obscene caricatures as James Gillray's *New Discoveries in Pneumatics*, satirizing the scientists Hippisley, Garnet and Davy (*left*).

Opposed to the scientists were the theologians, some of whom (then as now) put their faith in revelation rather than observation and experiment, basing their argument on what is now called 'intelligent design'. Shown here is the title-page of one of William Derham's similarly named books, *Astro-Theology* of 1719.

ASTRO-THEOLOGY:

OR A

DEMONSTRATION

OF THE

BEING and ATTRIBUTES

OF

GOD,

From a SURVEY of the

HEAVENS.

Illustrated with Copper Plates.

By W. DERHAM, Canon of *Windsor*, Rector of *Upminster* in *Essex*, and F. R. S.

The Third Edition Improv'd.

LONDON,

Printed by W. and J. INNYS, Printers to the Royal-Society, at the *Prince's Arms* at the West End of St. *Pauls.* MDCCXIX.

used to regarding science as a supreme form of knowledge, arrived at by careful objective experimentation and observation. But in the eighteenth century this was not the case. The Italian philosopher Giambattista Vico in his 1725 *Scienza nuova* (*The New Science*) put forward the idea that science was an unsatisfactory form of knowledge because it mostly dealt with entities of which we can have no direct knowledge. Vico argued that if one is seeking universal and eternal principles in a field of knowledge, qualities that allow us to call it a science, one must look to human history and human institutions. About physical objects we can only make up theories which are more or less probable. On the other hand, we can have an intuitive certainty about our understanding of the needs and desires that have united the human race across the ages, and which can be checked against common human experience. Vico's arguments were echoed throughout the century, and it became a commonplace that historical and literary knowledge produced judgements which were far more stable than those which came from knowledge of nature, and thus represented a superior intellectual outcome.

Problems also arose over the issue of causality. Here too, philosophers did not make things easy for the sciences. Statements that one thing causes another are clearly highly important in the sciences. Chemists like to be able to say that the presence of a particular substance causes a particular reaction. Yet the very existence of causality was challenged by the Scots philosopher David Hume. Hume argued in his *Essay on Miracles* that the only thing that compels us to connect events in terms of causation is previous experience. While scientific accounts of causal relationships could claim to be self-consistent, their truth value was based only on a constant similarity of sequences. It was thus a matter of inference, rather than self-evidently true. Our habit is to reason causally; but nothing guarantees that causal reasoning produces truth other than mere consistency with appearances, and nothing guarantees that these appearances will always appear in the same sequence. That the sun has risen for millions of days before today does not logically guarantee that it will rise tomorrow.

If philosophers never made things easy for the practitioners of the natural sciences, neither did the theologians. Especially in England, but also in France and Germany, a strong view emerged that science was not an autonomous body of knowledge, but a part of theology. Science could be understood as a subsidiary proof of the all-knowing, beneficent contriver, whose nature was reflected in his living creatures. The goal of science, from this viewpoint, was to look at nature and the universe as something created by God, and thus as only capable of being understood as the consequence of God's powers and purposes. As the English theologian William Derham wrote in his *Physico-Theology; or, A Demonstration of the Being and Attributes of God, from his Works of Creation*: 'The Creator doubtless did not bestow so much curiosity and exquisite workmanship and skill upon his creatures, to be looked upon with a careless or incurious eye, especially to have them slighted or condemned; but to be admired by the rational part of the world, to magnify his own power, wisdom and goodness throughout all the world, and the ages thereof ... my text commends God's works, not only for being great, but also approves of those curious and ingenious enquirers, that seek them out or pry into them. And the more we pry into and discover of them, the greater and more glorious we discover them to be, the more worthy of, and the more expressly to proclaim their great

GOD-LEERENDE NATUURKUNDE,
OF EENE
BETOOGING
VAN GODS WEZEN EN EIGENSCHAPPEN, UIT
DE BESCHOUWING VAN DE WERKEN
DER SCHEPPINGE.
MET KEURLYKE AANMERKINGEN EN
BEPROEFDE WAARNEEMINGEN.
DOOR DEN BEROEMDEN HEER,
WILLIAM DERHAM,
Rector te VPMINSTER, en Lid der Koninglyke
Maatschappye te LONDEN.
Dienende tot opheldering van B. NIEUWENTYT
Werreldbeschouwing.
Volgens den lesten Engelschen Druk vertaalt
DOOR
ABRAHAM VAN LOON,
Medicine Doctor te AMSTERDAM.
Met nodige Bladwyzers.

T E   L E I D E N,
By ISAAK SEVERINUS, Boekverkoper. 1728.

In translation these theological versions of cosmology spread throughout Europe. Derham's other book, *Physico-Theology*, was translated into several languages including Dutch (1728) and Hungarian (1793).

Creator.' In an age much concerned with the construction of a 'reasonable Christianity', natural theology could thus offer information about God without recourse to miracles, faith and revelation. Derham's book was one of many from both English Protestant and European Catholic authors. The title of John Ray's *The Wisdom of God Manifested in the Works of the Creation* could stand for many others of the time. Nature was seen, despite considerable evidence to the contrary, as evidence of God's benevolent ordering hand, and was therefore represented, using much evidence from scientific research, as ordered, as obeying laws, and as providing a benevolent habitat for man, who was thus enabled to carry out God's purposes. The progress of science in understanding nature was thus the process of understanding God.

Hume was quick to point out, however, that there were problems inherent in the way man perceived the world. Ideas were formed through sense impressions, and yet sense impressions themselves were fleeting, discontinuous, jumbled and confused. This probably meant that men were prevented from ever being able to truly perceive the natural order in a way they could guarantee was true rather than merely probable. Hume added to this objection a famous but far from influential critique of the basic premises of natural theology. He argued that reasoning from a creature to the nature of its creator was inherently invalid.

In spite of the cultural strength of the arguments of natural theology, the beneficence of God's created natural order was also often questioned. In particular, the huge earthquake that levelled the city of Lisbon in 1755 and caused 10,000 deaths seemed to restate in terms of the natural order the ancient problem of evil. Why should God have allowed so many innocent people to suffer through this catastrophe in nature? How could his intentions towards his creation be called beneficent? An enormous amount of writing was triggered by these questions, of which the most famous is probably Voltaire's short novel of 1759 called *Candide, or, Optimism*, in which Voltaire satirized those who, like the philosopher Leibniz, believed in the ultimate goodness of the world and God's intentions for it.

PHYSICO-THEOLOGIA,
AZ AZ,
AZ ISTEN'
LÉTELÉNEK és TULAJDONSÁGINAK
A' TEREMTÉS MUNKÁIBÓL VALÓ MEG-
MUTATTATÁSA.

IRTA
ÁNGLIÁBAN
DERHÁM VILIÁM
WINDSORI·KÁNONOK, ESSEX TARTOMÁNYBAN
UPMINSTERI PRÉDIKÁTOR, ÉS A' KIRÁLYI
TÁRSASÁGNAK TAGJA.

MAGYAR NYELVRE FORDITOTTA
SEGESVÁRI ISTVÁN.

Egy Tábla vajzolattal.

Nyomt. Betsben Nemes Trattner Tamás betüivel.

1 7 9 3.

John Ray found the hand of God in the works of nature, the orthodox Christian explanation. His influential *Wisdom of God* (1704) was soon translated into French (1723).

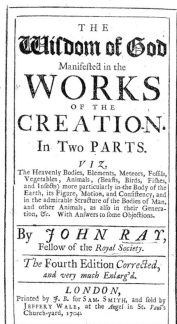

L'EXISTENCE
ET LA
SAGESSE DE DIEU,
Manifesteés dans les Oeuvres
DE LA
CREATION
PAR LE
SIEUR RAY,
Membre de la Societé Royale.
Traduit des l'Anglois.

A UTRECHT,
Chez JAQUES BROEDELET,
MDCCXXIII.

The advance of science

These were the philosophical contexts of science, which initially did as much to weaken its claims to truth as had the ridicule of Linnaeus' audience or the satire of *Gulliver's Travels*. By the end of the Enlightenment, however, the status of both science and medicine had advanced, as had their public visibility. Many scientific institutions had been founded, usually under direct royal patronage. These did little to increase the number of posts in science, but they showed that it had become sufficiently respected and visible for royal prestige to be lent to it. The St Petersburg Imperial Academy of Sciences, founded in 1724, for example, lay under the direct patronage of the tsar, Peter the Great. An Academy of Sciences had also been refounded in Berlin by Frederick the Great in 1746. The French Academy of Sciences was granted royal letters patent in 1699, which turned it into probably the most powerful scientific institution of the Enlightenment. The Royal Society of London was founded in 1660 as a private society, and granted letters patent in 1662 and 1663. All of these institutions worked first of all to fulfil the research mandates given to them by the sovereign. They were bound up in the attempts at modernization undertaken by all monarchies in this period under the pressures of international competition (see Chapter 1). They tested claims to patents, and new technologies and new scientific theories. They gave public sessions at which prize essay papers were read, controversies were carried forward, and some efforts were made to reach a wider audience. The academies were also important as arenas for the controversies, notably over such subjects as taxonomy, which formed a large part of scientific life in this period. Fundamental advances in knowledge also came from them. Catherine the

Great of Russia, for example, sent out scientists from the St Petersburg Imperial Academy of Sciences to map the vast unknown spaces of Siberia, and to report on its natural resources and indigenous peoples, while the voyages of Vitus Behring explored the north Pacific. The French Academy of Sciences tested and endorsed new machines and industrial processes as part of its mandate. The Royal Society of London functioned far more like a gentlemen's club, whose members reported not just on new machines, agricultural innovations and the classification of plants, but also on monstrous births, comets and popular superstitions. The academies also corresponded with each other. Peter Oldenburg, secretary of the Royal Society of London, for example, was renowned throughout Europe for the volume of his correspondence.

This contact between institutions thickened the strands of communication between scientists working in very distant parts of Europe in a way which made science into an international activity. Meteorological and astronomical projects were undertaken which depended on the mobilization of observers by the academies in many different countries. At the same time, scientific journals, often published by the academies, also allowed the communication of scientific information on an international basis. Science thus became a truly cosmopolitan activity. All this communication was in the last analysis underpinned by personal contacts between individual scientists. Nowadays, we do not regard personal letters as primarily concerned with the conveyance of non-personal news. For the scientists of the Enlightenment, however, this was

The catastrophic earthquake that struck Lisbon on 1 November 1755 destroyed more than a city and the lives of its citizens. It shook people's faith in the goodness and even the existence of God. How could he be both all-powerful and all-loving if he willed such things to happen? Voltaire made cruel fun of those who still believed that all was for the best in the best of all possible worlds.

LISABONA

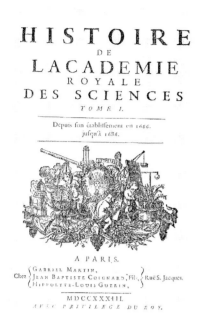

HISTOIRE
DE
LACADEMIE
ROYALE
DES SCIENCES
TOME I.

Depuis son établissement en 1666.
jusqu'à 1686.

A PARIS.

Chez {GABRIEL MARTIN,
JEAN BAPTISTE COIGNARD, Fils, Rue S. Jacques.
HIPPOLYTE-LOUIS GUERIN,

MDCCXXXIII.
AVEC PRIVILEGE DU ROY.

The prestige of science was confirmed by
the foundation of academies all over Europe –
London in 1660, Paris (*above*) in the 1690s, St
Petersburg in 1724, Berlin (*below right*) in 1746.
They were all under the patronage of royalty
(though the London Royal Society was not
state-run) and encouraged research and the
exchange of information. Parallel with them
were institutions dedicated to medicine. In 1774
Louis XVI laid the foundation stone of the
French Academy of Surgery, shown here in
a gouache by Gabriel de Saint-Aubin (*below*).

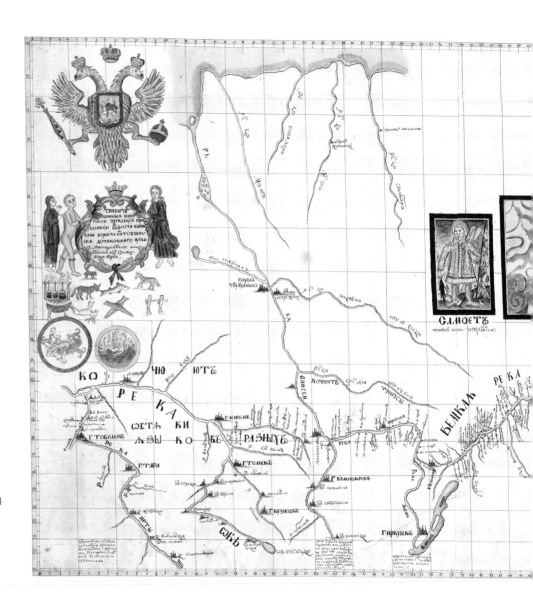

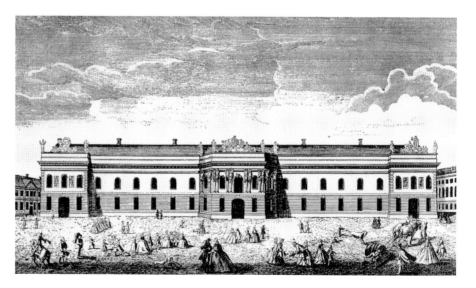

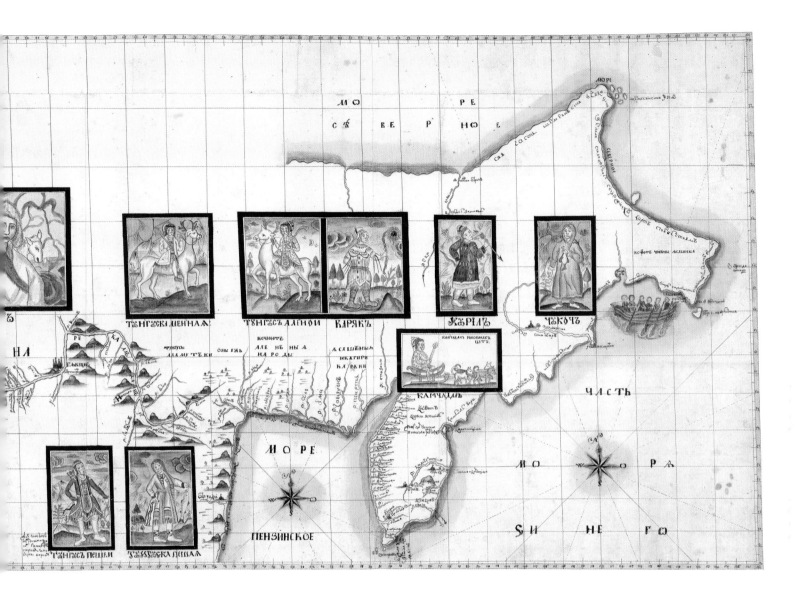

The text on the map includes labels such as МОРЕ СѢВЕРНОЕ, ТѢНГУСКА МЕННАА, ТѢНГУСЪ АЛЕНОИ, КАРЯКЪ, КУРІЛЪ, ЧЮКОЧЪ, КАМЧАДЛЪ, ТѢНГУСЪ ПЕЩЕН, ЧASSTUSCKA ПЕННАА, МОРЕ, ПЕНЗИНСКОЕ, ЧАСТЬ, МОРА, SИ НЕ ГО, НА

exactly their function. The letters read almost like modern scientific papers, and the responses from those who received them like the critical reactions featured on the correspondence pages of the modern journal *Nature*.

The strength of the links between men of science, however, did little to change the conditions in which science was carried out. In spite of the foundation of the academies, there were few other institutions which paid salaries for the full-time pursuit of natural knowledge. Royal map-making projects were one such, like the enormous project launched by Louis XIV of France to map the whole of his kingdom, which was carried on by the Cassini family for almost a hundred years. There were royal observatories, like those in Berlin and Paris, which subsidized astronomical research, and academies administering royal funds set out the terms on which explorers travelled, as the Royal Society did for James Cook (see Chapter 4). The royal botanical gardens in Paris, the Jardin des Plantes, was the home of research into natural history, especially under the directorship of the naturalist Georges Leclerc de

The unknown wastes of Siberia were explored by Russian expeditions during the 18th century. Vitus Behring's epic journey from Tobolsk to Kamchatka is illustrated on this map of 1729 (*above*).

Buffon. This was an age when the coming into being of great colonial empires meant that European science began to be increasingly distributed throughout the world. As the historian Richard Grove has noted, islands such as St Helena and Mauritius, equipped with European-style botanical gardens and herbaria, collected thousands of new exotic plant species to be fitted into the classification schemes of naturalists.

But such initiatives as the academies of sciences and the colonial botanical gardens were not able, and not intended, to offer employment to all those interested in science. In our times, almost all science receives some form of public funding. In the Enlightenment, this was available only to a tiny minority of those seriously pursuing scientific interests. Sometimes, access to posts in science was also blocked by the succession of dynasties like the Cassini family, astronomers and map-makers at the Paris Observatory from the middle of the seventeenth century until 1793, or the dynasties who directed the Observatory in Berlin. Such families controlled patronage in their particular field. Educational institutions in most countries had curricula which usually taught only small amounts of natural history and physical science. Science was very largely unprofessionalized. There were no university degrees in science, though there were in medicine. No agreed definition determined what should count as science and what should not. Probably the majority of scientific work was carried out by amateurs, that is, by devoted and knowledgeable practitioners of the natural sciences, often clergymen, who did not expect to find any place in a scientific institution, or receive any payment from one. It is noticeable that William Derham goes out of his way to praise the practitioners of science as men who could unveil the God-given character of nature. In doing so, he points to the way in which natural theology was involved in the raising of the status of the practitioners of science above the ridiculous figures satirized by Jonathan Swift. But he also unwittingly points out that science is not necessarily linked to a major Enlightenment idea, that of progress. For the natural theologians, scientists were there to reveal the works of God to man, not to

State patronage of scientific research, then as now, was based on the idea that such research might, in the end, prove useful socially or militarily. *Opposite:* Louis XIV visits the Académie Royale des Sciences in 1671. Every scientific pursuit is included – anatomical specimens on the walls, a telescope and an armillary sphere to represent astronomy and, in the frame being shown to the king, a plan of fortifications in the style of Vauban. Through the window one can see the botanical gardens and in the distance the Parisian Observatory, which still exists. Another engraving in the same series (*below*) illustrates research into physics and chemistry.

The Jardin des Plantes in Paris (*above right*), founded as early as 1635, was at the centre of French scientific studies, stimulated by the voyages of exploration all over the world from which specimens were brought back for cultivation at home. *Below:* Bernard de Jussieu plants a cedar of Lebanon, 1734. In time the Jardin came to include animals as well, paying them more scholarly attention than had been the case with traditional menageries. Jauffret's description (*above*) mentions 'two elephants'.

In England the equivalent of the Jardin des Plantes was Kew Gardens, founded in 1762, though not opened to the public until 1841. In this engraving of 1795 after J. Farrington (*below*), Syon House can be glimpsed across the river.

PROSPECTUS INTRA CAMERAM STELLATAM.

advance the works of man. It was not until the French Revolution that scientists were seen as a new priesthood, or had their expertise used on a large scale by the state, or were given important governmental positions.

Popular understanding

Science's visibility, however, was raised by far less weighty means than the solemnities of natural theology. This was an era in which popularizations came fast and furious upon each other's heels. Even popularizations of Isaac Newton's uncommonly difficult mathematical work began to appear: there was, for example, one by Voltaire. Many, such as Francesco Algarotti's 1735 *Il newtonianismo per le dame* (*Newtonism for Ladies*), were written for a female readership, showing too the development of a new female market for science. Children were not left out. In 1761 came a work on physics, *Tom Telescope's Philosophy of Tops and Balls*.

Institutions such as the Athénée in Paris gave lectures aimed at the general public. Individual, often itinerant, lecturers probably reached an even larger audience with sensational chemistry lectures full of smoke, explosions and foul smells, or electrical demonstrations full of sparks and bright flashes, or with demonstrations of magnetism.

The Royal Observatory at Greenwich, near London, was built by Charles II for John Flamsteed, the first Astronomer Royal, to the designs of Christopher Wren. It was from here that the meridian of longitude (0°) was measured. The instruments in this engraving are a quadrant, on the left, for measuring the altitude of the stars, a number of clocks set to different times, and a telescope with a screw to adjust the height.

Isaac Newton: Exploring the Cosmos and Capturing Light

Isaac Newton remains, with Albert Einstein and Marie Curie, one of the very few practitioners of science whose name has become a household word. His name is even linked to the appealing legend of the discovery of the laws of gravity through the apple falling on his head. Born into a farming family in 1642, Newton become a hero in his own time, and in realms far beyond the studies of the laws of light and the mathematization of the force of gravity which constituted his achievement. The well-known couplet by the contemporary poet Alexander Pope – 'Nature and Nature's laws lay hid in night;/ God said, Let Newton be: and all was light' – sums up the feelings of his contemporaries, both ordinary educated people of the time and the intellectual elite. Almost everyone had at least heard the titles of Newton's major works, his 1687 *Philosophiae naturalis principia mathematica* and *Opticks* of 1704. Even in 1749, 62 years after the publication of Newton's *Principia*, the philosopher David Hartley wrote in his *Observations on Man*: 'the proper method of philosophizing seems to be to discover and establish the general laws of action, affecting the subject under consideration, from … well-defined and well-attested phenomena, and then to explain and predict the other phenomena by these laws. This is the method of analysis and synthesis … followed by Sir Isaac Newton.' D'Alembert wrote, in the preliminary discourse to the *Encyclopédie*, that the latter had as its main objective 'classifying the workings of the human mind in order better to understand the truths of nature uncovered by Newton'.

In his own lifetime, and throughout the eighteenth century, Isaac Newton was treated as a cultural hero, not just for changing once and for all the nature of the cosmological sciences, but as someone whose work also had implications for the construction of a new science of man. Newton himself wrote at the end of his *Opticks*: 'And if natural philosophy in all its parts by pursuing this method shall at length be perfected, the bounds of moral philosophy will also be enlarged.'

But which method? Hundreds of simplifications of Newton's rarefied mathematics were produced for a wider public, among others by Voltaire. His companion, Mme du Châtelet, published what remains the only translation of the *Principia mathematica* into French. The Scots mathematician Colin MacLaurin produced the most widely read and influential synthesis of Newton's work on gravity. So widely known were these easy, sometimes even verbalized versions of Newton's mathematics that the subject even crops up in the popular dialogues on science for women written by Francesco Algarotti (*Il newtonianismo per le dame*, 1727), and in that of the Abbé Pluche.

Most of the popularizers, however, gave the impression that Newton had described the whole of the created universe, and described its order as a self-regulating system which could be defined by laws of motion. Newton's ideas were in fact more complex. While it was possible to describe the cosmos mathematically, it was not possible to use mathematics to answer first-order questions such as how the cosmos was actually kept in being and in motion. Newton himself denied that his work described a self-regulating universe.

Sir Isaac Newton (*above*) was pre-eminent for his work in two distinct areas: the structure of the cosmos and the nature of colour. Building on the discoveries of Copernicus (the heliocentric solar system), Kepler (the laws of planetary motion) and Galileo (the trajectory of moving bodies), he formulated a single theory of 'gravitation' that explained all these phenomena, from the fall of an apple to an eclipse of the sun.

The sun's light, which we see as white or colourless, is in fact a combination of every colour. A splendidly baroque *Allegorical Monument to Newton* of 1727–30 (*opposite*) by Pittoni and Valeriani illustrates the method of proving it. A ray from the sun shines through an aperture on the left and is reflected into a prism, where refraction splits it into its component colours on the extreme right.

Newton's prestige as the man who explained the universe inspired the visionary architect Etienne-Louis Boullée's fantasy *Cenotaph to Newton* (*below*), a huge globe – note the size of the trees around it – whose interior was a symbol of the cosmos.

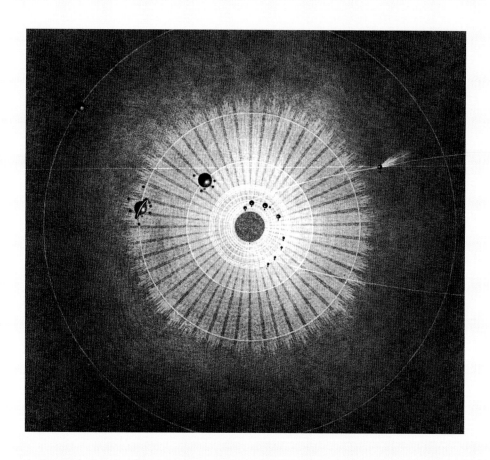

Voltaire was among those who expounded Newton's ideas to the enlightened public (*above*).

The Newtonian solar system became part of everyone's mental furniture, even if in a simplified form. This diagram of 1810 (*left*) represents the paths of the planets as circles, whereas they are in fact ellipses.

As he said: 'Motion is more apt to be lost than got, it is always upon the decay.' Energy, he thought, could only be restored to the cosmic system by periodic direct intervention by its Creator.

In all the glorification of Newton's work it is easy to forget how contentious was the scientific world in which he laboured. Conflict was perpetual, both within and without the Royal Society of London, England's premier scientific institution. The major bone of contention concerned scientific method. The Royal Society, led by Robert Boyle, had espoused a strongly experimental programme. Truth about natural phenomena came from experimentation, not from mathematics. But even Boyle's programme did not pass unchallenged. The political philosopher Thomas Hobbes asked Boyle searching questions about experimentalism. Hobbes saw no secure way, as the American historian of science Steven Shapin has pointed out, 'of proceeding from a pile of particulars (the results of experimentation) to causal knowledge that possessed the certainty appropriate to philosophy'. Quite the contrary: philosophy had to proceed from the correct knowledge of natural causes to knowledge of effects: 'State on certain grounds what the real cause is, and then you will be acting like a philosopher of mathematical representations. Decline to do so, and you will be a teller of stories about natural phenomena.'

The debate between Boyle and Hobbes was about the validity of experimental and mathematical sciences. Boyle himself, as Shapin notes, expressed serious reservations about mathematical idealizations, and his own experiential work is remarkably free of mathematical schemes and representations. He dealt in facts, not in the causal certainty of pure

OPTICKS:

OR, A

TREATISE

OF THE

REFLEXIONS, REFRACTIONS, INFLEXIONS and **COLOURS**

OF

LIGHT.

ALSO

Two **TREATISES**

OF THE

SPECIES and **MAGNITUDE**

OF

Curvilinear Figures.

LONDON,

Printed for Sam. Smith, and Benj. Walford,
Printers to the Royal Society, at the *Prince's Arms* in
St. *Paul's* Church-yard. MDCCIV.

Newton's treatise on light, published in 1704 (*opposite, below left*), was as decisive as his cosmological model and could more easily be understood by the lay public. It spawned a host of popular images – the French personification of *Opticks* (*right*), 'The Mirror and Spectacle Vendor' (*below*) and a weirdly decorated microsope of 1716 from Germany (*bottom*).

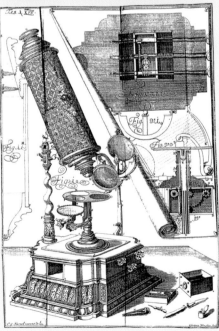

mathematics. 'Those who expected physical enquiry to yield causal certainty were thus deluded … Those who asserted that experimentally obtained facts had a similar level of causal certainty as pure mathematics were called dogmatists.' It was thus the case that Newton's work, both experimental and mathematical, was not immediately accepted on all sides as a towering achievement, but fell into the force-field between many different currents about what constituted legitimate science.

This was particularly so in the case of Newton's work with light, where his physical experiments with prisms were attempts to discriminate decisively between rival theories. In these inquiries into light, the results of the famous *experimentum crucis* were presented by Newton as mathematically true. It was already well known, as Shapin has pointed out, that sunlight refracted through a prism produced a spectrum of colours. Newton's *experimentum crucis* consisted in arranging two prisms in such a way that only one of the coloured rays produced by the first refraction was refracted a second time. The colour of the ray subject to the second refraction remained the same, and this proved to Newton that white light itself was made up of a mixture of different coloured rays. Newton's finding, however, was not easily accepted. In the contemporary state of disarray over the meaning of mathematical and experimental truth, it was a difficult matter to establish, as Shapin says, 'what this experiment established, how it established a theory of light, and with what certainty it did so'. Newton's *experimentum crucis* was difficult to replicate. The quality of prisms varied widely. His experiment smacked of dogmatism, and critics committed to experimentalism questioned whether a single one such as Newton's really proved anything. Newton retorted: 'it is not number of experiments, but weight to be regarded; & where one will do, what need of many?' The prominent Royal Society member Robert Hooke responded: 'I cannot think it be the only hypothesis [about the colour spectrum], nor so certain as mathematical demonstrations.'

However, Newton himself mixed experimentation and mathematics. In his *Principia mathematica*, the work in which he elaborated his theories of gravitation, he returned to this problem of the hypothesis: 'I have not as yet been able to deduce from phenomena the reason for these proportions of gravity, and I do not feign hypotheses. For whatever is adduced from the phenomena must be called an hypothesis: and hypotheses, when metaphysical, or based on occult qualities, or mechanical, have no place in experimental philosophy.' Earlier Newton had declared: 'God certainly does belong to the business of experimental philosophy.'

Newton's achievement in the *Principia mathematica* was to demonstrate that the same laws of gravitation controlled the orbits of planets and the fall of objects towards earth. Newton compared the force necessary to keep the moon in her orbit with the force of gravity at the surface of the earth, and found them almost the same. For some this seemed to put an end to the idea of a personal God who could intervene in nature, causing miracles. For others, Newton's theory seemed a guarantee of the very existence of God. Newton himself commented: 'This most beautiful system of the planets and comets could not proceed from mere mechanical causes.'

GABRIELLE·EMILIE·DE·BRETEVIL·MARQUISE·DV·CHASTELET·LORRAINE·

To mediate between the abstruse mathematical reasoning of Newton and the general public, interpreters and translators were needed. Emilie de Breteuil, Marquise du Châtelet, was perhaps the most brilliant. As well as writing an exposition of Leibniz's philosophy, she translated the *Principia* into French, a feat that no one has since tried to emulate. (This portrait is by Quentin de la Tour.)

The making of the theory of gravitation, however, was marred by disputes between Newton and the German philosopher Gottfried-Wilhelm Leibniz. Leibniz found gravitation to be an 'occult power', a force that no one had seen, and that acted at a distance, that is, without the presence of some intervening mechanism. Newton, Leibniz thought, also treated mass and velocity as real. In the days when occult forces everywhere were being ridiculed out of science, this was a serious charge. Leibniz printed his objections to Newton in his 1689 *Essay Concerning the Causes of the Motions of the Heavenly Bodies*. The new physical science which was emerging at the beginning of the Enlightenment tended increasingly to favour explanations through mathematical and mechanical laws.

Another bitter quarrel between the two men concerned whether Leibniz or Newton had invented the calculus. A note in the *Principia* seemed to imply that

IL NEWTONIANISMO
PER LE DAME
OVVERO
DIALOGHI
SOPRA
LA LUCE E I COLORI.

——— quæ legat ipfa Lycoris.
Virg. Egl. **X.**

IN NAPOLI

MDCCXXXVII.

Newtonism for Ladies (*above*), Count Francesco Algarotti's charmingly named attempt to make Newton's theory accessible to everyone.

Improved technology was essential for the scientific Enlightenment. *Below left:* the new compound microscope with its case. *Below right:* the lens-maker Peter Dolland and his assistant, painted by John Zoffany in 1772.

it was in fact Leibniz who discovered this profound mathematical insight. Newton's papers, however, make it clear that he had himself discovered the method in 1664, although he did not publish anything about it until 1704. Leibniz discovered the calculus in October 1675. He published on the differential calculus in 1684, and on the integral calculus in 1686. It seems that Newton discovered the calculus first, and Leibniz encountered it independently. Additionally, the notation we use today in calculus is Leibniz's, not Newton's. However, the priority dispute was taken up by the supporters of both men. The Royal Society established an investigative committee in 1712. It ruled that Newton had been the first to discover the calculus, but left room for Leibniz's argument that he had discovered it independently. This kind of dispute was almost inevitable given the scattered nature of the scientific enterprise, and the informal rules of its conduct. Today such a dispute would be settled unequivocally by first publication. In the early eighteenth century, it was not clear whether publication, conversation, letters or private notes established it.

As Alexander Pope recognized, Newton's achievement had both to do with cosmology, the making of a new world, and also with the basic image of the Enlightenment, that of light. The debate over the meaning of Newton's achievement was also a sign of its enormous importance for the extension of cosmic laws into all parts of the universe. It was also a vehicle for both doubt and affirmation in religion.

Newton's works were highly specialized and virtually impossible for the non-mathematician to understand. There was therefore a need for popularizations. One, by 'Tom Telescope' (1761), was 'adapted to the capacities of young gentlement and ladies', and tried to explain matters by reference to 'tops and bells' (*right*). An engraving shows a top in operation, presumably to demonstrate the stability of spinning objects. Another, published in 1759, for French readers (*below*), used a more sophisticated approach. Jean-Antoine Nollet, a member of the Academy of Science, lectured at the Collège de Navarre in Paris. He discovered the diffusion of liquids and invented an instrument called the electroscope in 1747.

The most thrilling of 18th-century experiments were the Montgolfier brothers' ascents in hot-air balloons (*opposite*). Among the spectators in 1783 was Benjamin Franklin, who left a vivid account of the occasion: 'When it was about two hundred feet high, the brave adventurers held out and waved a little white pennant.'

Frontifpeice

Lecture on Matter & Motion

THE
NEWTONIAN SYSTEM
OF
PHILOSOPHY
Adapted to the Capacities of young GENTLEMEN and LADIES, and familiarized and made entertaining by Objects with which they are intimately acquainted:
BEING
The Subſtance of SIX LECTURES read to the LILLIPUTIAN SOCIETY,
By TOM TELESCOPE, A.M.
And collected and methodized for the Benefit of the Youth of thefe Kingdoms,
By their old Friend Mr. NEWBERY, in *St. Paul's Church Yard*;
Who has alfo added Variety of Copper-Plate Cuts, to illuſtrate and confirm the Doctrines advanced.

O Lord, *bow* manifold are thy *Works! In Wifdom haft thou* made them all, the Earth is full of thy *Riches.*
Young Men and *Maidens, Old* Men and *Children, praife* the Lord. PSALMS.

LONDON,
Printed for J. NEWBERY, at the BIBLE and SUN, in *St. Paul's Church Yard.* 1761.

The biggest science-based show of all was undoubtedly the experiments with balloon flight which took place in Paris in 1783, and in many other cities in Europe in the same decade. Benjamin Franklin was an eyewitness. His account, contained in a letter written to the naturalist Sir Joseph Banks, is worth quoting at length: 'all Paris was out, either about the Tuileries, on the quays and bridges, in the fields, the streets, at the windows, or on the tops of houses, besides the inhabitants of all the towns and villages of the environs. Never before was a philosophical [scientific] experiment so magnificently attended. Some guns were fired to give notice that the departure of the balloon was near, and a small one was discharged, which went to an amazing height, there being but little wind to make it deviate from its perpendicular course, and at length the sight of it was lost. Means were used, I am told, to prevent the great balloons rising so high as might endanger its bursting. Several bags of sand were taken on board before the cord that held it down was cut, and the whole weight being them too much to be lifted, such a quantity was discharged as to permit it rising slowly … Between one and two o'clock, all eyes were gratified with seeing it rise majestically from among the trees, and ascend gradually above the buildings, a most beautiful spectacle. When it was about two hundred feet high, the brave adventurers held out and waved a little white pennant on both sides of their car, to salute the spectators, who returned loud claps of applause. The wind was very little, so that the object though moving to the northward, continued long in view; and it was a great while before the admiring people began to disperse. The persons embarked were Mr Charles, professor of experimental philosophy, and a zealous promoter of that science; and one of the messieurs Robert, the very ingenious constructors of the machine.' Franklin makes plain the mass enthusiasm generated by this experiment. Spectacle was the essence of the rise of science as a presence in society at large.

Electricity was among the wonders of the age. This coloured engraving shows a demonstration before a learned society in Amsterdam given by Professor van Swieden. Rubbing glass plates with a leather cushion generates a spark, to which the professor is pointing. To the left on the table behind the blackboard are a couple of Leyden jars, the first electrical accumulators.

Comparative anatomy made large strides before Darwin could use it as the basis for his theory. Both Buffon and Georges, Baron Cuvier were lecturing on the fossil skeletons of extinct animals in the late 18th century. Cuvier is seen here (*below*) at the Muséum d'Histoire Naturelle in Paris with an array of newly discovered skulls. He is credited with virtually inventing the science of palaeontology, though he stopped short of endorsing anything like the theory of evolution.

Throughout this century elites, usually educated primarily in the literature and history of the classical world, also became more familiar with science. It was not only Paris, London and St Petersburg which saw the foundation of academies with royal charters. In Spain, so-called Economic Societies were founded in many major cities outside Madrid with the objective of introducing agricultural reform and spreading new agricultural knowledge. In France, as the French historian Jacques Roger has noted, many major provincial towns such as Dijon and Metz also founded their own academies for the encouragement of a wide range of knowledge including science. Their elite members were thus kept abreast at least of major movements in science, and contributed to its diffusion throughout society. Offering prize competitions, the academies reached out to the larger world of the amateur scientist.

The laws of the cosmos

It was against this background that the science of the period was produced. It is possible to argue that the Enlightenment opens as much with the work of Isaac Newton as it does with the philosopher John Locke, who is often given this honour. Newton attempted in his 1687 *Philosophiae naturalis principia mathematica* (*Mathematical Principles of Natural Philosophy*) to produce mathematical descriptions of the cosmic order, of the motions of planets, the famous law of universal gravitation, and the idea of planetary space as infinite. Newton's achievement was transmitted down the century by a host of popularizers in most European

A fantasy called 'The First Lecture in the Sciences of Geography and Astronomy' appeared in the *Universal Magazine* in 1745 (*left*). It illustrates all the main cosmic systems, from the Ptolomeic (held by the man on the left), the armillary sphere (on the table) and the system of Tycho Brahe (on the wall, left), to the modern globe on the floor.

Not only men studied the physical sciences. Tsarist Russia was in the forefront of education for women. Ekaterina Ivanovna Moltchanova was a pupil at the very prestigious Smolny Institute in St Petersburg. Her portrait by Dmitri Levitzki (*below*, 1776) shows her interrupted in her reading of a book. On the table beside her is an air-pump, used to teach science at the institute, similar to that painted by Wright of Derby (see pp. 238–39).

countries. These popularizations played into the growing market for scientific knowledge. Each popularizer introduced his own distortions as he tried to produce verbal equivalents of Newton's complex and demanding mathematical formulas. Most gave the impression that Newton had described the whole of the created universe, and had represented its order as a self-regulating system which could be described by laws of motion. These physical laws, it was often implied, could be completely encapsulated by self-consistent mathematical systems. Newton's ideas were in fact far more complex. While it was possible to describe the cosmos mathematically, it was not possible to use mathematics to answer first-order questions as to how the cosmos was actually kept in being and in motion. Newton himself also denied that his laws really described a self-generating, self-regulating universe. As he said, motion 'is more apt to be lost than got, it is always upon the decay'. Energy, he thought, could only be restored to the cosmic system by the periodic direct intervention of the Creator.

Nor were the popularizers united on the ways in which Newton's work made an impact on other areas of thought. In the 1690s the theologian Richard Bentley preached sermons which enlisted Newton in the service of religion. Yet by 1734 the theologian and philosopher George Berkeley saw Newtonianism as conducive to heresy and atheism. There was even disagreement as to how Newton, who died in 1727, had actually produced his results. D'Alembert, in his 1751 introduction to the *Encyclopédie*, invoked Newton to show the supremacy of mathematical analysis in science, while others saw Newton's work as a triumph of pure observation. Later in the century some hoped that Newton's prestige could legitimate a 'science of man' which would discover the 'laws' of human behaviour just as Newton had discovered the laws of the physical universe. Even as late as 1802, the French utopian thinker Claude-Henri St Simon,

Planetary motion could be represented by an instrument called an orrery consisting of concentric rings placed to follow the paths of the planets. They could be made to move by turning a handle, and if a lamp was placed in the centre the phenomenon of eclipses became clear. Wright of Derby's painting of 1766 conveys all the fascination and wonder that this new knowledge of the universe could excite. The 'philosopher' presiding over the demonstration may be intended as a portrait of Newton.

Linnaeus based his classification of plants on the number and structure of the stamens and pistils (*below*). He arrived at a total of 24. Numbers 1–15 had isolated stamens, 16–20 had stamens and pistils growing together, 21–23 had male and female flowers, and 24 had hidden reproductive organs. *Bottom*: an illustration from his *Systema Naturae* (1735): the sunflower.

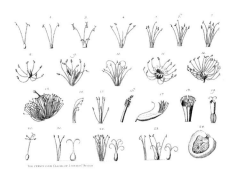

whom many have seen as one of the grandfathers of socialism, proposed a social system based on Newtonian principles of 'reason, order and universal law'.

Newton had little to say about living beings. Enlightenment science, however, devoted huge energy to the construction of systems of relationships between living beings to reflect the order of nature on earth. This was one of the most hotly contested of the major issues in Enlightenment science, and one which saw no conclusive victor emerge. Major questions still bedevilled natural history: for instance, whether taxonomy (the science of classification) could possibly make a representation of the real order of nature, in other words could produce a map of the classifications of living beings which was the same as the existing natural order; or whether classification was nothing but a heuristic device, which could never reliably display the real order of nature. Such thinking often challenged the very idea of classification itself, pointing out that individuals within species often varied so much that they called into question the whole idea that classification could really encompass the actual variety of the natural world. Naturalists who espoused this view believed that individuals were the only reality in nature.

Linnaeus, the Swedish naturalist whom we encountered at the beginning of this chapter, came to represent the most extreme statement of the first position. Strongly influenced by the ideas of natural theology, he and his pupils produced a new binomial system of classification, where living beings were placed in the order of nature by the classification of two features only, at least in the case of plants chosen for their reproductive characteristics, so much so that Linnaeus' system was often called the 'Sexual System' of classification. Linnaeus' approach to nature was thus also quite unhistorical. In his view of the natural world as a harmonious environment for man, he had little room for the idea of change.

Linnaeus' views were explicitly challenged by the French naturalist Georges-Louis Leclerc de Buffon. Buffon's best-known work was his *Histoire naturelle* (*Natural History*), a multi-volume work which began publication in 1749 and aimed to represent all living creatures. What really made for the work's success, however, was Buffon's extraordinarily clear and colourful writing, until very recently treated as a model of style in the French school curriculum. Buffon challenged the very possibility of classifying living beings. For him, classification was a mere heuristic device, not a way of revealing the actual structure of nature. Buffon also differed in another fundamental way from Linnaeus. He believed that the earth, and hence living beings, had a far longer history than the chronology of the Bible would admit. Buffon used fossil evidence and physical experimentation to argue for the greater age of the world. The world was not still in the state in which God had created it, and species did not emerge perfect and immutable from the divine hand. Theology and natural history clashed here, rather than working in the smooth partnership of natural theology. Buffon's physical experiments on the rates of the earth's cooling were condemned by the Paris theology faculty, the Sorbonne, because his work implied that the earth was far older than biblical chronology stated. This condemnation, however, did nothing to halt a gradual historicization of the discipline. Even man's own place in nature began to be questioned. Was man, God's highest creation, securely placed above the natural order, or was he actually part of it? Man had an immortal soul, but at the same time resembled primates rather strikingly. Did the earth too have a history? If God was benevolent, why had so many species become extinct? Looking at the natural order did not necessarily lead onto the certainties of natural theology.

It was the controversies emerging from the mid-Enlightenment onwards which began to make knowledge of nature seem increasingly important. In spite of philosophical objections and internal struggles between observational and experimental sciences, science was more and more successful in putting forward claims to both consistency and practical utility. By the end of the century, satires such as Jonathan Swift's against the scientists of Laputa had become rare indeed. Science was becoming acceptable in spite of the jeers of the unlearned and the *caveats* of the philosophers.

Enlightened medicine

Medicine had not stood still either. The role of hospitals changed radically; public health became a major medical concern; and institutional changes altered the way in which both doctors and patients related to each other. Changes in medical theory, practice and institutional structure in this period have attracted considerable attention, notably from the French philosopher Michel Foucault, and the historians Toby Gelfand and Jean-Pierre Goubert. One of the largest changes was the increasing tendency, most dramatically seen in Paris, to emphasize medical care through the removal of the sick poor to ever-larger hospitals. Expanded hospitals allowed the development of a new kind of medicine by bringing together for the first time large groups of patients exhibiting similar symptoms, and thus making possible a diagnostic practice which privileged the collection of symptoms rather than information from scattered patients about their personal experience of illness. It was in these hospitals that techniques such as palpation, percussion and ausculation were developed as part of a new diagnostic repertoire. Gone was the idea dominant still in country medicine in the mid-century that symptom complexes have an independent existence. The patient's personal medical history was dethroned from its position as a key to diagnosis. Such hospitals also made possible the collection of large numbers of corpses for autopsy, a precondition for the formation of the science of pathology. Poor patients, once viewed by the Church and the nursing orders (which still provided the major source of care in the hospitals) as souls deserving charity, became clinical material while alive, and objects for anatomical study when dead.

Eighteenth-century France, however, possessed many other sorts of medicine and many other sorts of medical practitioners. Village midwives, herbal healers, bone-setters and provincial pharmacists made up a range of affordable medical care which had no connection with the medical schools or with licensed practitioners. Historians have calculated that the number of the latter stood at fewer than one per thousand inhabitants of France. The fees charged by licensed practitioners who had attended university medical schools placed their assistance in any case beyond the reach of all but the prosperous middle classes. So medicine was not wholly professionalized and dependent on large hospitals. Though these are easily the most visible changes of the medical Enlightenment, for most people in fact this 'progress' was of little concern.

Georges-Louis Leclerc de Buffon, if not the greatest of European naturalists, made the most obvious impact on popular culture through his multi-volume *Histoire naturelle* (beginning in 1749), which aimed to include every living creature. He too aroused the hostility of the theologians by maintaining that the fossil evidence showed the earth to be far older than the Bible stated.

The Art of Anatomy

THE STUDY OF ANATOMY was fundamental to any medical advance. The Enlightenment was a period when much had already been discovered, but there still remained many important areas shrouded in mystery. Even the function of the heart in circulating blood had been discovered by William Harvey only in 1628.

The eighteenth century was rich in eminent anatomists, particularly in Germany (Albrecht von Haller – see p.275 – who related anatomy to physiology, which he called 'animated anatomy'), France (Marie-François-Xavier Bishat, who wrote a definitive *Anatomie générale* in 1800 but died at the age of 31) and Scotland (John Hunter, the famous teacher who had practical experience as an army surgeon, and Alexander Munro, who traced the connection between the muscles and the nervous system).

Now for the first time numerous expensive and often beautiful anatomical atlases were appearing, many of them specializing in particular organs, e.g., that of the Dutchman Bernhard Siegfried Albinus on the pregnant uterus, or of William Cheselden on bones. Even when the form and function of the major organs had been understood, there were still important discoveries to be made in such areas as the nerves and the glands. Scientists were also able to demonstrate the amazing ability of some animals to regenerate after injury: René Réaumur showed how lobsters could regrow their claws, and Lazzaro Spallanzani the tails of salamanders. In the 1790s Galvani and Volta (names that were taken into the scientific vocabulary) demonstrated the part played by electricity in stimulating the nerves and muscles. All this work was carried out in the face of hostility and in many countries legal prohibition against the dissection of human corpses.

From the very beginning anatomy was studied as seriously by artists as by doctors. For the former its value lay in achieving accuracy in their depiction of the nude body by understanding the structure of the muscles beneath the skin. Flayed figures known as *écorchés* were produced as aids to study, while naked bodies already starting to decay, called *transis*, had their place on tombs as stark reminders of death.

There is indeed always a latent ambiguity about these medical illustrations of the past. Are they science or art? Or both? Many works of sculpture and many anatomical drawings (by Leonardo above all) are reproduced in art books, while others languish in medical treatises. The distinction is further complicated by the fashion among anatomists for placing their figures in classical poses, as if they were alive and quite unaware that they are nothing but bones and muscles. One skeleton of a foetus in the Amsterdam Museum of Frederick Ruysch is wiping away tears. Studies by the London surgeon William Cowper

The anatomist Felice Fontana (*above*), previously in charge of the grand duke of Tuscany's Museum of Physics and Natural History, supervised the production of the wax models commissioned by Joseph II.

The female body displaying the musculature, veins, nerves and intestines (*opposite*).

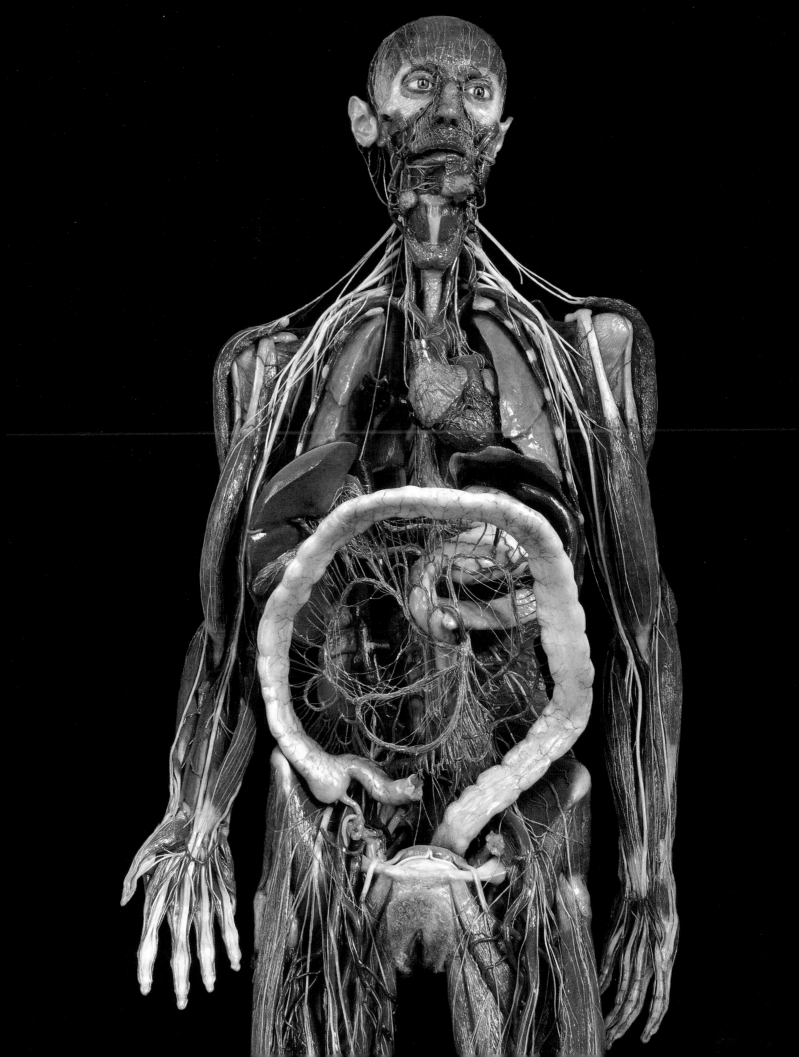

The neck and chest opened to show the heart and lungs (*opposite*).

The male body exposing the circulation of lymph and blood (*below*).

adopt positions taken from Raphael and Rubens. Everything depends on the attitude of the viewer. The issue arises particularly crucially in the case of some of the most amazing anatomical models ever made – the collection of wax figures commissioned by the emperor Joseph II and now in Vienna.

Its origins go back to 1786 when Joseph visited Florence and saw ones that had been made for the Florentine court. He was so impressed that he ordered an even grander collection for himself. The anatomists in charge were Felice Fontana (1730–1805) and Paolo Mascagni (1755–1815). The wax modeller was Clemente Susini (1754–1814), who took on 16 additional craftsmen to complete the task. In addition to the very stringent technical demands that had to be met, these men were also superb artists. Their work represents an aesthetically fascinating and at the same time extraordinarily precise study of the human body – muscles, heart, blood and lymph vessels, the brain, the uterus, etc. There were originally 1,192 objects in the so-called Josephinum, of which 995 now remain.

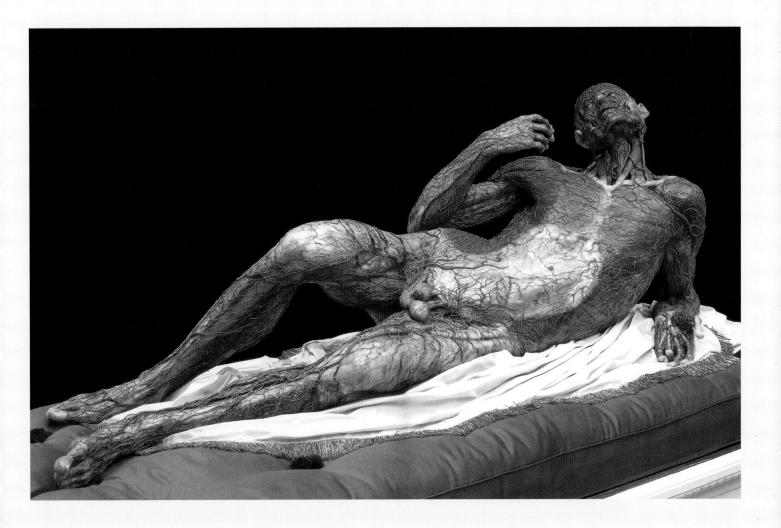

Care of the sick, no longer the responsibility of the Church, was central to Enlightenment thinking, and huge public hospitals were built at the expense of the state. A drawing by Benjamin Zix of 1805 (*right*) shows the ward of a hospital in Paris where wounded soldiers are being treated.

In Vienna Joseph II led enlightened thought in the creation of vast hospitals. Most of these buildings – shown here in a coloured engraving by J. and P. Schaffer (*below*) – still exist. In the distance is the circular structure (nicknamed the *Kugeltopf*, a kind of cream cake) intended for the treatment of the insane.

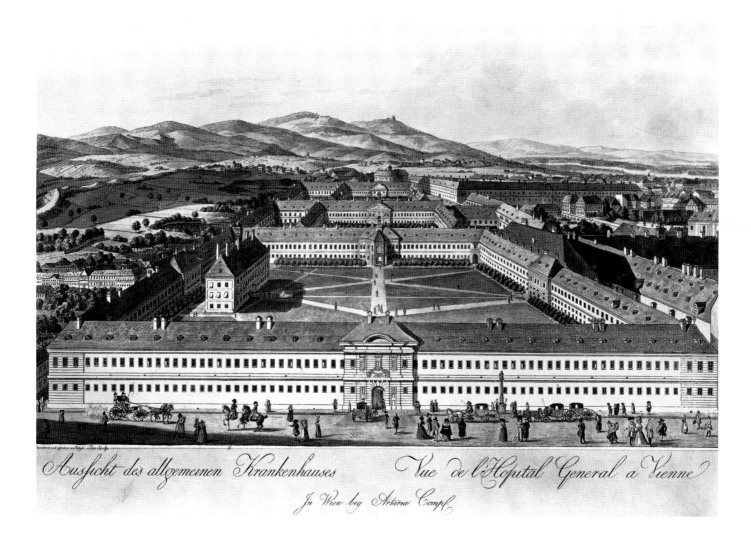

Ausficht des allgemeinen Krankenhauses *Vue de l'Hopital General a Vienne*

In Wien bey Artaria Compl.

Vaccination was one of the major advances in the history of medicine. An English doctor, Edward Jenner, noticed that milkmaids who had caught 'cowpox', a mild strain of smallpox that had transmuted to a disease of cows, were immune to smallpox itself. By artificially infecting patients with cowpox ('vaccination' is derived from the Latin *vacca*, 'a cow'), his discovery virtually wiped out that dreaded disease. Here, in a naive popular print (*left*), Jenner is shown vaccinating a child in 1796. Lady Mary Wortley Montagu was an early champion.

Drugs were manufactured with increasing sophistication and in increasing quantities, though the line between science and folk wisdom could still be a fine one. Shown here (*below*) is a French pharmacy.

As the century advanced, public and personal health, just as much the treatment of the new disease entities, increasingly began to lead medical research. This was the time when the modern concept of 'health' began to be defined. In its prescriptions for health, the medical profession, particularly in western Europe, aimed at a middle-class clientele, for which it produced a medical philosophy and a therapeutic regime totally distinct from the medicine available to the lower classes. Individualized health regimes for the middle classes were identified with the idea stemming from the Greek physician Galen of the 'six things non-natural'. The concept of the non-naturals was particularly suited to the increasing confidence of the middle classes all over Enlightenment Europe, which had often seized intellectual leadership. The non-naturals were factors external to man which inevitably and continuously influenced his physical well-being: air, food and drink, motion, rest, sleeping and waking, evacuation and retention. Therapeutic advice to the middle classes, contained in an increasing number of healthcare manuals absorbed by a wide reading public (see Chapter 2), emphasized the idea of health as a product of individual practice and control over the non-naturals. Just as it still is today in self-help books on weight control and other problems, health was conceptualized as a product of individual practice and control over the non-naturals. For the first time it was elevated to a moral ideal connected with responsibility for an autonomous self. Individual responsibility for health raised to a moral ideal paralleled other forms of self-discipline essential to middle-class success, or to social mobility. The idea that disease was divine punishment for sin and health a gift from God was replaced by the notion that the individual was himself responsible. Instead of being one of the accidents of life, 'health' became a good, even a right, to be actively striven for. The values of both health and personal hygiene emphasized not only the individual's active striving for health, but also his personal autonomy, his individual way of doing so. It was he and no other who took charge of his health. Here again, there are more than pre-echoes of modern 'take charge' ideals of health.

At the same time, doctors saw themselves as charged with a new task in public health which had nothing to do with the individual's acceptance of a regime of bodily management. Slaughterhouses and cemeteries, where bodies had been piled upon bodies, sometimes for centuries, gave off foul odours. Odours were seen as diagnostic by eighteenth-century doctors for the presence of disease-causing agents, which were blamed for the emission of miasma, or particles which rose into the air and dropped them. In the violent debates which often followed proposals to move burial grounds to the outskirts of the cities doctors found themselves also playing political roles which brought them into contact with city governments and with public opinion. As doctors increasingly found themselves involved in enforcing public-health measures in the countryside during epidemics or famines, their role also grew in rural areas previously virtually impervious to professional licensed practitioners, and their brand of medicine was increasingly identified with closely defined public-health issues. At this time too the science of statistics and probability came to maturity as an essential tool in calculating and understanding morbidity and the incidence of disease. These developments may explain why so many doctors came to the fore in the French Revolution, and why some, such as Pierre-Louis Cabanis, even proclaimed themselves part of a new priesthood.

Medical thinking about the constitution of living beings also underwent considerable changes in this period. The eighteenth century saw a strong challenge to the so-called 'iatro-medical ideas' which had dominated the medicine of the previous century, the major premise of which was that life can be reduced to the sort of dynamic functions exhibited by machines. No new orthodoxy, however, took its place. Just as in the case of taxonomy, several schools of thought battled for predominance, the most famous centred on the medical school of the University of Montpellier. Doctors like Boissier de Sauvages, Théophile de Bordeu and Paul-Joseph Barthez concentrated on the idea of the irreducible vitality of living beings, which could not be explained by reference to mechanical models. The Montpellier physicians sought the source of this vitality and analysed its manifestations, such as sensitivity, which had been ignored by the iatro-mechanists. Their medicine was dominated by their admission of the existence in living reality of dynamic and organic phenomena inexplicable by the physical and mechanical theories then available. For those who wished it to, the teachings of the Montpellier school also provided a physiology which duplicated most of the functions traditionally associated with the notion of the soul such as self-consciousness.

Another school of medical thought clustered around the German physician Albrecht von Haller. Working in Göttingen, Haller, whose work was known throughout Europe, distinguished through experimentation a force inherent in muscular fibre called irritability, and in nerve fibres called sensibility. Haller tried to leave a place in his physiology for the soul, which he defined as the only centre able to perceive the sensations carried to it by the nerve fibres. For the Montpellier physicians, however, this approach was unsatisfactory. Bordeu in particular regarded Haller's distinction between sensibility and irritability as too abstract. The Montpellier physicians emphasized a much more holistic view of the organism as a self-propelling, self-regulating entity, whose 'vital force' came from its interior, instead of from outside as a result of responses to stimuli. Bordeu emphasized the idea that organic beings seem to possess a peculiar

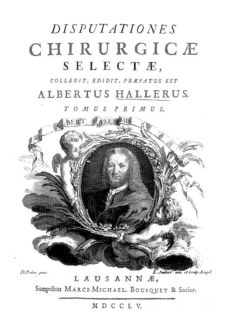

DISPUTATIONES
CHIRURGICÆ
SELECTÆ,
COLLEGIT, EDIDIT, PRÆFATUS EST
ALBERTUS HALLERUS.
TOMUS PRIMUS.

LAUSANNÆ,
Sumptibus MARCI-MICHAEL. BOUSQUET & Socior.
M DCC L V.

Albrecht von Haller of Göttingen
made important discoveries in physiology,
distinguishing between muscular fibres and
nerve fibres. His work was published in 1755
with a macabre frontispiece by P.F. Tardieu
showing a student defending a doctoral thesis
before a master.

capacity for acting in accordance with particular aims and ends, and live as a ceaseless reciprocal action in a complex dynamism. He saw the organism as possessing something like a force capable of executing functions that no blind mechanical motor could, and as fulfilling the functions necessary to keeping alive. He thus not only completely abandoned the approach of the iatro-mechanists, but his work also marked a significant abandonment of the idea that the soul had a physical location. Until Bordeu's work, the 'superior' functions of the body – self-consciousness, decision-making and the ordering of sense impressions – had been attributed to a 'soul', or to an intellectual centre of consciousness. In Bordeu, not only does the soul appear to be cut off from any actual psychic process, but the brain's supremacy as a conscious intellectual centre is replaced by a federation of many centres of perception. The brain remains the source of ideas but is no longer autonomous or completely dominant. It is its interaction with often autonomous ganglions which actively makes for the psycho-affective life of man. After this, it was impossible for any study of the 'superior' functions of man (reason and imagination, for example) to be separated from the study of bodily activities and functions. Such medical teachings, however, while they deepened the picture of the nature of man, also caused major confusion. Rationality and response, while still created in the brain, were now seen as emanating from an organ which had lost its undisputed dominance over other parts of the body. The soul itself had been increasingly eased out of physiology under the pressure of experimental work aimed firmly at the answering of answerable questions, of which the nature of the soul was not one. Bordeu's physiological research was thus far removed from ideas based on the non-naturals and on the development of the idea of hygiene and health. For medical thinkers of the latter persuasion, the body was controllable, able to be managed by a dominant brain and self-consciousness, through advice, moderation and common sense.

If the physiological bases of the personality became increasingly confused by the end of the Enlightenment, so did the theories of medical practitioners themselves. Increasingly the licensed medical community made proposals for intervention in the remote world of rural communities hostile to its claims and suspicious of its motives. Middle-class, urban medicine became ever more eager to spread precepts of hygiene and disease control into the countryside, particularly in times of local epidemics. More generally, the writings of economists and political commentators identified poor health among a rural population plagued by under-nourishment, epidemics and malaria as a major cause of slow economic progress and failure to increase agricultural productivity.

The picture of science and medicine at the end of the Enlightenment is thus utterly different from that at the beginning. The ridicule of science and its fierce controversies has very much lessened, though not entirely disappeared. European science was now present on a worldwide basis. Academies of science both controlled and encouraged scientific agendas. Exploration had filled European cabinets with hitherto unknown species. Science had gained visibility with the increasing opportunities for the relatively well-to-do to witness scientific entertainments; it had become part of a genteel regimen of relaxation. Medicine had enlarged its institutional basis, set diagnostics on a new path, and given itself more visibility by its concern for individual health and public hygiene. As a result, medical men prepared the way for their prominence in the politics of the French Revolution. The Montpellier physicians and the work of Albrecht Haller had begun to lay the foundations of a science of life. For the ordinary person, the worker in the town or the peasant in the countryside, however, little may have changed except for the intervention of physicians in times of dearth and epidemic. At the intellectual level, however, the changes in science had been enormous. No longer could it be described as an activity principally concerned with extracting sunbeams out of cucumbers.

Surgery was still a gruesome and dangerous process but spectacular advances both in the technology of the instruments used and in knowledge of anatomy aided the surgeon's skill. The *Universal Magazine* illustrates this progress.

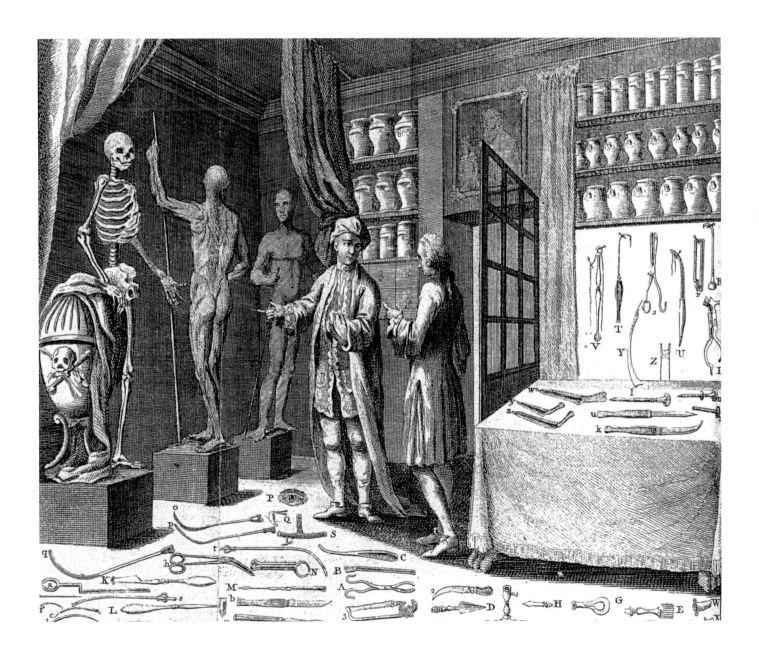

8

Epilogue:
The Legacy
of the
Enlightenment

It is a truism that we interpret the past to find clues to the present, or look there for moral values which we think have vanished from our own times. Of no time in history, except perhaps the classical period of Greece and Rome, is this more true than of the Enlightenment. No other age in history bears the name of a philosophical movement rather than the name of a ruler or of a war. Our own age has moved too into a unique relationship with the Enlightenment, seeing it as at once the bearer of light and the cause of colossal evil. This fascination is manifest even at the level of popular culture: Leonard Bernstein's *Candide*, Peter Weiss' *Marat-Sade*, Peter Shaffer's *Amadeus*, with its following film, Jonathan Miller's staging of *Don Giovanni*, the stage play and then the film of *Liaisons Dangereuses*: the list could be extended. The history of entire epochs has been evaluated, as we will see, by reference to the Enlightenment, which has also been dragged into definitions of modernity and post-modernity.

The re-evaluation of the Enlightenment began in the Enlightenment itself. Opponents, often clerics, often Jesuits such as the Abbé Barruel, interpreted it as the completion of the Protestant Reformation of the sixteenth and seventeenth centuries: the Reformation had allowed a dangerous liberty of thought, and this liberty of thought was leading to a chaos of opinions within society that could only weaken Church and monarchy. This opinion is somewhat similar to that of Immanuel Kant (see Chapter 1), who pointed out the problems arising from the unfettered use of critical reason.

Counter-Enlightenment thinkers also pointed to the profoundly rationalistic strand in the Enlightenment, its refusal to accept truths based on revelation or miracle. For them, the consequent Enlightenment campaigns for religious toleration in particular were seen as devastating to religion, because toleration implied that all religions were equal and that the truth of any was immaterial. For counter-Enlightenment thinkers, this was to say that the 'truth' or 'falsehood' of any statement was merely relative, that no unseen world existed, and that no appeal could be made to any higher political, religious or moral source than man himself. Man had set himself at centre stage. As the Abbé Barruel wrote: 'The school of Raynal, Voltaire, of Jean-Jacques, of Helvetius, of Diderot, is one of rebellion, of insubordination, of anarchy.' In 1787, the provincial writer Rigoley de Juvigny lamented: 'Philosophy has penetrated everywhere, has corrupted everything … The outcome of this distressing revolution has been the general depravation of morals. And indeed how could morals remain pure when an all-consuming luxury corrupts them? When everything gives off a spirit of independence and liberty that leads us to sever the ties that bind us to state and society, making of us egoists who are as indifferent to evil as to good, to virtue as to vice? When an ungrateful and false philosophy seeks to snuff out filial piety in our hearts, the love that we possess from birth for our kings, the attachment we owe to our country … ? When, in a word, we have lost all idea of duty, of principle, every rule of conduct, and every sentiment of religion?'

Counter-Enlightenment: Church and monarchy

De Juvigny was right to point out the connection between religious reform and political loyalties. In France, the coronation ritual described the king as eldest son of the Church and in that ceremony he took oaths to extirpate heresy from his kingdom, words of little comfort for his Protestant and Jewish subjects.

MÉMOIRES
POUR SERVIR
À
L'HISTOIRE
DU JACOBINISME;

Par Mr. *l'Abbé* BARRUEL.

Première Partie.

A LONDRES,
De *L'Imprimerie Françoise*,
Chez PH. LE BOUSSONNIER & Co. No. 122
Wardour Street, Oxford Street.
Se vend chez A. DULAU & Co. No. 107 *Wardour
Street*, Soho.
Et chez
De Boffe, *Gerard Street*. Boosey, *Royal Exchange*.
Booker, *Bond Street*. Et chez P. Fauche, à *Hambourg*.

1797.

The enemies of the Revolution saw the Enlightenment as a conspiracy to undermine the state. The Abbé Barruel's 1797 book (*above*), printed in England, put the case most strongly.

The opposite view was expressed in numerous prints and pamphlets. Perée's engraving of 'Regenerated Man' of 1797 (*opposite*) shows him, heroically nude, holding the Declaration of the Rights of Man and trampling on the ruins of religion and tyranny, while a bolt of lightning strikes the crown.

PREVIOUS PAGES
Was the French Revolution the logical consequence of the Enlightenment or a tragic perversion of its values? Both views were held at the time and have continued to be held ever since. Certainly many key ideas of the Revolution were derived from Enlightenment thinking, as were belief in reason and disdain for superstition. On the other hand, it was possible to see the Enlightenment as opening the door to extremism, fanaticism and bloodshed. 'The Feast of the Supreme Being', celebrated in Paris in 1794, symbolized aspiration rather than achievement. The Tree of Liberty crowns the hill-top. In the foreground Agriculture, holding a Phrygian cap, enters with the fruits of the earth.

DE LA DÉCADENCE

DES LETTRES
ET DES MŒURS,

DEPUIS LES GRECS ET LES ROMAINS
JUSQU'A NOS JOURS.

PAR M. RIGOLEY DE JUVIGNY,
Conseiller honoraire au Parlement de Metz,
de l'Académie des Sciences, Arts & Belles-
Lettres de Dijon.

DÉDIÉ AU ROI.

A PARIS,
Chez MÉRIGOT le jeune, Libraire, Quai des Augustins,
au coin de la rue Pavée.

M. DCC. LXXXVII.
Avec Approbation, & Privilége du Roi.

'A general depravation of morals',
according to Rigoley de Juvigny, was the only
result of the Enlightenment. His book (*above*)
was published two years before the Revolution,
which he must have seen as a confirmation
of everything he had predicted.

For Hegel (*opposite*) the Revolution was
philosophically a failure, since it was unable
to provide a substitute for the religion that it
destroyed. Men's minds became focused on
the World rather than the Spirit.

These were words which had lain behind many of the religious policies of Louis XIV, who died in 1715. If Louis XV took things more lightly, it is clear that Louis XVI on the other hand was profoundly moulded by the ideology of Christian kingship. It was this which largely contributed to his execution in January 1793. For him, as for counter-Enlightenment thinkers, throne and altar really were inseparable.

Those who saw attacks on religion as attacks on the monarchy regarded the Enlightenment not as a commitment to social and legal reform, but as a largely religious movement. Many viewed it as the final throes of the Protestant Reformation of the sixteenth century. In the opening years of the nineteenth century even the great German philosopher Hegel saw the Enlightenment as a failed attempt to close the Reformation and preserve its promised freedoms of mind and spirit. Whether his interpretation was correct is not important. What is important is that he too, like counter-Enlightenment thinkers of his time, saw the Enlightenment as a movement which had destroyed the unseen world and reduced man's life on earth to precisely and only that. As he wrote in the *Phenomenology of Spirit*: 'Formerly, they had a heaven adorned with a vast wealth of thoughts and imagery. The meaning of all that is hung on the thread of light by which it was linked to that of heaven. Instead of dwelling in a this-world presence, men looked beyond it, following the thread to an other-worldly presence, so to speak. The eye of the spirit had to be forcibly turned and held fast to the things of this world; and it took a long time before the lucidity which only heavenly beings used to have could penetrate the dullness and confusion in which the sense of worldly things was enveloped, and so make attention to the here and now as such – to what has been called "experience" – an interesting and valid exercise. Now, we seem to heed just the opposite: our senses are so fast rooted in earthly things that it requires just as much force to raise them. The Spirit shows itself so impoverished, that, like a wanderer in the desert craving for a mouthful of water, it seems to crave for its refreshment only the bare feelings of the divine in general.'

Hegel, as Louis Hinchman has argued, alleged that the Enlightenment failed to produce any set of beliefs which could possibly replace religious faith. In fact, it had, he thought, moved the grounds of debate about religion away from questions of the *truth* of religion, which had obsessed the Reformation era of the sixteenth and seventeenth centuries, to the mere *utility* of religion in providing social stability. The Enlightenment simply saw the world as an outcrop of other phenomena such as the laws of nature which were knowable by man. In that case, religion ceased to have an independent status as relating to a world of faith only partially knowable by man, and became totally assimilated to human needs and human understanding. Once man became an end in himself, as Hegel alleged that he had in Enlightenment thought, once he lost religious aspiration, he became trapped in solipsism, unable to judge himself aright, or to form non-utilitarian ties to other human beings. Thus Hegel, like Kant, saw the Enlightenment as an uncompleted project for intellectual freedom. But for Hegel, the Enlightenment had betrayed itself, left unfulfilled its religious mission to complete the Reformation, because of the nature of man, autonomous and self-sufficient, dependent only on experience for the formation of ideas.

Counter-Enlightenment thinkers would have agreed, as the historian Darrin MacMahon has pointed out. Their propaganda would not only have made

the utilitarian point that religion was necessary for social cohesion, but also discussed the cultural costs of the 'disenchantment of the world' which Hegel pointed to, a world in which no appeal could be made to a higher source, and in which there were no non-utilitarian grounds for morals. In such a situation, no justification could be made for the valorization of history and family, nor for the (allegedly dangerous) idea of abstract rights.

Counter-Enlightenment thinkers from the middle years of the eighteenth century were also sharpening their ideas about the Enlightenment attack on religion. The idea that the Enlightenment was an actual conspiracy, by *philosophes*, rather than a general tendency of thought, grew up around these years, fostered by conservative journals such as the Jesuit *Journal de Trévoux*, and Jesuit thinkers and historians such as the Abbé Barruel. Barruel's massive work *Mémoires pour servir à l'histoire du Jacobinisme* was one of the most influential books of its time. It too put forward the idea that the *philosophe* 'conspiracy' had not only caused the ruin of religion, with all that that implied, but had also caused the French Revolution itself. Novels such as the best-selling *Le comte d Valmont, ou les égarements de la raison* (*The Count of Valmont, or the Vagaries of Reason*) influenced opinion more subtly. The idea of a *philosophe* conspiracy fitted only too well with the 'paranoid style' (to use a phrase coined by well-known American historian Gordon Wood) of court politics in this era. Real plots and conspiracies had marked the history of the monarchy, and all in public life were still on the qui vive for fresh ones. Nor was this simply a quirk of absolutist monarchy in France. The American colonists justified their break from Britain by alleging that a plot had been formed against them by George III. It was thus not hard to see the *philosophes* as conspirators. Counter-

Jesuit thinkers, unsurprisingly, agreed with those who saw the Enlightenment as a threat not only to religion but also to social order. The *Journal de Trévoux* publicized this view from 1701 to 1762 (*above*).

A moral tale, *Le Comte de Valmont*, was published anonymously in 1774. Its message was that religion was the only basis for ethical conduct. The frontispiece (*right*) illustrates the hero being led astray by Passion, but recalled to virtue by Truth.

Enlightenment thinkers attacked all collective organizations such as the Freemasons as conspirators, and were delighted to find actual conspiracy in the actions and thoughts of the group known as the *Illuminati* in the German states, who indeed wished to take over the monarchy and Church in the name of the Enlightenment.

The French Revolution of 1789 was immediately proclaimed a *philosophe* conspiracy by the anti-Enlightenment. The assertion of abstract rights with the proclamation of the Rights of Man and Citizen in 1789, the abolition of the monarchy in 1792 and the execution of the king and queen in 1793, appalled many. Attacks on the property and hierarchy of the Catholic Church confirmed the idea that the Revolution long plotted by the *philosophes* was indeed a continuation of the Protestant Reformation. The proclamation of a break with the past, and the abolition of the Christian calendar, seemed to signal all that the anti-Enlightenment had most feared about the elimination of tradition and history of which monarchy and Church had been the twin pillars. The institution of religious tolerance for Protestants and Jews worked to the same effect.

The Revolution was a profound shock for the opponents of the Enlightenment. Opinions polarized, as we can see from reading what a pro-Enlightenment German journalist wrote in the *Oberdeutsche Allgemeine Literaturzeitung* in 1793: 'Then the disorders in France erupted, and now they again reared their empty heads and screeched at the top of their voices, "Look there at the shocking results of the *Aufklärung*! Look there at the philosophers, the preachers of sedition!" Everyone seized this magnificent opportunity to spray their poison at the supporters of *Aufklärung*.'

'Natural Law, or the Empire of Reason', another illustration to *Valmont*. Everything is sacrificed to the love of order and the common good (*below left*). Two deathbeds teach the same lesson – first that of the impious, a bitter end without the consolations of religion (*below middle*), then that of the Christian soul, comforted by the image of Christ (*below right*).

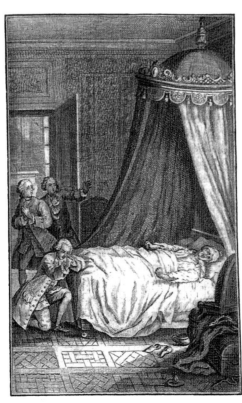

DÉCLARATION

DES DROITS DE L'HOMME
ET DU CITOYEN.

Le peuple François convaincu, que l'oubli et le mépris des droits naturels de l'homme, sont les seules causes des malheurs du monde, a résolu d'exposer dans une déclaration solemnelle ces droits sacrées et inaliénables afin que tous les citoyens pouvant comparer sans cesse les actes du gouvernement avec le but de toute institution sociale, ne se laissent jamais opprimer et avilir par la tyrannie, afin que le peuple ait toujours devant les yeux les bases de sa liberté et de son bonheur, le magistrat la regle de ses devoirs, le législateur l'objet de sa mission.
En conséquence, il proclame, en présence de l'Être suprême, la déclaration suivante des droits de l'homme et du citoyen.

ARTICLE PREMIER

Le but de la société est le bonheur commun.
Le gouvernement est institué pour garantir à l'homme la jouissance de ses droits naturels et imprescriptibles.

2. Ces droits, sont l'égalité, la liberté, la sureté, la propriété.

3. Tous les hommes sont égaux par la nature et devant la loi.

4. La loi est l'expression libre et solemnelle de la volonté générale, elle est la même pour tous, soit qu'elle protège, soit qu'elle punisse; elle ne peut ordonner que ce qui est juste et utile à la société, elle ne peut défendre que ce qui est nuisible.

5. Tous les citoyens sont également admissibles aux emplois publics. Les peuples libres ne connoissent d'autres motifs de préférence dans leurs élections, que les vertus et les talens.

6. La liberté est le pouvoir qui appartient à l'homme de faire tout ce qui ne nuit pas aux droits d'autrui: elle a pour principe, la nature, pour règle, la justice; pour sauve-garde la loi; sa limite morale est dans cette maxime; ne fais pas à un autre ce que tu ne veux pas qu'il te soit fait.

7. Le droit de manifester sa pensée et ses opinions, soit par la voie de la presse, soit de toute autre maniere, le droit de s'assembler paisiblement, le libre exercice des cultes, ne peuvent être interdits.
La nécessité d'énoncer ses droits, suppose ou la présence ou le souvenir récent du despotisme.

8. La sureté consiste dans la protection accordée par la société à chacun de ses membres pour la conservation de sa personne, de ses droits et de ses propriétés.

9. La loi doit protéger la liberté publique et individuelle contre l'oppression de ceux qui gouvernent.

10. Nul ne doit être accusé, arrêté, ni détenu que dans les cas déterminés par la loi et selon les formes qu'elle a prescrites.
Tout citoyen appelé ou saisi par l'autorité de la loi doit obéir a l'instant: il se rend coupable par la résistance.

11. Tout acte exercé contre un homme hors des cas et sans les formes que la loi détermine, est arbitraire et tyranique: celui contre lequel on voudroit l'exécuter par la violence, a le droit de le repousser par la force.

12. Ceux qui solliciteroient, expédieroient, signeroient, exécuteroient ou feroient exécuter des actes arbitraires sont coupables, et doivent être punis.

13. Tout homme étant présumé innocent jusqu'à ce qu'il ait été déclaré coupable, s'il est jugé indispensable de l'arrêter, toute rigueur qui ne seroit pas nécessaire pour s'assurer de sa personne, doit être sévèrement réprimée par la loi.

14. Nul ne doit être jugé et puni qu'après avoir été entendu ou légalement appelé, et qu'en vertu d'une loi promulguée antérieurement au délit. La loi qui puniroit des délits commis avant qu'elle existat, seroit une tyrannie; l'effet rétroactif donné à la loi seroit un crime.

15. La loi ne doit décerner que des peines strictement et évidemment nécessaires; les peines doivent être proportionnés au délit et utiles à la société.

16. Le droit de propriété est celui qui appartient à tout citⁿ de jouir et de disposer a son gré de ses biens et de ses revenus, du fruit de son travail et de son industrie.

17. Nul genre de travail, de culture, de commerce, ne peut être interdit à l'industrie des citoyens.

ART DIX-HUITIEME

Tout homme peut engager ses services, son temps; mais il ne peut se vendre, ni être vendu: sa personne n'est pas une propriété aliénable. La loi ne connoit pas de domesticité; il ne peut exister qu'un engagement de soins et de reconnaissance, entre l'homme qui travaille et celui qui l'emploie.

19. Nul ne peut être privé de la moindre portion de sa propriété sans son consentement si ce n'est lorsque la nécessité publique légalement constatée l'exige, et sous la condition d'une juste et préalable indemnité.

20. Nulle contribution ne peut être établie que pour l'utilité générale. Tout les citoyens ont droit de concourir à l'établissement des contributions, dans surveiller l'emploi, et de s'en faire rendre compte.

21. Les secours publics sont une dette sacrée. La société doit la subsistance aux citoyens malheureux, soit en leur procurant du travail, soit en assurant les moyens d'exister a ceux qui sont hors d'état de travailler.

22. L'instruction est le besoin de tous. La société doit favoriser de tout son pouvoir les progrès de la raison publique, et mettre l'instruction a la porté de tous les citoyens.

23. La garantie sociale consiste dans l'action de tous, pour assurer à chacun la jouissance et la conservation de ses droits cette garantie repose sur la souveraineté nationale.

24. Elle ne peut exister si les limites des fonctions publiques ne sont pas clairement déterminées par la loi, et si la responsabilité de tous les fonctionnaires n'est pas assurée.

25. La souveraineté réside dans le peuple, elle est une et indivisible, imprescriptible et inaliénable.

26. Aucune portion du peuple ne peut exercer la puissance du peuple entier; mais chaque section du souverain assemblée, doit jouir du droit d'exprimer sa volonté avec une entiere liberté.

27. Que tout individu qui usurperoit la souveraineté, soit à l'instant mis a mort par les hommes libres.

28. Un peuple a toujours le droit de revoir, de réformer et de changer sa constitution. Une génération ne peut assujettir à ses loix les générations futures.

29. Chaque citoyen a un droit égal de concourir à la formation de la loi, et a la nomination de ses mandataires ou de ses agens.

30. Les fonctions publiques sont essentiellement temporaires, elle ne peuvent être considérées comme des distinctions ni comme des récompenses, mais comme des devoirs.

31. Les délits des mandataires du peuple et de ses agens, ne doivent jamais être impunis. Nul n'a le droit de se prétendre plus inviolable que les autre citoyens.

32. Le droit de présenter des pétitions aux dépositaires de l'autorité publique ne peut, en aucun cas, être interdit, suspendu, ni limité.

33. La résistane a l'oppression est la conséquence des autres droits de l'homme.

34. Il y a oppression contre le corps social lorsqu'un seul de ses membres est opprimé: il y a oppression contre chaque membre lorsque le corps social est opprimé.

35. Quand le gouvernement viole les droits du peuple, l'insurrection est pour le peuple, et pour chaque portion du peuple, le plus sacré et le plus indispensable des devoirs.

As this quotation also implies, supporters of the Enlightenment found their position weakened as the Revolution in France lurched through ever more violent and radical phases. Favourite Enlightenment words such as 'virtue' began to take on new and terrifying meanings. Civil war broke out in France in 1793. The supporters of throne and altar faced revolutionary troops. Appalling atrocities were committed on both sides. Political terror, resulting in the execution of thousands, began to be used from 1792. Hundreds of alleged counter-revolutionaries were massacred in the prisons of Paris that autumn. The Terror made it seem that all the worst prognostications of the counter-Enlightenment had come true. It is not surprising that after Napoleon's seizure of power in 1799 reaction against both the Enlightenment and Revolution was the order of the day. As Napoleon himself thundered in 1803, the language of the *philosophes* was 'this impious language that teaches the people to disdain the faith of their fathers, this seditious language that teaches them to revolt against authority; this corrupting language that outrages morality, encourages vice and removes all impediments to the passions … this philosophy, in short, that sullies nearly every one of the pages of the *philosophes* of the eighteenth century … a code of atheism … a code of immorality … a code of bloody revolt'.

Anti-Enlightenment thinkers could also derive considerable comfort as they looked outside France to the revolutionary movements which overtook other states. Even in largely peaceful Germany, the prince-bishopric of Mainz was overthrown in 1795, and although the spring republic which was proclaimed in its place lasted only a few weeks, it became a paradigm for the ideology of

The height of revolutionary violence came with the Terror under Robespierre. This popular print of 1794 (*above*) makes the point that his victims – the piles of skulls – came from the clergy, the parliament, the nobility, the Constituent Assembly, the legislature and the Convention, but the greatest sufferers were the people.

The Rights of Man as formulated in 1793 (*opposite*). 'Article No. 1. The purpose of society is the common good. Government is instituted to guarantee to man the enjoyment of his natural and inalienable rights. No. 2. These rights are liberty, safety and property.'

Napoleon (*left*) as first consul rejected both the Enlightenment and much of the Revolution's 'code of atheism … of immorality … of bloody revolt'.

revolution in Germany. German critics of the old regime had looked to the European republican tradition, and taken heart from the establishment of the new American republic after its battle with the tyrannous monarchy of King George III. German writers with Enlightenment allegiances had consistently denounced the abuses of arbitrary power by their princes, of which the most notorious was the forced shipping to America (to fight on the English side) of young German men pressed into the army. These forces were sold to King George as though, as many contemporary writers remarked, they had been so many slaves.

Words of war, wars of words

These wars of words were increasingly polarized. Prussian participation in the First Partition of Poland, in 1772, caused an outcry, as the Poles were redistributed between Prussia, Austria and Russia against their will. The German writer Johann Gottfried Seume, who had himself been shipped to America as a pressed man, declared his allegiance to the Enlightenment: 'Enlightenment is the correct, complete, exact insight into our own nature, our relationships, the bright term defining our rights and duties.' By the 1790s, it was commonplace to remark, as did the writer Karl Friedrich Reinhard, that both *Aufklärung* and *lumières* had been transformed into 'words of war'. Seume, looking to the French Revolution for a model, thundered that it had the glory in world history of having brought the principles of reason into public law. If we let these principles die, he continued, every part of the world would deserve its little Bonaparte. Seume, Reinhard and the writers and thinkers who, like Georg Forster, took part in the Mainz Republic held hard to these ideas, even when the increasingly violent course of the revolution in France seemed to deviate sharply from its earlier stages when it had still been possible to see its achievements as the realization of decades of enlightened criticism.

Against this background, it is possible to produce a new interpretation of Kant's essay on *Aufklärung* (see Chapter 1), which comes to grips with the ambiguity of his relation to the revolutionary era of the German Enlightenment. Kant's idea that public criticism was only legitimate in the private realm (a part of his essay neglected by nearly all post-modernist interpreters) now looks like an attempt to slow down the increasing momentum of criticism in the German states. '*Sapere aude!* Yes, but only a few will do so' led to knowledge by a guardian class. Kant's essay has little or nothing to say to the increasingly fierce outbursts of criticism in the name of Enlightenment. This cuts it off from one strand in German history, that leading to the foundation of the GDR, which always proclaimed its roots in the Mainz Republic and the German Jacobins, who had been strongly influenced by the revolutionaries who had established the French Republic under the banners of freedom and reason. Kant concludes, however, with the difficulties of bringing about Enlightenment under an absolute ruler. This too the Mainz republicans understood. The Mainz Republic, in spite of its short life-span, is important because it demonstrated the revolutionary potential of any Enlightenment which would dare to break through the contradictions, ironies and caveats of Kant's account, to actualize some of its major ideas, such as freedom and reason.

Yet 1795 was already late in the history of the Revolution in France. A weak government ruled over a bankrupt France surrounded by external

One who never lost his belief in either the Enlightenment or the Revolution was Johann Gottfried Seume, who died in 1810 but whose autobiography was posthumously published in 1813. He had been conscripted into the Hessian army and shipped to America, which perhaps nourished his respect for liberty.

Goethe too was a man of the Enlightenment. His watercolour of 1790 shows the French frontier with the slogan: 'Travellers, this land is free.'

enemies, and with wavering support at home. It was no surprise, when Napoleon Bonaparte seized power in 1799, that his first task should have been to restore order. This meant undoing many of the more extreme measures of the revolutionary period, such as its attack on the French Catholic Church. In 1802, Napoleon concluded a concordat with the Pope which ended the schism between the Catholic Church and the French state. In the same year the French novelist and statesman François René de Chateaubriand published his well-timed *Génie du christianisme* (*The Spirit of Christianity*). For long probably the best-known and best-selling defence of Christianity in general and Catholicism in particular, this used arguments drawn both from natural theology (see Chapter 7) and from poetry and painting to make the case for the truth of religion. Chateaubriand's attitude to the Enlightenment was predictable. Voltaire, he wrote, 'had the sad art of making atheism fashionable among a capricious and likeable people … religion was attacked in every way possible, from pamphlets to large volumes, from epigrams to sophisms. Authors of religious books were covered with mockery, while at the same time books that Voltaire and his friends laughed at together were praised to the skies. Voltaire was so superior to his disciples that he even laughed at their antireligious excesses. However, this destruction of religion spread right through

France, to provincial academies, the seats of bad taste and in-fighting. Society women and grave philosophers alike preached unbelief. Everyone seemed to accept that Christianity was only a barbarous system whose collapse could not come soon enough for human liberty, the progress of Enlightenment, ease of living, and the elegance of the arts and crafts.'

Chateaubriand established the age of Louis XIV as a standard against which to judge the Enlightenment in general, and Voltaire in particular. He links it with the Enlightenment's attacks on the bases of religion, singling out *Candide* for particular attention. In this novel, the eponymous hero and his companions stagger from one overwhelming disaster to the next. They are witnesses to the 1755 earthquake in Lisbon, in which more than 10,000 people were killed and most of the city was destroyed. This and their own misfortunes make them confront the question of evil: why does God allow bad things to happen to good people? If he does, can he be either benevolent or all-powerful? The only coherent answer to this question in the novella is given by the Manichaean, Martin.

For Chateaubriand, on the other hand, Christianity mobilized the deepest human feelings, such as attachment to one's native land. In a passage which well demonstrates the powerful and emotional language of the *Génie*, he considers: 'if someone asked us what it was that kept us linked to the place where we were born, we would hardly know what to say. Perhaps it is the smile of a mother, a father, or a sister; the old teacher who brought us up, or childhood friends, or even the most simple and trivial things: a dog barking in the night, the nest of swallows by the window, the church tower … these little things show the reality of Providence. They could not possibly be the source of patriotism, and the great virtues which are born from it, if a supreme will had not ordered it so.' This passage, with its emotional penetration, is

The fall of Mainz to the French revolutionary armies in October 1792 (*opposite*) led to the founding of the short-lived Republic of Mainz by a group of radical German sympathizers (*above*). It was the first such republic outside France. One of its memers was Georg Wedekind, whose own version of the Rights of Man – following the French model – was published in 1793 (*below*).

Napoleon inherited a divided nation, which he succeeded in uniting, but at the cost of founding a new despotism. In spite of his scathing criticism of the *philosophes*, he did fundamentally believe in the Enlightenment. A contemporary allegory (*right*) shows him leading France back from the brink towards Justice and Plenty, while Discord and Faction plunge into the abyss.

The Catholic Church resumed its place in French official life when Napoleon signed a Concordat with the Vatican in 1802. In the same year Chateaubriand published his *Génie du christianisme* (*below*), which to a large extent argued against the work of Voltaire and the *philosophes*.

GÉNIE

DU CHRISTIANISME,

OU

BEAUTÉS

DE

LA RELIGION CHRÉTIENNE;

PAR

FRANÇOIS-AUGUSTE CHATEAUBRIAND.

Chose admirable ! la religion chrétienne , qui ne semble avoir
d'objet que la félicité de l'autre vie , fait encore notre
bonheur dans celle-ci.
MONTESQUIEU, *Esprit des Lois* , Liv. XXIV , ch. III.

Nouvelle Édition à laquelle on a inséré les notes formant
l'appendice à la fin de chaque Volume.

TOME PREMIER.

A PARIS,

CHEZ MIGNERET, IMPRIMEUR,
RUE DU SÉPULCRE, F. S. G. Nº. 28.

AN X.—1802.

typical of Chateaubriand's style; it is this quality, rather than the novelty of its theological arguments, that explains the impact of his writing.

Continuities

It is a mistake, however, to see the *Génie* only as a series of disingenuous, perfectly timed arguments for the supremacy of Catholicism and the existence of God. The underlying problem with which it wrestles is that of continuity. Chateaubriand himself had once spoken for an entire generation when, in his autobiography, he described the French Revolution as 'a river of blood which separates for ever the old world in which you were born from the new world on whose frontiers you will die'. This sense of the French Revolution as a dark and threatening chasm in time, so different from the joyful *novus ordo seculorum* of the triumphant American Revolution of 1776, contributed crucially to negative revaluations of the Enlightenment. Having acknowledged the magnitude of the historical discontinuities caused by the upheavals of the Revolution and the attacks of the Enlightenment on the traditions of religion and monarchy, where should the post-revolutionary world find its own ground? Chateaubriand, like many of his generation, tried to find a happier past by asserting continuity in 1802 not with the eighteenth but with the seventeenth century and its writers such as the tragedian Racine, the comic writer Molière and the famous preacher Bossuet. This was not easy to accept. The Abbé Barruel's theses on the continuities between the Enlightenment and the French Revolution seemed to be only too well borne out by the events of post-1815 Europe. The wave of revolutionary movements which swept through Europe in the 1820s and 1830s, and which were in fact, especially in southern Europe, influenced by secret societies of political activists, seemed to provide vivid empirical evidence of the link between conspiracy, revolution and mutant forms of 'Jacobinism'.

Indeed, Barruel was far from alone in his attempt to find continuities between the Enlightenment, the French Revolution and contemporary upheavals. In 1856, Alexis de Tocqueville published his *L'ancien régime et la révolution française* (*The Old Regime and the French Revolution*). Tocqueville, a liberal politician worried by the revolution of 1848 and the increasingly authoritarian turn of French politics after Napoleon III's seizure of power in 1852, was no conservative figure looking back with regret to a time when throne and altar stood unchallenged. He argued that there were indeed continuities between the eighteenth century and the Revolution, but he saw them as lying not only with the thinkers of the Enlightenment, but also with the increasing power of the centralized state, which had continued to grow unabated in both the *Ancien Régime* and the revolution. He believed that this development in fact spanned the huge chasm between pre- and post-revolutionary worlds which had seemed so unbridgeable to Chateaubriand. It was this growth of the state, Tocqueville argued, which would extinguish liberty, as much as had the mob rule of the Revolution. He argued that, catapulted into practical politics after 1789, the men of the Enlightenment, whom he viewed as inexperienced utopian thinkers, had been unable to provide any ideological bulwark against the growth of political terror or the centralization which went with it: 'the philosopher's cloak provided safe cover for the passions of the day, and political ferment was canalised into literature, the result being that our writers now became leaders of public opinion, and played for a while the part which normally in free countries falls to the professional politician.' In fact, their utopian idealism both before and after 1789 had created a situation where debate and legitimate differences of opinion could not be maintained, and terror therefore became the only way to exercise power, leading to a vast increase in dictatorial central government.

Other leading nineteenth-century historians also concerned themselves with problems of continuity between the Enlightenment and the Revolution. Louis Blanc's *Histoire de la révolution française* (*History of the French Revolution*) of 1847 makes a sustained attempt to trace the ideas of the Enlightenment throughout the Revolution. This, however, is a difficult if not impossible task. The Enlightenment hardly produced a unified body of thought. While the revolutionaries themselves often alluded to Voltaire and Rousseau – two thinkers who had often been at loggerheads during their lifetimes – their own thinking often proceeded in directions which would have horrified those whose names they used to legitimate their actions. It is debatable, for example, whether Rousseau would have appreciated the use to which his *Social Contract* was put in order to justify the employment of terror during the Revolution. While much use was also made of appeals to Enlightenment ideals of progress or reason, few could have foreseen in 1789 the extent of the changes which were to occur by 1792.

Did the years 1789–99 see one revolution or many, each with a different relationship to the Enlightenment and with its own complex debates?

'Saint Napoleon' had been an Early Christian martyr in the Roman army. His image was used to glorify the emperor and his (apparent) submission to the Church.

The Vision of Matthias Koeppel

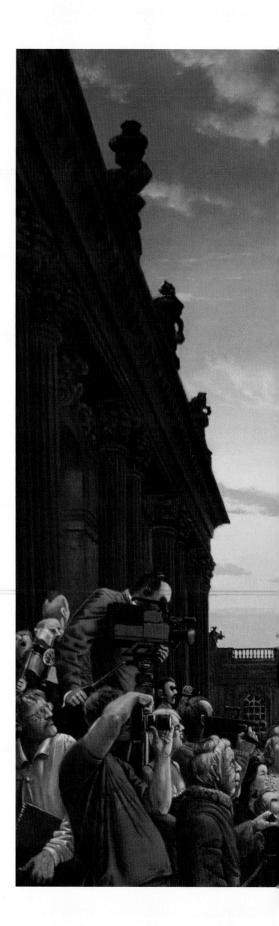

THESE TWO RELATED OIL PAINTINGS, created in the aftermath of German reunification in 1990, are meditations on the presence of the Enlightenment in the present. The first (*right*) shows the reburial of Frederick II in 1991. Contrary to his own wishes, the king had been buried in the Garrison Church in Potsdam, and only after many intervening staging posts did his coffin at last return to Sans Souci, where he had asked to be buried on his death in August 1786. Frederick's reburial caused enormous controversy. It was seen as an attempt to revive in federal Germany the militaristic attitudes of the Prussian state, which, it was alleged, had begun with Frederick's wars. Few paused to reflect on the king's policies of religious toleration. Koeppel paints a huge squad of journalists at maximum distance from the catalfalque of Frederick II, and yet also linked to him by the famous arcade at the rear of Sans Souci. The catafalque is in the traditional royal colours of black and white.

Both these pictures leave at least half the canvas bare of figures, filled with an enormous sky-scape of pink, grey-blue white and rose. Like the Dutch landscape masters of the seventeenth century, who specialized in such scenes, Koeppel leaves the complex action in this picture under a question mark. How important is it all really?

When, however, one looks closely at the action of the picture *Sans Souci/ Sans Souci 1993*, set on the huge staircase before the palace (see Chapter 6), it is crammed with eighteenth-century images. The dancing lady with a tambourine, for example, is the famous dancer La Barbarina, with whom the king was much taken. A famous portrait by Anton Pesne, painted around 1745, shows her against the background of the same famous arcade. On the stairs leading up to the palace, one sees a tiny figure, taken from a portrait of Frederick II's brother Prince Heinrich, painted by Anna Dorothea Therbusch in 1773. No doubt many more of these painted quotations could be found.

The most important one is that of Frederick himself, standing foregrounded in his favourite black suit and hat. This is also taken from a portrait, painted by Johann Christoph Franke between 1775 and 1785, which is one of the iconic representations of Frederick II. The king turns half towards us as our eyes are swept up the grand staircase to the top of the terraces leading to the front of Sans Souci, welcoming us into the world not so much of Koeppel's imagining as almost a scrapbook of the eighteenth century, in which we are invited to wander and make our own relationships with the figures there depicted.

The Lying in State of Frederick the Great. Two centuries after his death Frederick's body was at last in 1991 laid to rest at Sans Souci, as he had originally ordered. In 1786 he had been interred in the garrison church of Potsdam next to his father whom he hated.

Two modern thinkers, Theodor Adorno (*right*) and Max Horkheimer (*below*), reopened the debate in 1947. In their view the Enlightenment, by substituting reason for religious faith, led to the treatment of human beings as objects and to the divorce of knowledge from ethical values.

In the long term

Much twentieth-century assessment of the Enlightenment remained surprisingly close to the themes of the counter-revolutionary thinkers of the nineteenth century. In 1947, for example, the philosophers Max Horkheimer and Theodor Adorno published their influential *Dialectic of Enlightenment*. Writing in the immediate aftermath of a world war and the Holocaust, the authors asked 'why mankind, instead of entering into a truly human condition, is sinking into a new kind of barbarism'. This happened, in their view, because of a paradox which lay at the heart of Enlightenment thinking: 'The Enlightenment had always aimed at liberating men from fear, and establishing their sovereignty. Yet the fully Enlightened earth radiates disaster triumphant. The programme of the Enlightenment was the disenchantment of the world: the dissociation of myths, and the substitution of knowledge for fancy.' Like the earlier counter-revolutionary writers, Horkheimer and Adorno also see the Enlightenment as a sign of religious crisis, with myth and revelation removed from any thinking worthy of the name. The Enlightenment project of the 'disenchantment of the world … the dissociation of myths and the substitution of knowledge for fancy' made it difficult, even where an outward conformity with religion was reached, to focus aspirations of harmony and fulfilment on the 'regions Beyond', but instead 'redefined them as criteria for human aspiration'. This allowed what Horkheimer and Adorno famously baptized 'the administered life', a 'rational' organization of men, nature and knowledge itself for the achievement of the objectives of this world. It was this which they saw as contributing not only to the general character of life in the twentieth-century West, but also specifically to the organization and management of the Holocaust, where the treatment of human beings as mere objects to be administered and consumed by a rational technological system reached its starkest expression.

The second important idea which Horkheimer and Adorno brought to the study of the Enlightenment was that its view of rationality had the effect of turning knowledge into a commodity, and thereby of breaking down the traditional connection between knowledge, truth and wisdom. 'Once viewed as a commodity to be bought and sold, Knowledge itself became merely a means to an end and culture became wholly a commodity disseminated as information without permeating the individuals who acquired it.' Technology was a particular culprit: 'technology does not work by concepts and images, by the fortunate insight, but refers to method, the exploitation of others' work and capital. What men want to learn from nature is how to use it in order wholly to dominate it and other men … on the road to modern science, men renounce any claim to meaning.' These comments encapsulate much of Hegel's thinking of more than one hundred years before, discussed above. Much has been said about the 'information revolution'. Horkheimer and Adorno's argument that knowledge now started to function as a form of goods upon a market, ceased to be internalized by individual people, and became divorced from truth values and from ethical questions, may seem to be supported by the dramatic growth in the circulation of books and news in the eighteenth century (see Chapter 2). But it is hardly substantiated by the ethical concerns that so mark Enlightenment writings. Religious toleration and the making of the benevolent state are two conspicuous examples in this context. Yet the building of the latter was accompanied by a new stress, especially in the German states and England, on efficiency. It was this new stress which caused Frederick II of Prussia to describe himself as the 'first servant of the state'. Similarly, the struggle for religious toleration was, as its opponents saw very clearly, the result of an abandonment of any concern with the truth of any particular religion, an outcome which would have been almost inconceivable in the seventeenth century.

Horkheimer and Adorno's account has many faults. It cannot decide whether it is philosophy or history, it contains a long and much-derided account of the Greek hero Ulysses as the first bourgeois, and its decision to jump from the eighteenth to the twentieth century, without assessing the far more obvious impact of the nineteenth century on the horrors of the twentieth, is strange, to say the least. It is justified, though insufficiently discussed, by seeing the philosopher Nietzsche as a transitional figure, with ambiguous attitudes towards Kant's essay. Nonetheless, it looks as though Horkheimer and Adorno's negative interpretation of the Enlightenment might, for all its faults, carry a measure of truth.

Another important interpretation of the Enlightenment is far more positive. The German philosopher Jürgen Habermas opposed many of Horkheimer and Adorno's ideas in his 1962 *Struckturwandel der Offentlichkeit* (*The Structural Transformation of the Public Sphere*), adopting many of their insights into the Enlightenment consumption of culture, but without drawing their negative conclusions. For him, other potentialities of the Enlightenment were still alive in the modern world and pointed in directions to be pursued in the making of modern society. Habermas based his ideas of the Enlightenment on the famous essay by Immanuel Kant (see Chapter 1) with which we opened this book. He emphasized Kant's perception that, far from being closed and over, the Enlightenment had still to be pursued and brought to completion.

The Enlightenment, he argued, contained the potential to emancipate individuals from restrictive particularism in order to be able to act as human

A contrary view is held by Jürgen Habermas, who sees the Enlightenment as the seedbed of modern quasi-moral concepts, such as 'public opinion'. He comes close to Kant's original analysis.

beings, linked to other human beings by common values such as freedom, justice and objectivity. These values were indeed important to the Enlightenment. But in discussing the Enlightenment's potential to change the world, Habermas is too ready to assume the existence of universal values, and that those values are necessarily those central to the Enlightenment. This position also means that Habermas contradicts Enlightenment writers such as Herder who decried the attempts of his time to override cultural distinctiveness born of differences of race, religion, language or place of birth.

Habermas argues that the Enlightenment saw the creation of a 'public realm' where opinions were discussed and transformed through newspapers, books, plays and pictures into what we would now call 'public opinion'. In Habermas' view this was the creation of the middle classes who organized and consumed the flow of cultural materials. Far from seeing this, as Horkheimer and Adorno had, as the beginnings of a 'culture industry' which would degrade knowledge

To women the Enlightenment showed the way to assert their equality with men, the first step on the road to intellectual and legal emancipation. Mary Wollstonecraft's *Vindication of the Rights of Women* was the pioneering work. Statements which now, largely thanks to her example, seem mere truisms required revolutionary courage to put into words at the time: 'For man and woman, truth, if I understand the meaning of the word, must be the same.'

into a mere instrument of control, Habermas views the creation of the public realm as a means of liberation, as providing a space where men could escape their roles as subjects and gain autonomy in the exercise and exchange of their own opinions and ideas. In interpreting the culture of the Enlightenment Habermas is thus also demonstrating the possibility of historical analysis filled with positive moral meaning for the present.

In this his work unexpectedly converged with that of the French philosopher Michel Foucault, who engaged with Habermas in debate over the meaning of the Enlightenment. Foucault also saw Kant's essay as providing a crucial definition of the Enlightenment. Abandoning earlier positions in which he had seen a great gap between the Enlightenment and modern thinking, Foucault adopted Kant's view that the Enlightenment had been incomplete, and used Kant's essay as a starting point for a new understanding of the idea of critical reason as an agent of change. Habermas and Foucault united in agreeing on the importance of the Enlightenment for a re-evaluation of the present.

The feminine perspective

We have concentrated up till now on the prolonged history of the opposition to the Enlightenment. But this is not the whole story. The Mainz Republic demonstrated the strength of the revolutionary potential in the Enlightenment, though as it did so it also confirmed all the fears of the anti-Enlightenment. Yet contemporaries produced important uses and justifications for the Enlightenment. In an absolutely different context from the Mainz Republic, the writer, traveller and educationalist Mary Wollstonecraft fought fiercely to save the Enlightenment from contemporary daily practice as it related to women. Wollstonecraft's father was an unsuccessful gentleman farmer, and she made her way out of her humble situation by her writing and by the sort of educational work then allowed to women. She became a governess and worked in the family of the Irish peer Lord Kingsborough. Afterwards, she set up her own school for girls, wrote book reviews, essays, an account of her travels in Sweden, and became part of the circle of Joseph Johnson, a radical printer and publisher, and of Dr Price, a famous dissenting minister, public speaker and supporter of liberal causes ever more unfashionable as the French Revolution became more violent. Wollstonecraft was lucky to live in the first era in which it became possible for a woman to earn something of an independent living. After many adventures she ended her life as the wife of the radical political thinker William Godwin, and died in 1797 giving birth to their daughter, Mary, future wife of the poet Shelley and author of the novel *Frankenstein*. Wollstonecraft's 1792 *Vindication of the Rights of Women* caused a furore and has often been seen as one of the foundation texts for modern feminism. At the end of 1792, she moved alone to Paris and stayed there during the height of the Terror. It was there that she began a liaison with the American entrepreneur Gilbert Imlay, by whom she had a daughter. Two suicide attempts followed, on Imlay's desertion and infidelity.

In the *Vindication*, Wollstonecraft describes the way in which eighteenth-century women were most often educated, without the study of classical languages, history and literature in which their brothers were steeped. Their educations instead concentrated on the domestic arts, in the expectation that their destiny would be as wives and mothers. Wollstonecraft argued against

'We know how to fight and win, we know to to use other weapons than the needle and scissors. O Bellona, companion of Mars, should not all women follow your example and march forward with a step equal to that of men? Goddess of force and courage! at least you need not blush for Frenchwomen.' A French print of *c.* 1791. In the event, however, the Revolution did little to improve the status of women.

the folly of such an educational division, pointing out that educated mothers are better at their maternal tasks because they are better able to inform their children about the outside world. In this sense, although we have no evidence that Wollstonecraft ever read Kant's essay, she is asking women to leave behind their 'self-imposed immaturity'. She also denounced the legal and financial inferiority of women. She several times compared the position of women to that of slaves, in the sense of their complete dependence and lack of rights.

All these protests about the position of women expressed a complex relationship with the Enlightenment itself. She welcomed the Enlightenment idea of the universality of reason. And yet she asked, 'Who made man the exclusive judge, if women partake with him of the gift of reason?' There was always a contradiction between how the Enlightenment often described itself, as a system of universal values, which Wollstonecraft accepted and admired, and how the Enlightenment worked in practice to give different characteristics to men and to women. She was confused by the idea of gender. As she wrote: 'For man and woman, truth, if I understand the meaning of the word, must be the same; yet for the fanciful female character, so prettily drawn by poets and novelists, demanding the sacrifice of truth and sincerity, virtue becomes a relative idea, having no other foundation but utility, and of that utility, men pretend arbitrarily to judge, shaping it to their own convenience.'

Sexuality confused Enlightenment thinking. Wollstonecraft pointed out that it was founded on ideals such as reason and virtue which were said to be innate in or attainable by all human beings. Yet rationality was precisely what was denied to women by writers such as Rousseau, and virtue for women was defined in an exclusively sexual sense. As Wollstonecraft pointed out, however, such manoeuvres can only lead to a dangerous moral relativism, which will also retard the progress of the Enlightenment. Wollstonecraft's writings are an attempt to rescue the Enlightenment from the stresses imposed upon it by gendered thinking and gendered practice.

Enough has now been said to show the great range of interpretations of the Enlightenment, from Barruel's view that it was a mere front for a Masonic conspiracy against throne and altar, to Habermas' suggestion of a connection between it and human liberty, to Mary Wollstonecraft's attempt to rehabilitate the Enlightenment through attention to the rights of women. So great is this range of interpretation, and so great are the attempts of recent historians to show the Enlightenment as a social phenomenon (see Chapters 1 and 2) that the term 'Enlightenment' itself might be thought to have become diffuse to the point of meaninglessness. It is easy to understand this view. But we may also think of 'Enlightenment' not as a historical expression which has failed to encompass a complex historical reality, but rather as a capsule containing stress points, debates and concerns, which however differently formulated do appear to be characteristic of the way in which ideas, opinions and social and political structures interacted in the eighteenth century. Those characteristics included major contradictions, and fierce internal struggles. When Rousseau, for example, in his *First* and *Second Discourses* challenged the idea of the onward progress of man to ever greater civilization, he opened a major rift in Enlightenment thinking. Every person who wished to be thought enlightened had to position himself in between these paradoxes and contradictions. It was in such positioning that the Enlightenment was created.

FRANÇAISES DEVENUES LIBRES.

. . . . Et nous auſſi, nous ſavons combattre et vaincre.
Nous ſavons manier d'autres armes que l'aiguille et le fuſeau. O Bellone !
compagne de Mars, a ton exemple, toutes les femmes ne devroient-elles pas
narcher de front et d'un pas égal avec les hommes ? Déeſſe de la force et
du courage ! du moins tu n'auras point à rougir des *FRANÇAISES*.

Extrait d'une Prière des Amazones à Bellone.

Timeline

1700 Berlin Academy of Sciences founded

1704 Newton's *Opticks*. Death of Locke

1709 Berkeley's *New Theory of Vision*

c.1710 Watteau's *Pilgrimage to the Isle of Cythera*

1711 *Spectator* begins publication

1713 Statue of Hercules at Wilhelmshöhe

1715 Death of Louis XIV. Accession of Louis XV

1716 Death of Leibniz

1719 Defoe's *Robinson Crusoe*. Death of Addison

1724 St Petersburg Academy of Sciences founded

1725 Death of Peter the Great

1726 Swift's *Gulliver's Travels*

1727 Death of Newton

1728 Vico's *Scienza nuova*

1729 Death of Steele

1732 Zedler's *Universal Lexicon*

1735 Linnaeus' *Systema natura*

1737 Göttingen University founded. Algarotti's *Newtonianismo per le dame*

1739 Hume's *Treatise of Human Nature*

1740 Vitus Behring's last voyage. Richardson's *Pamela*

1741 Handel's *Messiah*

1745 'Yew Tree Ball' at Versailles

1746 Berlin Academy of Sciences founded

1747 Sans Souci at Potsdam begun. Richard's *Clarissa*

1748 La Mettrie's *L'Homme machine*. Montesquieu's *De l'esprit des lois*

1749 Buffon's *Histoire naturelle*

1750 Tiepolo begins frescoes at Würzburg

1751 *Encyclopédie* begins publication

1754 Condillac's *Traité des sensations*

1755 Johnson's *Dictionary* Lisbon earthquake

1756 Seven Years' War begins

1759 Voltaire's *Candide*. Johnson's *Rasselas*

1761 Rousseau's *Julie*

1762 Rousseau's *Emile* and *contrat social*. Death of Lady Mary Wortley Montagu

1763 Neues Palais, Potsdam

1764 Beccaria's *Essay on Crimes and Punishments*

1766 Lessing's *Laokoön*

1768 Cook's first voyage to the Pacific

1769 Hargreaves' patent for the Spinning Jenny

1770 Raynal's *Histoire philosophique*

1771 Ledoux's Salines at Chaux begun

1774 Goethe's *Sorrows of Young Werther*. Death of Louis XV. Accession of Louis XVI

1776 American War of Independence. Adam Smith's *Wealth of Nations*. Death of Hume. Death of Rousseau. *Göttinger Taschencalender* first published. Blumenbach's *On the Natural Variety of the Human Species*

1778 Johann Gottfried Herder's *Von Erkennen und Empfinden*

1779 Death of Cook. Campe's Philanthropins founded

1780 Death of Maria Theresa

1781 Kant's *Critique of Pure Reason*. Schiller's *Die Rauber*

1782 Rousseau's *Confessions* (posthumously published). Laclos' *Liaisons dangereuses*

1783 Berlin Academy of Sciences offers a prize for a definition of 'Enlightenment'. First balloon ascent in Paris

1784 Death of Diderot. Death of Johnson

1786 Death of Frederick the Great

1787 Bernardin de St Pierre's *Paul et Virginie*

1789 *Life of Olaudah Equiano*. Fall of the Bastille; beginning of the French Revolution

1791 Foundation of Republic of Haiti. Mozart's *Magic Flute*. Boswell's *Life of Johnson*. Paine's *Rights of Man*

1792 Wollstonecraft's *Vindication of the Rights of Women*

1793 Execution of Mme Roland. Execution of Louis XVI and Marie Antoinette. Macartney mission to China

1794 Death of Condorcet. Execution of Lavoisier

1795 Mainz Republic

1776 Death of Catherine the Great

1799 Napoleon seizes power. Death of Lichtenberg. Mme Roland's *Advice to my Daughter*

Men and Women

Representative 'Enlightenment People' could belong to any number of categories, from philosophers, writers and scientists to statesmen, hostesses and artists. This selection has been made to include as wide a cross section as possible in order to emphasize the different ways in which the movement that later historians have chosen to call 'the Enlightenment' might manifest itself.

Joseph Addison

Joseph Addison was born in 1672, the son of the rector of Milston, Wiltshire. He was educated at Charterhouse and then Oxford, where he received his degree in 1691. In 1699 he made a Grand Tour of the main European capitals, part of the education of an eighteenth-century gentleman. Addison's work combined politics with poetry and other literary writing. He was elected to parliament in 1707, and in 1709 he went to Dublin as secretary to the lord lieutenant of Ireland. In 1710 he founded *The Whig Examiner* to counter the Tory views of *The Examiner*, a periodical managed by Jonathan Swift. From 1709 to 1711 Addison wrote for *The Tatler*, and then co-edited *The Spectator*. *The Spectator* ran daily for 555 numbers (the last issue was on 6 December 1712), and although by modern standards it had a fairly small circulation, it was widely read by important people of the time. Addison and his friend Sir Richard Steele wrote 90 per cent of the *Spectator*'s essays. Their goal was to bring philosophy into schools and libraries and into fashionable society. They covered such topics as literary and philosophical questions, good and bad manners, and life in the country and in town. Addison was the author of *Cato: A Tragedy* (1713), was appointed secretary of state (1717) and retired the following year with a generous pension. He died in 1719.

D'Alembert (Jean Le Rond)

D'Alembert, born in 1717, the illegitimate son of the writer and *salon* hostess Claudine de Tencin (1682–1749), rapidly became famous as a mathematician. He was a member of the *salons* of Mme Geoffrin and Mme du Deffand, where he encountered his lifelong passion, Julie de Lespinasse. With Diderot, he co-edited the *Encyclopédie*, and wrote its 'Preliminary Discourse', an important reflection on the nature and organization of knowledge. He wrote about 1,400 articles for the *Encyclopédie*, some of which led him into controversy with Rousseau and the musician Rameau. After 1758, he withdrew from the *Encyclopédie*, and began to write musical and literary criticism. In 1779 he became perpetual secretary of the Royal Academy of Sciences in Paris. D'Alembert has often been seen as one of the last thinkers capable of contributing over the whole range of knowledge. He died in 1783.

Cesare Beccaria

Cesare Beccaria was born in 1738. Best known as the author of the 1764 treatise *Dei delitti e dei pene* (*Of Crimes and Punishments*), Beccaria had a huge impact on Enlightenment thinking on law, crime and capital punishment, which is denounced in his work, along with judicial torture and arbitrary justice. He argued that punishment was a necessary self-defence mechanism of society, rather than an infliction legitimated by divine sanctions against sin. His work was widely translated and had a major impact on practice, especially in smaller states such as Tuscany, and even in France, where judicial torture began to be dismantled in the 1780s. Beccaria died in 1794.

François Boucher

François Boucher was born in 1703. After working for a short time in decorator-painter François Lemoyne's studio, where he was probably influenced by the older master's love of the Venetian decorative painters (bright colours and voluptuous forms), Boucher learned the fundamentals of engraving and engraved many drawings by Antoine Watteau. In 1723 he won the Prix de Rome awarded by the Royal Academy, but declined the prize of a year's study in Rome. Later, in 1725, he saved enough money to travel to Italy with painter Carle Vanloo. In 1733 Boucher married Marie Jeanne Buzeau and had three children. Boucher was admitted as a full member to the French Academy in 1734 with the diploma piece *Rinaldo and Armida* and soon attracted the attention of Mme de Pompadour, who virtually adopted him as her official painter. Thanks to her patronage, Boucher enjoyed the favour of Louis XV. In 1755 he became inspector of the Gobelins tapestry works, the following year became its director, and was appointed first painter to the king and director of the French Academy in 1765. Boucher executed more than 1,000 paintings, at least 200 engravings and well over 10,000 drawings in various media. Although prolific, he was inventive with his landscapes, portraits, genre themes, and mythological and religious scenes. In 1760 his work was attacked by Denis Diderot for its lack of serious purpose. He died in 1770.

Georges-Louis Leclerc, Comte de Buffon

Buffon was born in 1707 at Montbard, of a family of high-ranking legal officeholders. After an important tour of Italy, he took up residence in Paris, and was a member of both the Académie Française and the Academy of Sciences. His impact on the Enlightenment stemmed primarily from his writings on natural history (*Histoire naturalle, générale et particulière*, 15 vols, 1749–67). Buffon saw nature as having a history far older than that suggested by biblical chronology, and his support for the idea that man was intrinsically *within* the natural order led to condemnations by the theology faculty of Paris in 1749. As director of the Jardin Royal or botanical gardens, Buffon also played an important role in increasing the accessibility of natural history to the general public. He died in 1788.

Fanny Burney

The English novelist and diarist Fanny (Frances) Burney was one of the most popular novelists of the late eighteenth century and an important chronicler of English morals, manners and society. Born in 1752 to Dr Charles Burney (a distinguished historian of music), she began to write at a young age. Her first novel, *Evelina, or The History of a Young Lady's Entrance into the World*, was published anonymously in 1778 and won her acceptance into the *salons* of the famous. Her other novels include *Cecilia* (1782), *Camilla* (1796) and *The Wanderer* (1814). Between 1787 and 1791 she served as second keeper of the robes to Queen Charlotte. In 1793 she married General d'Arblay, a French refugee, and lived in France with him from 1802 to 1812. Burney's life in the late eighteenth century is recorded in her diaries, journals, notebooks and correspondence. She published three volumes of the *Memoirs of Dr Burney* (begun in 1814). She died in 1840. After her death her own voluminous diaries were published: seven volumes of *The Diary and Letters of Madame d'Arblay* (1842–46), two more volumes of *The Early Diary of Francis Burney* (1907), and fuller versions in the late twentieth century.

Catherine II, Empress of Russia

Catherine II, born into a German princely family in 1729, became the empress of Russia on the death of her husband, Tsar Peter, in 1762. She was influenced by Voltaire, Montesquieu and the *Encyclopédie*, and corresponded with Voltaire, Diderot and with the *salon* hostess Mme Geoffrin. She tried in many ways to Europeanize Russia, but her relationship with the Enlightenment has often been questioned, as she systematically advantaged the nobility and steadily increased the numbers of serfs. Her territorial conquests at the expense of Turkey and Poland also seem to have had little to do with the general Enlightenment support for peaceful international relations. Nonetheless, her reputation was high among *philosophes*. Catherine was probably most influenced by Enlightenment thinkers in her project for a general lawcode for Russia. She died in 1796.

Jacques-Louis David

The French painter Jacques-Louis David was born to a well-to-do bourgeois family in 1748. He studied with Boucher, and then under Joseph Vien. In 1774 David won first prize in the Prix de Rome competition with his painting *Antiochus Dying for the Love of Stratonice*. In 1775 he went to Rome with Vien who had just been appointed director of the French Academy there. Some works from this time include the painting *Belisarius Asking for Alms* (1781) and *Andromache by the Body of Hector* (1783). He was admitted to the French Academy with the former. With the Revolution in full swing, David abandoned his classical approach and began to paint scenes describing contemporary events, such as *The Oath of the Tennis Court* (1791) glorifying the first challenge to royal authority in France. He also executed many portraits and was involved in politics (he was elected to the National Convention in 1792). *Gardens of the Luxembourg* (1794) and *The Rape of the Sabine Women* (1789) are two other paintings from

this period. Later David would be named 'first painter' to Napoleon, and would execute many portraits of the emperor. After Napoleon's defeat at Waterloo and the restoration of the Bourbons, David fled to Switzerland, and then settled in Brussels where he painted until his death in 1825. David's style, focusing on the barest essentials and refusing to be influenced by the 'frivolous' Rococo style, had an impact on many young painters. He was himself influenced by the historian Johann Winckelmann and the artist Anton Raphael Mengs. He taught Ingres.

Denis Diderot

Denis Diderot was born in 1713. He achieved fame in his lifetime largely as the co-editor of the *Encyclopédie*, and to a lesser extent as a playwright, art critic and commentator on current issues. Many other of his works became known only posthumously, such as the *Supplément au Voyage de Bougainville*, published in 1796. Diderot came from a family of provincial artisans and workshop owners, orthodox believers who saw their son take minor orders in 1726. Diderot quickly rejected belief in the existence of a personal god, and instead saw nature itself and matter as full of energies, constantly in transformation. In apparent contradiction to this implicit determinism, Diderot also preached a secular morality of benevolence and civic virtue, as well as satirizing what he regarded as social prejudices against adultery and sexual repression. Rejecting the religious life, he earned a living as a lawyer's clerk, writer and private tutor, until his marriage in 1743. In 1773–74 he visited Russia at the invitation of the empress Catherine, but left disillusioned. Many of his ideas are discussed in his extensive correspondence. Diderot died in 1784.

Jean-Honoré Fragonard

Born in 1732, Jean-Honoré Fragonard worked as an apprentice in Jean-Baptiste Chardin's studio between 1747 and 1748, and began studying with François Boucher in 1748. In 1752 he won the Prix de Rome (a prize awarded by the Royal Academy of Painting and Sculpture that allowed study at the French Academy in Rome), and then studied in Italy from 1756 to 1761, specializing in landscapes. Fragonard returned to France in 1761 and was

soon accepted into the Royal Academy in 1765 on the basis of a serious history painting which was typical neither of his taste nor temperament. Fragonard's later paintings, which were designed to provide pleasure for highly sophisticated patrons, constitute the final expression of the Rococo style. Between 1765 and 1770 he created several portraits such as *The Swing*, in which the sitters wear fanciful costumes and which are of an erotic or suggestive nature. These types of pictures were harshly criticized by Denis Diderot, a leading philosopher of the Enlightenment. Despite such criticism of the Rococo style as well as of some of his specific paintings, Fragonard's work continued to be in demand. In the 1770s he received many commissions, including for such work as *Loves of the Shepards* for patrons like the Comtesse du Barry, Louis XV's mistress. The artist managed to avoid imprisonment during the Revolution in 1789. From 1794 to 1797 he helped to create and administer the new National Museum in the palace of the Louvre. He died in 1806.

August Hermann Franke

August Hermann Franke was born in 1663. After attending the University of Leipzig, he was attracted to Dresden to become the disciple of the famed religious reformer Philip Spener. With Spener behind him, he went on to preach as well as educate. In the process he converted many to the way of thinking of the Pietists, as his group of reformed Christians came to be known. His success earned him persecution from orthodox Lutherans, however, and his enemies succeeded in prohibiting his Bible study classes and, later, in getting him removed from the church in Erfurt where he was preaching. Spener sent Franke to Halle, promising him a position as a professor of Greek and oriental languages at the university soon to be founded at the city. As Halle became the Pietist headquarters, Franke utilized the movement to help the poor there. He laboured to get them food, jobs and, most famously, free education. He established several free schools as well as his well-known orphanage, which not only cared for orphaned children, but also fed and educated thousands of poor students free of charge. Franke's establishments became the model for similar institutions throughout Germany, providing the poor with greater access to organized relief and schooling. He died in 1727.

Benjamin Franklin

Benjamin Franklin was born in 1706 in Boston into a large (he had 12 siblings) pious puritan family. Rejecting his father's Calvinist theology, he was influenced by the more secular world view of Sir Isaac Newton and John Locke. Owing to his family's poverty, Franklin was unable to attend school; however, he became an apprentice in a newspaper print shop and read widely. In 1724 he moved to London, became a master printer and lived among aspiring authors. Returning to America, he acquired his own press and published the newspaper *Poor Richard's Almanac*. Franklin was later clerk of the Pennsylvania Assembly, postmaster of Philadelphia, ran a bookshop and had partnerships with various printers worldwide. He was so successful that he retired at the age of 42. In 1727 he became involved in civic-minded projects (organizing the Junto, a club of aspiring tradesmen that encouraged city improvements such as setting up a library, fire company, a college and an insurance company). Next his attention turned to science. In his famous kite experiment, he proved that lightning is a form of electricity. Other achievements included creating a theory of heat, charting the Gulf Stream, ship design, meteorology, and inventing bifocals and a harmonica. In 1756 he was elected to the Royal Society of London. Franklin's time was also taken up with politics. He was elected to the Pennsylvania Assembly in 1751, spent nearly 40 years as a public official and a leader in the Quaker Church. During the French and Indian War (1754–63), he worked with British commanders to win a North American empire for Britain, and for 30 or more years he aligned himself with politicians such as William Pitt. Franklin then played a central role in the great crises that led to the Declaration of Independence. He served as representative and peace commissioner in Europe for many years, and attended the Constitutional Convention (1787) to draw up the constitution of the United States. He died in 1790.

Frederick II, King of Prussia
Frederick II was born in 1712. After a difficult early life, he succeeded his father as king in 1740; in this year he seized the rich province of Silesia from Austria, and thus plunged Europe into the War of the Austrian Succession. In 1756 his aggression again triggered the international conflict known as the Seven Years' War. He played a leading role in the partition of Poland in 1773. During his reign, the Prussian economy was modernized, while the powers of the aristocratic class increased and serfdom remained. Frederick surrounded himself with *philosophes* such as La Mettrie, the Marquis d'Argens and Maupertuis, whom he engaged to head the new Academy of Sciences in Berlin. Voltaire visited him in 1750. Frederick

himself wrote extensively on his own life and times, and more generally on politics and kingship, pieces which were admired by the *philosophe* Grimm, but condemned by Diderot in his 1771 *Pages contre un tyran*. He died in 1786.

George III
Born in 1738, George III was the eldest son of Frederick, Prince of Wales. Frederick died in 1751, leaving George his heir. Hence he ascended the throne when his grandfather died in 1760. George III married, as was expected of him, a German Protestant princess, Charlotte Sophia of Mecklenburg-Strelitz (1761). George struggled to find a minister in whom he had confidence and who could also control the government. Eventually he appointed Lord North 'prime minister', an office he held from 1770 to 1782. During the first two decades of his reign, George III was faced with several major issues. Most significant were those created by the political reformer John Wilkes and by the American colonies. Prosecuting Wilkes made him personally unpopular and diminished the public's confidence in his government. In 1782 North's ministry fell when the American colonies won their independence. The king's concerns in his later years included continuing ministerial struggles, issues of financial and administrative reforms, quarrels with his two eldest sons (George, Prince of Wales and Frederick), and anxiety over his own health. George III experienced four major attacks of mental incapacity from 1788 to his death in 1820. In his last years he was also totally blind and deaf. When George III experienced his fourth bout of mental incapacitation in 1811, Prince George became regent.

Johann Wolfgang Goethe
Johann Wolfgang Goethe, born in 1749, is widely regarded as the most influential writer of the German Romantic period, and also by many as Germany's single greatest literary

figure. Despite an early desire to devote his energies to the study of the classics, at 16 Goethe went to Leipzig University at the urging of his father to study law (1765–68). This did not stifle his literary ambitions, however: he wrote lyric poetry, plays and fiction, in addition to practising law. Several of his works served to fuel the *Sturm und Drang* (Storm and Stress) movement, which opposed Enlightenment rationality. His wildly popular novel *The Sorrows of Young Werther* (1774), for example, provided the model for the Romantic hero. In 1775 Goethe became a court official at Weimar, where he came to be in charge of mines, roads, finance and war. He was also the president of the treasury from 1782. He continued to grow as a writer and also busied himself with scientific pursuits, including alchemy and the formulation of a theory of light in opposition to Newton's. He also proved the existence of the intermaxillary bone in man, evidence he used to demonstrate the continuous nature of anatomy across species, human and animal (although the bone had previously been discovered in Paris in 1780). In 1791 he was freed from most of his court duties to devote himself more fully to writing. He continued, though, to function as the court's general supervisor for arts and sciences and as director of the court theatres for many years, publishing his masterpiece, his drama in two parts *Faust*, in 1808 and 1832. In his later years, Goethe was revered as a living cultural icon, and artists and statesmen from around the world made the pilgrimage to Weimar to meet with him. Goethe died in 1832.

Francisco de Paula José de Goya y Lucientes
Born in 1746, Goya began drawing at a young age thanks to the encouragement of a priest. The young artist was apprenticed to José Luzan y Martinez for four years (1759–63). He then went to Madrid, where he failed to make a successful career. In 1775 he married Josefa Bayeau, sister of Francisco Bayeau. Bayeau was director of the San Fernando Academy and used his influence to help his brother-in-law. Some of Goya's subsequent work includes a set of Rococo-style cartoons created for the Royal Tapestry Factory of Santa Barbara and a series of etchings from paintings by Diego Velázquez. Goya was

named court painter (1779), was appointed lieutenant director of painting in the academy, then painter to the king (1785) and elected to the membership of the San Fernando Academy in 1788. Goya executed many portraits for the royal family and nobility before a grave illness left him totally deaf (1792). Many of his works reflect his horror of cruelty and his compassion for its victims. Other later work includes several series of etchings: *Los caprichos* (1796–98), *Los desastres de la guerra* (*Disasters of War*) (1814), *Los proverbios* (1813–15; 1817–18) and *The Tauromachia* (1815–16). Goya retired to Bordeaux in 1825 and died of a stroke in 1828.

Jean-Baptiste Greuze

Born in 1725, Greuze studied painting in Lyon and went to Paris in around 1750. He then entered the Royal Academy and worked with Charles Joseph Natore, a well-known decorative painter. Greuze became known for his sentimental paintings of peasants or lower-class people seen in humble surroundings; examples are *The Village Bride* (1761), *The Father's Curse* (1765) and *The Prodigal Son* (1765). His work constituted a reaction against Rococo frivolity in art. Denis Diderot, leading philosopher of the Enlightenment, hailed him for his serious concern with moral subjects. The artist's simple paintings were popular with all classes of society. Greuze survived the French Revolution, but his fame did not. He died in 1805 in poverty and obscurity.

Johann Gottfried von Herder

Born in 1744 in East Prussia of a strongly Pietist family, Herder became a pupil of Immanuel Kant at the University at Königsburg. Ordained in 1767, he moved to Riga and published his *Fragments on a New German Literature*, in which he argued for an independent German literature. In 1769 he travelled to France and, returning to Germany, met Lessing in Hamburg and became court preacher to Count Schaumburg-Lippe. In 1774 he published *Another Philosophy of History*, which combated cosmopolitanism and rationalism. In 1776 he left for Weimar, where he met Goethe and published on Hebrew poetry and his *Ideas on the Philosophy of Human History* (1784–91). Some of these ideas were reconsidered, under the impact of the French Revolution, in his *Letters on the Progress of Humanity*. He died in 1803.

Baron d'Holbach (Paul-Henry Thiry)

Born in 1723, D'Holbach was of Swiss origin and made a fortune as a financier in Paris. He gathered around him a group which included D'Alembert, Diderot, Buffon, Raynal and Rousseau. He attacked organized religion and argued for the sole reality of the material world. Much of his work was clandestinely published to avoid censorship, but he also wrote articles for the *Encyclopédie* on religion and on earth sciences. His 1770 *Système de la nature* was his most famous work, and was attacked by Voltaire and Frederick II of Prussia. D'Holbach died in 1789.

Thomas Jefferson

Thomas Jefferson, third president of the United States (1801–09), was born in 1743 into Virginia planter society. He involved himself in natural history, exploration (especially the expeditions of Zebulon Pike, and Lewis and Clark [1804–06]), and founded the University of Virginia. Elected to the Virginia House of Burgesses (1769–76), he served as chairman of the committee that composed the Declaration of Independence. He inserted anti-slavery passages into the Declaration which were removed at the insistence of delegations from Georgia and South Carolina. Governor of Virginia between 1779 and 1781, he was US minister in France 1785–89. His presidency saw the expansion of the USA through the 'Louisiana Purchase', a vast undefined territory westwards of the Mississippi river. A lifelong slave-holder, he prohibited the importation of slaves, but not slave-holding or the slave trade internal to the USA. His interest in architecture is shown in his own house, Monticello, and the buildings of the University of Virginia at Charlottesville. His only published work, *Notes on the State of Virginia*, a compilation of information about the geology and natural history of the state, as well as remarks on the problem of slavery, was published in 1787. Jefferson died in 1826.

Samuel Johnson

Samuel Johnson was born the son of a bookseller in 1709. He was educated at the Lichfield Grammar School, and then later studied with a clergyman. In 1728–29 Johnson attended Pembroke College, Oxford, but he was embarrassed by his poverty and unable to complete his degree. After several attempts at academic odd jobs, Johnson went to London in 1737 to make a career as a man of letters. He worked at a variety of literary tasks, publishing a biography of his friend Richard Savage, a series of periodical essays – *The Rambler* (1750–52) and *The Adventurer* (1753–54) – and a dictionary of the English language (1755). Johnson's moral tale *Rasselas, Prince of Abyssinia* appeared in 1759 and later, in 1762, he accepted a pension of £300 a year from George III. In 1764 Johnson and the painter Joshua Reynolds founded a club whose members eventually numbered some of the most eminent men of the time (including economist Adam Smith, historian Edward Gibbon, and politicians Edmund Burke and Charles James Fox). His last two major literary works were an eight-volume edition of the works of Shakespeare and a ten-volume series (known as *The Lives of the Poets*) of biographical and critical studies of 52 English poets. Johnson died in 1784.

Sir William Jones

Sir William Jones was born in 1746 in England. Jones had already demonstrated a keen interest in languages as a young man and his interest persisted throughout his time at Oxford, where he studied oriental literature, emerging with a knowledge of languages such as Italian, Spanish, Persian, Arabic, Hebrew, Chinese and Portuguese (by his death, he knew 13 languages in all). After gaining some standing as an orientalist, Jones decided to pursue a more profitable occupation. He passed the bar in 1774 and went on to become a supreme court judge in Bengal, India, in 1783. He was knighted soon after. Thankfully, his interests in oriental studies did not end with his success in the field of law. He studied Sanskrit, founded the Bengal Asiatic Society, translated many key Indian texts and in general advocated the importance of looking to the East for wisdom. As the father of comparative philology, he also noted the similarity of Sanskrit to Latin and Greek. Jones died in 1795.

Immanuel Kant

Born in 1724, Immanuel Kant came from a strongly Pietist background in Prussia. After studying at the University at Königsburg, he became professor of mathematics and philosophy there in 1756. Kant was influenced by D'Alembert and Rousseau, as well as by the Scots philosopher David Hume. His most famous work, the *Critique of Pure Reason*, appeared in 1783. In 1784 he took part in a prize competition to answer the question 'What is Enlightenment?', and in 1795 published a *Project for Perpetual Peace*. Though Kant's reflections on the basis of rationality proceeded from Locke's rejection of innate ideas, he asked whether reason or the soul should be autonomous or independent of sense impressions. Kant died in 1804.

Julien Offroy de La Mettrie

Julien Offroy de La Mettrie was born in 1709 in Caen and educated by Jesuits. He studied medicine at Leiden. His medical interests led him to a materialist position affirmed in his 1748 *L'Homme machine* (*Man the Machine*) and his *Discourse on Happiness*. La Mettrie was much influenced by Epicurean philosophy, of which he published an analysis in 1750. These views attracted hostility from Catholics and Protestants alike, and La Mettrie was forced to leave Leiden for Berlin, where he was welcomed by Frederick II. Nor was much *philosophe* opinion in his favour, as his thinking ran counter to belief in free will and the idea that morality was somehow 'natural' and therefore innate. He died in 1751.

Johann Caspar Lavater

Johann Caspar Lavater was born in 1741 in Zurich, the thirteenth child of a doctor who also held important positions in the city government. In 1763 a one-year journey to Pomerania in northern Germany brought him the friendship of Moses Mendelssohn and the poet Klopstock. In 1774 he made a similar trip along the Rhine and met Goethe, who initially supported his physiognomic theories but later argued against them. In 1772 he published his most famous work, the *Physiognomische Fragmente*. The book was highly controversial and in the end received little support from the intellectual community. Its theory, that qualities of character (e.g., 'contentiousness' or 'affection') might be localized on features of the exterior of the skull, was important for later researchers in brain localization. Contemporaries, however, pointed out the arbitrary nature of Lavater's definition of character qualities, and queried the idea that the exterior formations of the skull had any relationship to the configuration of the brain itself. Lavater was strongly opposed to the French Revolution and was fatally injured during the French siege of Zurich in 1799. He died in 1801.

Antoine Laurent Lavoisier

French chemist Antoine Laurent Lavoisier was born in 1743. Among his early works are an essay on the problems of urban street lighting (1766). He received a provisional appointment to the Academy of Sciences (1768) and invested in the *Ferme Générale*, which collected taxes for the royal government (1768). Thanks to his position as commissioner of the French Gunpowder Commission (1775–92), Lavoisier enjoyed both a house and a laboratory in the Royal Arsenal. His most significant contributions to science are the formulation of the oxygen theory of combustion (which attacked the then-current phlogiston theory), and the creation of a new programme for reforms of chemical nomenclature (1787). He is often called the founder of the modern science of chemistry. In addition, his pioneering work in the field of physiology (studying the process of body metabolism and respiration) served to inspire similar research for generations to come. As the Revolution gained momentum from 1789 on, Lavoisier's world crumbled around him: the *Ferme* was suppressed (1791), he was forced to resign from his post on the Gunpowder Commission (1792) and all learned societies, including the Academy of Sciences, were suppressed (1793). At the end of 1793, the arrest of all the former tax collectors was ordered. Lavoisier and 27 of his former colleagues were guillotined on 8 May 1794.

Georg Christoph Lichtenberg

Georg Christoph Lichtenberg was born in 1742. After studying mathematics, astronomy and natural science at Göttingen, Lichtenberg became a philosophy professor there in 1770. His career evolved and he became a writer, mathematician, inventor and the first experimental physicist in Germany. As a critic and wit he became very well regarded. Among countless others, he took many of the *Sturm und Drang* writers and Sentimentalist poets in his sights. His *Waste Book*, a collection of random thoughts that he had recorded over the years, was published after his death and has been enjoyed by many as an intriguing portrait of a fertile mind. Lichtenberg also became a staunch Anglophile in the course of his lifetime, and he promoted England as the greatest country in existence. His studies of electricity led him to invent 'Lichtenberg Figures', an ancestor of modern xerography. He died in 1799.

Carl Linnaeus

Carl Linnaeus was born in 1707. He began his higher education by studying medicine at both the universities of Lund and Uppsala. His knowledge of the sexuality of plants, however, gained him a position as a lecturer in botany at Uppsala. He eventually took his degree in medicine at the University of Hardewijk in 1735, but continued to write essays on botany and to mingle with the top naturalists of the day. After several years away from his native Sweden, Linnaeus returned to establish a prominent medical practice in Stockholm. He became a botany professor at Uppsala in 1741. His most famous contribution to science was his systematic method for identifying plants and animals using the hierarchy of genus, class and order. He also conceptualized ecology as a specific field of scientific research. Linnaeus was appointed chief royal physician in 1747 and was made a knight in 1758. He died in 1778.

John Locke

Born in 1637, Locke is the author of the *Essay Concerning Human Understanding* (1690) and one of the key figures of the early Enlightenment. This work was of fundamental importance because it criticized Descartes' doctrine of innate ideas and thus opened the way for much subsequent thinking by Hume, Condillac, Kant and others on the meaning of human intelligence. Locke was also seen as a pioneer in the struggle for religious tolerance as a result of his 1689 *Letters on Toleration*, as well as his *The Reasonableness of Christianity* of 1695. His influence on Voltaire was very strong, as it was on Rousseau, whose *Emile ou de l'éducation* (1762) was affected by his 1693 *Thoughts Concerning Education*. The Enlightenment also gained from Locke's *Second Treatise on Civil Government* the basis of its thinking on the idea of the contractual nature of society and government. Locke died in 1704.

Toussaint L'Ouverture

Leader of the only successful slave revolt in the Caribbean, Toussaint L'Ouverture was born in 1743 near Cap François on the French possession of St Domingue (now Haiti), of slave parents. His life was defined by resistance to slavery. He took part in the slave insurrection of 1791, which resulted in the collapse of the slavery system on the island by 1793. He led forces against the British occupation of the island in 1798, and defeated a mulatto (mixed-race) revolt in 1799. By 1801 he and his forces controlled the whole island, and resisted Napoleon's attempts to re-establish slavery. In 1802 he was overcome by a French military force under General Leclerc. He was captured and died in prison in France in 1803.

Moses Mendelssohn

Moses Mendelssohn was born in 1729. He was the first major Jewish figure of the Enlightenment. He profited from the climate of religious toleration enforced by Frederick II to form an intellectual circle and publish widely, while at the same time composing in Hebrew, including a valuable commentary on Maimonides. Mendelssohn contributed to contemporary debates on religious toleration and Jewish emancipation, though insisting on the necessity for cultural diversity and avoiding uniformity. He contributed to the 1784 debate on the definition of 'Enlightenment' and wrote widely on aesthetics. Mendelssohn's work demonstrates the capacity of Enlightenment debates to mobilize thinkers across ethnic and religious lines. He died in 1786. He was the grandfather of the composer.

Anton Raphael Mengs

Anton Raphael Mengs was born in Bohemia in 1728, the son of a painter. His father had high expectations for him and was a strict tutor as well. Between 1741 and 1744 Anton was taken to Rome to study. He was appointed Saxon court painter in 1746, then returned to Rome where he continued to study ancient and Renaissance art, converted to Catholicism, married and established himself as one of the leading painters in the city. He was most in demand as a portraitist of members of the gentry on the Grand Tour. Mengs was influenced by his study of ancient sculpture, Michelangelo, Raphael and Correggio, although his work retained some of the vitality and freshness of the Rococo style. His best-known works include the ceiling fresco *Apotheosis of St Eusebius* (1757) for the church of S. Eusebio in Rome and the ceiling fresco *Parnassus* (1761). In 1761 Mengs was appointed court painter in Madrid and he produced frescoes for the royal palaces of Madrid and Aranjuez and many religious paintings, allegorical works and portraits. In 1769 he painted the ceiling fresco *Allegory of History and Time* in the Camera dei Papiri in the Vatican Library. He died of tuberculosis in 1779. Mengs' works were influential in the rejection of baroque ideas and the triumph of Neoclassicism in the late eighteenth century in Rome.

Baron de la Brède et de Montesquieu (Charles-Louis de Secondat)

Montesquieu was born in 1689, a member of a prominent family among the legal nobility of France. He himself was president of the *parlément* or sovereign appeal court of Bordeaux from 1726. The year 1721 saw the appearance of his first major work, the *Persian Letters*, a

satire on the institutions of France, which also presented a less than usually idealized view of the orient. *De l'esprit de lois* (*On the Spirit of the Laws*) (1748) was equally a best-seller, and was one of the most widely translated and diffused works of the Enlightenment, especially after it attracted the hostility of the Church and was placed on the Index in 1751. Montesquieu argued for the inevitability of different systems of government, because of the way in which states are moulded by climate, geography, history, extent and by the '*morale*' of their inhabitants. He died in 1755.

Isaac Newton

Born in 1642, Newton published his theory of universal attraction, or gravitation, in his *Philosophiae naturalis principia mathematica* (1687). A fellow of Trinity College, Cambridge, and master of the Royal Mint, he pursued fundamental research in optics and was often seen, especially in Europe, as an exemplar of empirical, rationalist research. However, Newton also believed in alchemy and in numerological interpretations of biblical prophecy. He died in 1727.

Tom Paine

The journalist and revolutionary propagandist Tom Paine was born in England in 1737. He moved to Philadelphia in 1774 and was a writer and then editor on the *Pennsylvania Magazine*. He received recognition with the publication of his 79-page pamphlet *Common Sense* (1776), a powerful exhortation for American independence. It was an immediate success and helped prepare Americans for the Declaration of Independence a few months later. His other influential writings include *The Crisis Papers* (13 of which appeared between 1776 and 1783) in which Paine attacked Tories, profiteers, inflationists and counterfeiters. Later he defended republican principles and urged Englishmen to overthrow their monarchy in *The Rights of Man* (1791). The English government reacted by outlawing Paine, and he fled to France where he took part in drawing up a new constitution. Paine's most controversial writing was *The Age of Reason* (1794), a direct attack on the irrationality of religion and a defence of deism. Returning to America in 1802, he was ostracized by those around him. He died in 1806.

François Quesnay

François Quesnay was born in 1694. After an eventful early life, he became a surgeon employed first by the duke de Villeroi, then by Louis XV. His quarters at Versailles became a meeting place for Diderot, Turgot

and Mirabeau. He is most associated with the new economic theory called Physiocracy which was discussed in Quesnay's articles for the *Encyclopédie*. Physiocracy sees land as the sole source of wealth, and advocates strong monarchy to guarantee the operation of a free market in land and agricultural products. His major works were his *Droit naturel* of 1765 and his *Maximes générales du government économique d'un royaume agricole* of the same year, theories that influenced Karl Marx. He died in 1774.

Abbé Raynal (Guillaume-Thomas)

Born in 1713, Raynal was a priest in minor orders who until 1750 earned a living as a tutor and journalist. The publication of his *Anecdotes littéraires* in 1750 secured Raynal's place among the Paris intelligentsia. In 1770 he produced the work on which his modern reputation rests, the *Histoire philosophique et politique des établissements et du commerce des Européens dans les deux Indes*, one of the first major histories of European colonialism, a vast compendium of geographical and economic knowledge, as well as an argument for the morality of commerce and the immorality of slavery. This book, produced with the help of Diderot, produced such fame for Raynal that he left Paris for the provinces to try to reduce the inconvenience of publicity. He was an opponent of the French Revolution. Raynal died in 1796.

Samuel Richardson

The English novelist Samuel Richardson was born in 1689. An apprentice printer to John Wilde for seven years, Richardson learned his trade well and, after serving as an overseer to a printing shop, set up on his own in 1720. Within 20 years Richardson had built up one of the largest and most lucrative printing businesses in London. He published a wide variety of material including his own novels and did official printing for the House of Commons. His first known work, published in 1733, was *The Apprentice's Vade Mecum* (a conduct book addressed to apprentices), which was followed by *A Seasonable Examination* (1735), a pamphlet supporting a parliamentary bill to regulate the London theatres. He also wrote a guide to letter-writing for various occasions. However, Richardson's best-known works are two epistolary novels, *Pamela* and *Clarissa*. The first was published in two volumes in 1740 and became so popular that Richardson followed it up with a sequel in 1741. His next major piece of writing, *Clarissa*, was published in seven volumes in 1747–48. It is a massive work (more than a million words and the longest novel in the English language), containing 547 letters. His third and final novel, *Sir Charles*

Grandison, was published in 1753–54. Richardson died in 1761.

Jean-Jacques Rousseau

Jean-Jacques Rousseau was born in 1712 in Geneva, where he was raised by his father, a watchmaker. Leaving Geneva, he entered on a vagabond existence, converted to Catholicism in Turin, and became linked to Mme de Warens at Chambéry from 1736 to 1738. Focused at this period on music, he arrived in Paris in 1742 and became friendly with Diderot. The 1740s saw him moving increasingly to writing, beginning with articles for the *Encyclopédie*. In 1750 Rousseau's *Discours sur les sciences et les arts* won a prize competition at the Academy of Dijon, which was followed in 1755 by the *Discours sur l'origine de l'inégalité parmi les hommes*. Disputes with Voltaire and Diderot followed. Other major works were his novel *Julie ou la nouvelle Héloïse* (1761); *Emile ou de l'education* and *Du contrat social* (1762). His autobiography, the *Confessions*, appeared posthumously between 1782 and 1788. He believed in following nature and in the innate goodness of human beings. His influence, particularly that of the *Social Contract*, actually increased during the French Revolution. Rousseau died in 1778 and was buried on an island in the middle of a lake at Ermenonville, some miles north-west of Paris, the estate of his last protector, Count Louis-René Girardin. It became a place of pilgrimage for his admirers, and was painted many times, notably by Hubert Robert. The planning of the island, in which Robert probably assisted, in the open style of the 'English Garden', was intended to recall the landscapes around Lake Geneva described in Rousseau's *Julie*, and was influenced by his philosophy of the nobility and transparency of nature. In the garden surrounding the lake were placed statues devoted to philosophy and to friendship, and a small pantheon, modelled on the Temple of the Sybil at Tivoli. The pantheon was inscribed with the names of Enlightenment heroes such as Franklin and Newton. This beautiful site may still be visited.

Friedrich Schiller

Friedrich Schiller was born in 1759 to an army captain and the religious daughter of an innkeeper. As a boy, he attended the duke of Württemberg's military academy and then studied medicine. He wrote his final dissertation on the interrelationship between man's spiritual and physical natures at the same time that he was working on his first play, *Die Räuber* (1781). Schiller worked as a medical officer to a regiment stationed in Stuttgart for several years. He earned very little money and took out loans in order to publish *Die Räuber*. Other early works include a collection of poetry, *Anthology auf das Jahr 1782*, and the dramas *Die Verschwörung des Fiesko zu Genua* (1783) and *Kabale und Liebe* (1784). He also wrote *Die Schaubühne als moralische Anstalt betrachet* (1784) and *Don Carlos, Infant von Spanien* (1785). Schiller's hymn *An die Freude* was later set by Beethoven in his Ninth Symphony. Schiller and Goethe formed a strong relationship beginning around 1794. In 1798–99 Schiller completed his trilogy on Albrech von Wallenstein, a leader in the Thirty Years' War. Schiller's importance in German literature is not confined to his poetry and drama. He also did notable work in history, philosophy and aesthetics. Schiller died in 1805.

Adam Smith

Adam Smith was born in 1723. Probably the most famous economic thinker of the Enlightenment, Smith's work is still used to justify modern economic ideologies. From 1748 he was a member of an intellectual circle including David Hume, Hugh Blair, the philosopher of 'common sense', and the historian of the Spanish empire William Robertson. Smith's first book, the 1759 *Theory of Moral Sentiments*, made him famous. He spent 1763–65 in France, and came to know not only Voltaire, but also Physiocrat thinkers such as Turgot. The latter believed that land was the basis of wealth. From 1767 to 1776, Smith concentrated on producing theories of the division of labour, of money, and of the liberty of trade and commerce. These studies were the basis of his most famous work, published in 1776, *The Nature and Causes of the Wealth of Nations*. Adam Smith died in 1790.

Giovanni Battista Tiepolo

The Italian artist Giovanni Battista Tiepolo is known for his brightly coloured works and frescoes filled with figures floating on clouds. Born in Venice in 1696, as a youth Tiepolo was apprenticed to a mediocre but fashionable painter. By the age of 20, he had exhibited his work independently and won recognition in the art world. In 1716 he became a member of the painters' guild, and in the 1720s he carried out many large-scale commissions on the northern Italian mainland. From the 1730s on, he devoted himself mainly to secular themes (mythology and allegories that glorified Venice and its noble families). He worked on several frescoes, including the *Apotheosis of Francesco Barbaro* (1761) and the frescoes in the Kaisersaal and in the great stairway of the Residenz, Würzburg (1751–53). In 1762, answering King Charles' request, he painted the frescoes for the new royal palace in Madrid. As the style of Neoclassism became more popular, Tiepolo's work began to be viewed as frivolous and out of date. In 1767 the artist secured one last major commission to paint seven large altarpieces for the church of S. Pascal at Aranjuez. However, shortly after they were finished the altarpieces were taken down and replaced by canvases by Mengs and others. Tiepolo died in 1770.

Anne-Robert-Jacques Turgot

Anne-Robert-Jacques Turgot was born in 1727. He began his career as an officeholder in the Paris *parlément* and collaborated on the *Encyclopédie*, writing articles mainly on economics. He became *intendant*, or royal civil governor, of the province of the Limousin in 1761 and finance minister from 1774 to 1776. One of the few Enlightenment thinkers to have held high office in France, his economic ideas closely resembled those of the Physiocrats such as Quesnay, though he was also influenced by Adam Smith. His career in government was undermined by his support for a free market in wheat, which led to high prices and riots all over the Île de France, the so-called *Guerre des Farines*, in 1775. He was also opposed to the existence of the artisan guilds, which he saw as a restriction on free trade. Turgot died in 1781.

Voltaire (François-Marie Arouet)

Born in 1694, Voltaire was one of the dominant figures of the Enlightenment, due to his satirical wit, his enormous output, his capacity to mobilize public opinion and his relations with the great. Born into a legal family and educated by Jesuits, he was quickly introduced at court and began his literary career as a dramatist, and made an important stay in England (1726–29), turning to history with his *Charles XII* (1731), to political comment with the *Lettres anglaises* (1734) and to scathing moral philosophy with

Candide (1759). The favour of Mme de Pompadour made him court historian and he was invited to Berlin by Frederick II in 1750–53. He used his prestige to save the lives and reputations of the Calas and Sirvin families, and produced in 1763 his *Treatise on Toleration*. Voltaire died in 1778.

Josiah Wedgwood

Born in 1730 in England, Wedgwood helped transform pottery production into a major industry and also devised some new forms of pottery himself. After establishing himself by working in the family pottery business and later becoming a partner of the prominent potter Thomas Whieldon, he opened his own factory in Burslem in 1759. Ten years later he opened another which he named 'Etruria' where he notably built his employees their own village as a contribution to society. Also, with the help of partner Thomas Bentley, he applied modern marketing techniques to his business, which successfully expanded its influence. By looking to antiquity as a model, Wedgwood invented unglazed black basalt ware and blue jasper ware with white raised designs. He died in 1795.

John Wesley

John Wesley was born in 1703. Best known as a great evangelist and as the founder of Methodism, he wrote a great deal during his lifetime, including hymn collections, histories, biographies and journals. After studying at Oxford, Wesley was ordained first as a deacon (1725) and then himself became a fellow at Oxford (1726), teaching Greek. He was ordained as a priest in 1728. After a failed mission to Georgia (1735–38), Wesley had a revelation while reading *Luther's Preface to the Epistle of the Romans* at a meeting in London. He felt strongly that his salvation was a certainty, and was moved to transmit that certainty to others. Most regular clergy were unnerved by his extreme passion, however, and denied him access to their churches. He went on to found the first Methodist chapel (1739) and the Moorfields Foundry, the Methodist headquarters. Wesley died in 1791.

Benjamin West

Benjamin West was born in 1738 in America. Even though surrounded by Quakers who tended to frown upon art, West's work seems to have been encouraged from a young age and the young boy gained a reputation as a child prodigy. His first paintings (from the 1750s) include *The Death of Socrates* and *Landscape with Cow*. In 1759 West studied in Rome where he was introduced to such famous artists as Gavin Hamilton and Anton Raphael Mengs. In 1763 he arrived in London and focused on painting portraits. He was commissioned by the archbishop of York to paint *Agrippina with the Ashes of Germanicus* (1767). King George III commissioned a painting on the theme of nobility, *Regulus Leaving Rome* (1769), and the king and West soon became good friends. West's other well-known paintings include the battle scene *The Death of Wolfe* (1771) and his *Christ Healing the Sick* (1811), a painting bought by the British Institute for 3,000 guineas, the largest sum paid in England up to that time for a contemporary work. In 1792 he was elected president of the Royal Academy. Benjamin West died in 1829. He played an important role in the history of American art by training gifted younger American painters of the time. He was known for being friendly and helpful to any artist looking for some help.

Johann Joachim Winckelmann

Born in 1717 in Germany, Winckelmann began his career with an education in theology and medicine at both Halle and Jena universities. However, in 1748 he decided that art history was his true path and travelled to Rome to become librarian to a cardinal there. He would also find a calling as an archaeologist, and in 1763 he was appointed superintendent of Roman antiquities. Perhaps his most influential work was *History of the Art of Antiquity* (1764), which helped to steer art and architecture towards Neoclassicism. He met his end by murder in 1768 in Trieste.

Mary Wollstonecraft

Mary Wollstonecraft was born in 1759 in London and began her career as a teacher and headmistress of a school in Newington. There, along with her sister Eliza, she first came to grips with the realization that the girls she was trying to educate were being put in an inferior position to men by society. She expressed her concerns in *Thoughts on the Education of Daughters* in 1787, in which she proclaimed that Enlightenment ideals demanded that women be given a decent education. She went on to become the governess to Lord Kingsborough's family and, following that, went to France for a number of years to observe and write about the political and social upheaval there. When she returned home, she joined a radical group, whose members included William Godwin, Tom Paine, Henry Fuseli and Joseph Priestley. Among her many writings, undoubtedly the most famous is *A Vindication of the Rights of Woman* (1792), a feminist classic. She eventually married Godwin and died in 1797 while giving birth to her daughter Mary, who would gain fame for writing *Frankenstein*.

Count Nikolaus Ludwig von Zinzendorf

Born in 1700 in Dresden, Germany, Zinzendorf's religious sensibilities were shaped by the Pietism of his godfather Spener and of Franke's Paedagogium in Halle. He went on to become educated as a jurist at Wittenberg, also studying theology. He worked as a public official from 1721 to 1727 before abandoning that path to become the leader of a group of Moravians who were exiled because of their religious beliefs. He allowed the group to stay at his estate, where they founded a community called *Hernnhut* ('The Lord's Keeping'). He refounded the Moravian Church and became its bishop when he was ordained in Tübingen in 1734. He considered Moravians to be part of the Lutheran Church and focused on 'Jesus mysticism' and the importance of 'religious community'. His actions put him at odds with more orthodox Christians and he was exiled from Saxony in 1736. He continued to labour to expand the influence of Moravianism, founding congregations all over the world. He was also a prolific writer, producing more than 100 books and numerous Moravian hymns. Zinzendorf died in 1760.

Enlightenment Places

There are a few places where the atmosphere of the Enlightenment still lingers. The following selection is necessarily personal, and the reasons for including a site vary widely. The exercise, nevertheless, has its reward if it brings the reader closer to the experience of living in that very special epoch.

Botany Bay

In April 1770, the explorer Captain James Cook discovered a small harbour on the south-eastern coast of Australia, which he at first called 'Stingray Harbour' and then, possibly to tease the two botanists aboard his vessel, Daniel Solander and Joseph Banks, 'Botany Bay'. Twenty years after Cook, a difficult problem afflicted the British government: how to dispose of the large numbers of felons sentenced to exile every year under a brutal penal code. Banks gave enthusiastic testimony to parliament on the possibilities of Botany Bay as a place of settlement for the convicts, and under the leadership of Captain Arthur Phillip, the First Fleet of 11 ships and 1,400 people left England in May 1787 and arrived at Botany Bay in January 1788. It was immediately obvious that sandy soil and poor water supply, in spite of Banks' praises, made Botany Bay impossible as a site of settlement for the convicts. Nothing daunted, Phillip sailed up the coast until he found a promising harbour, and named it Sydney Cove after the Home Secretary. A short ceremony was held to mark the landing of the convicts here on 26 January, which has become Australia Day, a day which marks of the founding of the first white polity in the Pacific World, or indeed anywhere else in the known world in this period.

It is possible to see the foundation of Australia not so much as a convict settlement, as an Enlightenment society, dedicated, as were many others, to a social experiment through the making of a new ordered society. Convicts had never before been formed into a colony, and the challenge before Phillip was the very Enlightenment one of obtaining mastery over the natural world. He was also working out, just as global explorers had in other parts of the world his relations with the Aborignes or indigenous people, with whom he enjoined his men to stay in good relations. In all these ways, Sydney Cove was an Enlightenment society.

The British Museum

In 1753 parliament passed the British Museum Act, which established in London the first fully publicly accessible library and museum in the world. It opened to the public in 1759. Its holdings were originally composed of several collections of books, manuscripts and objects such as natural-history specimens. George II donated the royal library in 1757. The collections were increased by the gifts and bequests of Sir Hans Sloane, who died in 1753, the Harley Manuscripts presented by the Earl of Oxford, and the Cotton Manuscripts which had been presented to the nation by John Cotton in 1700. Other collections were added to the museum: those of the antiquaries and collectors of classical objects Sir William Hamilton, Richard Payne Knight, Charles Towneley and Charles Cracherode. Its first home in the seventeenth century was Montague House, now demolished. The present building was created by Robert Smirke from 1823.

Public access to the museum was an important indicator of the way in which Enlightenment England had created an extensive reading public which was also avid for genteel spectacle. As Sir Hans Sloane wrote in his will bequeathing his collections to the museum: 'nothing tends more to raise our ideas of the power, wisdom and goodness and providence and other perfections of the Deity … than the enlargement of our knowledge in the works of nature … I do will and desire that for the promoting of these noble ends, the glory of God and the good of man, my collection in all its branches may be if possible kept and preserved together whole.'

Ironbridge

The iron bridge which spans the Severn Gorge at Coalbrookdale, an icon of industrialization designated a World Heritage Site in 1986, has given its name to the industrial communities working around it. Construction began in 1776, and helped to turn the surrounding small-scale iron-founding and lead-smelting businesses into mass-production industries. The bridge itself was built after startling demonstrations by local floods of the fragility of brick and wood bridges. A surprising amount of the eighteenth-century buildings – furnaces, workers' houses and a chapel – around the bridge can still be seen today. Ironbridge symbolizes the industrialization which marked the last half of the eighteenth century in north-western Europe.

Kew Gardens

To the south of London, Kew Gardens had their origin in gardens full of exotic plants first owned by Lord Capel of Tewkesbury, which were enlarged and extended in the mid-century by Princess Augusta, the widow of Frederick, Prince of Wales. Sir William Chambers erected several structures for her in the gardens, of which the best known is the Chinese pagoda completed in 1761, which consists of a series of floors reaching to 163 feet high, gradually decreasing in area, each one hung with silver bells. George III enriched the gardens, advised by Sir Joseph Banks, who became director of Kew gardens in 1797. Like Linnaeus, Banks sent out plant collectors to many parts of the world, some of whose trophies were kept in Banks' private collection, others given to Kew. A herbarium was also created, and became probably the largest collection of dried plants and seeds anywhere. Other seeds and specimens were obtained by swapping duplicates with other great botanical collections, such as the Muséum National d'Histoire Naturelle in Paris, from amateur collectors, such as East India Company officials in India and on the Cape of Good Hope. Kew thus functioned not only as a beautiful and instructive strolling ground for the public, but as a central collecting point for plants obtained globally.

Lunatic Asylum, Williamsburg, Virginia

In the autumn of 1773, the Public Hospital for Persons of Insane and Disordered Minds in Williamsburg, Virginia, received its first patient. It was the only institution in the British North American colonies which specialized in attempting to treat the disorders of the mind. Founded in the years around the American revolt against British rule, the institution was a response to the fears and uncertainties of those years, fears and uncertainties which spread into social fears about insanity and the insane. The building and endowment of the hospital had first been proposed by the lieutenant-governor of Virginia Francis Fauquier in 1766. A member of the board of the Greenwich Hospital for Foundling Children and of the Royal Society, Fauquier combined all the Enlightenment virtues of activity in the world and investment in the rational thought of science. He wished to end the practice of confining both the permanently and temporarily insane in the public gaol. In the eighteenth century other more pacific places organized around the idea of cure rather than confinement began to be founded in England: the Lunatic Hospital in Manchester, also in 1766, St Luke's in London in 1751, and St Luke's in Newcastle on Tyne in 1764. Fauquier's request was thus fully in tune with current trends. It took, however, until 1773 for the legislation to be enacted to establish the Public Hospital. It was not designed to offer long-term care, or asylum to the merely destitute or the chronically disturbed who offered no harm to themselves or others.

Therapeutic possibilities were limited. Patients occupied bare cells and slept on the ground on thin mattresses. Powerful drugs, dunking, bleeding, blistering and restraining devices were used. Electrostatic generators were used to shock patients. These devices were believed to refocus the patient's attention and drain the system of harmful fluids. Above all, patients were exhorted to reconsider what was then assumed to be their choice to live as an insane person.

Monticello

Monticello was the name given by Thomas Jefferson to the house and estate he built near Charlottesville, Virginia, between 1769 and 1793. Jefferson regarded architecture as one of his few relaxations. As he said, 'Architecture is my delight, and putting up and pulling down one of my favourite amusements.' Jefferson constructed Monticello as a Palladian villa, an adaptation of Plate XLI of Book II of Leoni's *Palladio*. Its appearance shows a Palladian porch tacked onto a Neoclassical villa. Monticello was probably the first building in this style in the American colonies, and its existence shows the global spread, not only of plants, animals and people in this period, but also of architectural designs and thinking about the management of interior spaces. It was this style in which Jefferson also built the University of Virginia buildings.

Jefferson's interiors were crammed with objects that focused on the American present. The dining room was crowded with busts of Washington, Franklin and La Fayette, Voltaire and Turgot, and the patriot naval commander Paul Jones. In the front hall were objects, including a mammoth, brought back by Lewis and Clark from their famous 1804 transcontinental journey of discovery. More puzzling is the colossal bust of Jefferson himself which was also placed in the hall, on the pedestal of which are represented the 12 tribes of Israel and the 12 signs of the Zodiac. The room also contained a reclining statue of Cleopatra, balanced by one of a reclining Venus in the grounds.

Charles Wilson Peale's Museum, Philadelphia

Charles Wilson Peale, an outstanding artist and lay scientist, was a close friend of Thomas Jefferson. He founded a dynasty of artists, whose leading members were his sons Rubens and Rembrandt Peale. Peale's museum was a wooden building. A sign over the door bore the words 'School of Wisdom'. Inside, Peale had crammed shelves and display cases with natural-history specimens, shells, eggs and dried plants, stuffed birds and animals, books and pictures, including one recording his own excavation of a prehistoric animal on the Ohio river. Stuffed alligators hung from the ceiling. Stuffed mountain lions were displayed in realistic poses. Curiosities and wonders such as a stuffed five-legged cow suckling a two-legged calf, pantaloons made from a whale's intestines, a mammoth and the shoes and socks made for the 'Irish Giant' O'Brien (8 feet high) were also on display. There was a collection of paintings of famous Americans – the paintings were for sale – and a silhouette machine.

The Peale Museum retained some of the characteristics of the 'cabinets of curiosities' of the seventeenth century, with their jumbles of rocks, books, jewels, narwhal horns and stuffed crocodiles. But it was also a national museum in the sense that a great many of the exhibits, including the pictures for sale, made it the first art gallery in North America displaying the products of the American colonies and showing their famous men to Americans themselves.

Pompeii and Herculaneum

In AD 79, an eruption of Vesuvius, near Naples, buried the two Roman towns of Pompeii and Heraculaneum in mud and ashes. Herculaneum was only seriously excavated from the 1730s, at the order of the king of Naples And for Pompeii, it was the 1760s before serious excavation began. Much was already known about the events of AD 79. But the excavations came as a revelation, offering insights into the daily life of Rome only a little after the death of Christ, because instead of isolated monuments and statues, excavators found a complete town. Workers on the excavations were able to reconstruct kitchens and shops, schools and bath houses. An important consequence was the impact of the style of Roman buildings, furniture and clothes on contemporary styles. Imitated in the Enlightenment, they were the direct ancestors of Neoclassical style. The art historian Winckelmann, remarked that the antiquities of the Bay of Naples including Pompeii and Herculaneum were 'different from all antiquities on earth, a coast which was once the fairy land of poets and the favourite retreat of great men'.

Stourhead

The gardens at Stourhead, near Salisbury in Wiltshire, which may still be seen, were laid out by the wealthy banker Sir Samuel Hoare from 1741. Their use of imagery, and the way they organize the reactions of the walker through the gardens, reveal much about how the Enlightenment responded to both its classical and medieval pasts. Stourhead was (and is) laid out as a circuit of walks along a river bank. Hoare's guests would walk down from the house to a lake, across a five-arched stone bridge of Palladian design, then take the path along the water's edge, their view guided not only to the temples but also to a grotto with statues, and on the way back would pass a temple of Flora, and a pantheon, and then see the newly built medieval village and church nestling behind the house. The walk concludes with a visit to a temple of Apollo, actually a reconstruction of the ruined circular temple of Venus at Baalbec in North Africa. Around the lake are stones with inscriptions of lines from Ovid and Virgil's *Aeneid*. Hoare clearly regarded the passage through the grotto as corresponding to Aeneas' descent to Avernus, and made it clear to visitors by an inscription on the temple of Flora that his lake could be taken as an allegory of Lake Avernus.

Vauxhall Gardens

Vauxhall Gardens opened in London in 1728. Originally regarded as a place of rowdy behaviour, drunkenness and masked balls which cloaked all kinds of intrigue, the Gardens became over the following decade, thanks to the efforts of their owner, John Tyers, a far more genteel affair, brought to a height in 1738 by Tyers' purchase and display of a statue of Handel by the famous French sculptor Roubillac. This statue shows Handel not as a mighty musical genius (which many in Britain in fact regarded him as) but in informal dress, improvising on a small harp. A contemporary guidebook noted: 'His harmony has charmed even … the crowd into the profoundest calm and most decent behaviour.'

Vauxhall was a new kind of public venue, to which there was no equivalent in France, a place where high and low, in fact anyone who could pay the price of admission, could mingle in respectable and orderly surroundings. In this structural sense, Vauxhall Gardens closely resembled the coffee houses as places for discussion and instruction.

Suggestions for Further Reading

Many original works, such as those, for example, by Voltaire, Condorcet, Locke and Hume, are now translated and available in full on the Internet. The same goes for most of the *Encyclopédie*. Accordingly, this bibliography will concentrate on secondary works, and those primary sources not yet so available.

Introduction

BLANNING, T.C.W., *The Eighteenth Century: Europe 1688–1815*, Oxford, 2000

DOYLE, WILLIAM, *The Old European Order 1660–1800*, Oxford, 1981

FITZPATRICK, MARTIN, PETER JONES, CHRISTA KNELLWOLF and IAIN McCALMAN, *The Enlightenment World*, Abingdon and New York, 2004

OUTRAM, DORINDA, *The Enlightenment*, Cambridge, 2005

PORTER, ROY, *The Enlightenment*, London, 1990

WILLS, JOHN E., *1688: A Global History*, New York and London 2001

1 What Was the Enlightenment?

BARNARD, F.M., *Herder's Social and Political Thought*, Oxford, 1965

BOYLE, NICHOLAS, *Goethe: The Poet and the Age*, Oxford, 1991

ISRAEL, JONATHAN, *Radical Enlightenment: Philosophy and the Making of Modernity, 1650–1750*, Oxford, 2001

OUTRAM, DORINDA 'The Enlightenment our Contemporary', in Clark, William, Jan Golinski and Simon Schaffer, *The Sciences in Enlightenment Europe*, Chicago, 1999, 32–43

PORTER, ROY, *The Creation of the Modern World: the Untold Story of the British Enlightenment*, New York, 2000

REISS, HANS, ed., *Kant's Political Writings*, Cambridge, 1992

SCHMIDT, JAMES, *What Is Enlightenment? Eighteenth-Century Answers and Twentieth Century Questions*, Berkeley, 1999

2 The Sociable Enlightenment

BREWER, JOHN, NEIL MacKENDRICK and J.H. PLUMB, eds, *The Birth of a Consumer Society: The Commercialisation of Eighteenth-Century England*, London, 1982

BREWER, JOHN, *The Pleasures of the Imagination: English Culture in the Eighteenth Century*, Chicago, 1997

D'ALEMBERT, JEAN LE ROND DE, *Preliminary Discourse to the Encyclopedie* (1751), ed. Richard N. Schwab, New York, 1993

DARNTON, ROBERT, *Mesmerism and the End of the Enlightenment*, Cambridge MA, 1968

DARNTON, ROBERT, *The Business of Enlightenment: A Publishing History of the Encyclopedie, 1775–1800*, Cambridge MA, 1979

DARNTON, ROBERT, *The Literary Underground of the Old Regime*, Cambridge MA, 1982

DARNTON, ROBERT, *The Great Cat Massacre and Other Episodes in French Cultural History*, New York, 1984

MELTON, JAMES VAN HORN, *The Rise of the Public in Eighteenth-Century Europe*, Cambridge, 2001

RAVEL, JEFFREY S., *The Contested Parterre: Public Theatre and French Political Culture 1680–1791*, Ithaca and London, 1999

ROCHE, DANIEL, *Everyday Things: The Birth of Consumption in France, 1600–1800*, Cambridge, 2000

3 Marriage, Children and Gender: The Enlightenment Family

BOUCE, PAUL GABRIEL, ed., *Sexuality in Eighteenth-Century Britain*, Manchester, 1982

CROWLEY, JOHN E., *The Invention of Comfort: Sensibilities and Design in Early Modern Britain and Early America* (Baltimore, 2001)

EARLE, ALICE MORSE, *The Diary of Anna Green Winslow, a Boston Schoolgirl of 1771*, Boston MA, 1894

FAIRCHILDS, CISSIE, *Domestic Enemies: Servants and their Masters in Old Regime France*, Baltimore, 1984

HULL, ISABEL V., *Sexuality, State and Civil Society in Germany, 1700–1815*, Ithaca, 1996

KATES, GARY, *Monsieur d'Eon Is a Woman: A Tale of Political Intrigue and Sexual Masquerade*, New York, 1995

LASLETT, PETER, *Life and Illicit Love in Earlier Generations*, Cambridge 1977

McCUBBIN, ed., *'Tis Nature's Fault: Unauthorised Sexuality in the Enlightenment*, Cambridge, 1987

THOMAS, KEITH, *Man and the Natural World: A History of the Modern Sensibility*, London and New York, 1985

SHORTER, EDWARD, *The Making of the Modern Family*, New York, 1975

STONE, LAWRENCE, *Family, Sex and Marriage in England, 1500–1800*, Harmondsworth and New York, 1979

THORNTON, PETER, *Authentic Domestic Interiors 1620–1920*, London, 1984

TRAER, JAMES F., *Marriage and the Family in Eighteenth-Century France*, Ithaca NY, 1980

4 The Global Enlightenment

ARMITAGE, DAVID, 'Is There a Pre-History of Globalisation?', in *Geographies of the Eighteenth Century: The Question of the Global*, ed. Dror Wahrman, Bloomington, 2004

AXTELL, JAMES, *Natives and Newcomers: The Cultural Origins of North America*, Oxford, 2001

BEAGLEHOLE, J.C. (ed.), *The Journals of Captain James Cook on his Voyages of Discovery*, 2 vols, Cambridge and London, 1962

BOUGAINVILLE, LOUIS DE, *Voyage autour du monde*, 2 vols, 1772 (translated by J.R. Forster, London, 1772)

FORSTER, JOHAN REINHOLD, *Observations Made during a Voyage around the World*, 1778, ed. Nicolas Thomas, Harriet Guest and Michael Dettelbach, Honolulu, 1996

FROST, ALAN, 'The Pacific Ocean: The Eighteenth Century's "New World"', in *Captain James Cook: Image and Impact*, ed. Walter Veit, Melbourne, 1979, 5–49

GERBI, ANTONELLO, *The Dispute of the New World*, Pittsburgh, 1973

HONOUR, HUGH, *Chinoiserie: The Vision of Cathay*, London, 1966

JACOBSON, DAWN, *Chinoiserie*, London and New York, 1993

LAWSON, PHILIP, *The East India Company: A History*, Harlow and New York, 1993

MACARTNEY, LORD, *An Embassy to China, Being the Journal Kept by Lord Macartney during his Embassy to the Emperor Ch'ien-lung, 1793–1794*, ed. J.L. Cramner-Byng, London, 1962

OUTRAM, DORINDA, 'On Being Perseus: New Knowledge, Dislocation and Enlightenment

Exploration', in Livingstone and Withers, 281–84

SMITH, BERNARD, *European Vision and the South Pacific*, New Haven and London, 1985

SWIFT, JONATHAN, *Gulliver's Travels into Several Remote Nations of the World* (1726), ed. Albert J. Rivero, New York, 2002

5 Exploring the Self

COX, STEPHEN D. *'The Stranger within Thee': Concepts of the Self in Late Eighteenth-Century Literature*, Pittsburgh, 1980

CRAFT-FAIRCHILD, CATHERINE, *Masquerade and Gender: Disguise and Female Identity in Eighteenth-Century Fictions by Women*, University Park PA, 1993

HOFFMAN, R., MECHAL SOBEL and FREDRIKA TEUTE, *Through a Glass Darkly: Reflections on Personal Identity in Early America*, Chapel Hill, NC, 1997

LAMB, JONATHAN, *Preserving the Self in the South Seas, 1680–1840*, Chicago, 2001

ROUSSEAU, JEAN-JACQUES, *Julie, ou la nouvelle Héloïse* (1761), ed. Michel Launay, Paris, 1967

SOBEL, MECHAL, *Teach Me Dreams: The Search for Self in the Revolutionary Era*, Princeton, 2000

STRICKLAND, STUART, 'The Ideology of Self-Knowledge, and the Practice of Self-Experimentation', *Eighteenth Century Studies*, 31 (1998), 453–71

6 Authority and Architecture

BINDMAN, David, *Hogarth*, London, 1985

BREWER, JOHN, *The Sinews of War: War, Money and the English State, 1688–1783*, Cambridge MA, 1988

COLLEY, LINDA, *Britons: Forging the Nation 1707–1837*, London, 1992

CROW, THOMAS, *Painters and Public Life in Eighteenth-Century Paris*, New Haven and London, 1985

DIDEROT, DENIS, *Diderot on Art*, trans. and ed. John Goodman, London, 1995

HERMANN, WOLFGANG, *Laugier and Eighteenth-Century French Theory*, London, 1962

HONOUR, HUGH, *Neoclassicism*, London, 1968

IRWIN, DAVID, *Neoclassicism*, London, 1997

RAEFF, MARC, *The Well-Ordered Police State: Social and Institutional Change through Law in the Germanies and Russia, 1600–1800*, New Haven, 1983

ROSENAU, HELEN, *Boullée and Visionary Architecture*, London and New York, 1976

SCOTT, H.M., *Enlightened Absolutism: Reform and Reformers in Late Eighteenth-Century Europe*, Basingstoke, 1990

FRANCO VENTURI, *The End of the Old Regime in Europe 1768–1776: The First Crisis*, trans. R. Burr Litchfield

VIDLER, A., *Ledoux*, London 1984

YOUNG, HILARY, ed., *The Genesis of Wedgwood* (exhibition catalogue), Victoria and Albert Museum, London 1998

7 Science and Medicine

BAKER, K.M., *Condorcet: From Natural Philosophy to Social Mathematics*, Chicago, 1975

CLARK, WILLIAM, JAN GOLINSKI and SIMON SCHAFFER, eds, *The Sciences in Enlightenment Europe*, Chicago, 1999

DOUTHWAITE, JULIA, *The Wild Girl, Natural Man, and the Monster: Dangerous Experiments in the Age of the Enlightenment*, Chicago, 2002

DRAYTON, RICHARD H., *Nature's Government: Science, Imperial Britain and the 'Improvement' of the World*, New Haven and London, 2000

FOUCAULT, MICHEL, *Madness and Civilisation: A History of Insanity in the Age of Reason*, trans. Alan Sheridan, 1973

FOUCAULT, MICHEL, *Birth of the Clinic: An Archaeology of Medical Perception*, trans. Alan Sheridan (*Naissance de la clinique*, Paris, 1963), London, 1976

GILLISPIE, CHARLES COULTON, *Science and Polity in France at the End of the Old Regime*, Princeton, 1980

GROVE, RICHARD, *Green Imperialism: Colonial Expansion, Tropical Island Edens and the Origins of Environmentalism*, Cambridge 1995

JORDANOVA, LUDMILLA, *Sexual Visions: Images of Gender in Science and Medicine between the Eighteenth and Twentieth Centuries*, Hemel Hempstead, 1989

LIVINGSTONE, DAVID and C.J. WITHERS, *Geography and Enlightenment*, Chicago, 1999

PORTER, ROY, ed., *Patients and Practitioners: Lay Perceptions of Medicine in Pre-Industrial Society*, Cambridge, 1985

RISKIN, JESSICA, *Science in the Age of Sensibility: The Sentimental Empiricists of the French Enlightenment*, Chicago, 2002

ROSEN, GEORGE, 'Cameralism and the Concept of Medical Police', *Bulletin of the History of Medicine*, 27 (1953), 21–42

SCHIEBINGER, LONDA, *The Mind Has No Sex? Women in the Origins of Modern Science*, Cambridge MA, 1989

STEVEN SHAPIN, *The Scientific Revolution*, Chicago, 1996

TERRALL, MARY, *The Man Who Flattened the Earth: Maupertuis and the Sciences in the Enlightenment*, Chicago, 2002

WESTFALL, R., *Never at Rest: A Biography of Isaac Newton*, Cambridge, 1980

8 Epilogue: The Legacy of the Enlightenment

GORDON, DANIEL, *Postmodernism and the Enlightenment: New Perspectives on Eighteenth-Century French Intellectual History*, New York and London, 2001

HABERMAS, J., *The Structural Transformation of the Public Sphere: An Enquiry into a Category of Bourgeois Society*, Cambridge MA, 1989

HORCKHEIMER, MAX and THEODOR ADORNO, *Dialectic of Enlightenment*, New York, 1972

HOY, D.C., ed., *Foucault: A Critical Reader*, Oxford, 1986

MCMAHON, DARRIN, *Enemies of the Enlightenment: The French Counter-Enlightenment and the Making of Modernity*, New York, 2001

RABINOW, PAUL, ed., *The Foucault Reader*, New York, 1984

Sources
of Illustrations

AKG = Archiv für Kunst und Geschichte, London
BAL = Bridgeman Art Library, London
MBA = Musée des Beaux-Arts

akg images, London 6, 8–9, 10, 11, 19, 32, 35, 37, 38, 57, 78, 85 (top), 91, 142, 206, 208–9, 212, 227, 230, 232, 234 (top), 246 (bottom right), 290, 295, 296–7, 300 (both), 301

AKG/Erich Lessing 225, 233 (all), 234, 235

AKG/Monheim 210, 211, 231

AMSTERDAM:
Rijksprentenkabinet 72, 73, 108, 137 (bottom)
Scheepvartmuseum 138 (both)

ARLES: Musée Reattu 116

Arxiu/Mas, Inst. Amatler 106

BAL 17, 18, 19, 21, 46, 58–59, 76–77, 90–91, 95, 96, 97, 104, 109, 110–111, 114, 126, 128–9, 131, 133, 135, 151, 180–81, 204–205, 222–223, 241, 243, 246, 256, 259, 264–65, 267

BERLIN:
Kupferstichkabinett 27, 74 (both), 82 (top), 83, 225
Staatliche Museen 37, 38 (right), 78

BOSTON: Museum of Fine Arts 107 (top)

Brandstätter Verlag Vienna, photos Alexander Koller 267, 270, 271

BRATISLAVA: Melske Galerie 222–223

CAMBRIDGE: Fitzwilliam Museum 110–111

CANBERRA: National Library 131

Castle Howard, private collection 169 (right)

Cesky Krumlov: castle 192 (top)

CHANTILLY: Musée Condé 185 (bottom), 267

Chatsworth, Duke of Devonshire 95 (bottom)

CHICAGO: Art Institute 18 (top)

Corsage, Barclay & Simmonds Ltd 29

Courtauld Institute of Art, London, photo 86 (top)

Christie's Images 147, 159, 166

DERBY: Museum and Art Gallery 264–265

DETROIT: Institute of Art 180–181

DIJON: MBA 54–55

DRESDEN:
Kupferstichkabinett 31 (bottom), 64–65
Porzellansammlung 62 (right)

DUBLIN: National Gallery of Ireland 95

DÜSSELDORF: Goethemuseum 283

EXETER: Royal Albert Memorial Museum 133

R.B. Fleming photos/BL 96, 99 (all)

F. Foliot photos/BN, Paris 6, 17, 47, 61, 84, 85 (bottom), 148 (left), 149 (right), 250 (top), 278–79, 286, 287 (both), 292, 293, 305

FRANKFURT AM MAIN:
Freies Deutsches Hochstift 32
Goethe Museum 307

FREIBERG: Bergakademie 20

GENEVA: Musée J. J. Rousseau 101

GÖTTINGEN: Universitätsbibliothek 246–47

GREENWICH, London: National Maritime Museum 170–171

The Hague: Gemeendemuseum 260–261

B. Hajos 229 (bottom)

HALLE: Frankeschen Stiftungen 124

HAMBURG: Kunsthalle 18 (bottom)

M. Hamm 38 (left)

HULL: City Museum 151

JENA: Karl Zeiss Archives 233 (all)

Kippenberg Collection 289

KLEVE: Stadtisches Museum 93

KRONENBORG: Seafaring Museum 137

Emily Lane 45, 214, 215, 216, 218, 219 (both)

LE MANS: Musée de Tesse 94 (bottom)

LIÈGE: Musée de l'Art Wallon 8–9

LILLE: Musée des Beaux-Arts 19 (top)

Lincoln, Usher Gallery 17

LONDON:
Board of the Grand Lodge of England 87
British Library 25, 26, 96, 99 (all)
British Museum 64, 179
Tate Gallery 68, 69 (left)

LOS ANGELES: J. P. Getty Museum 41, 121 (top and bottom), 140 (all), 155, 156 (all), 157, 160, 161, 251, 305, 306, 307, 308, 310, 312

MADRID: Prado 20 (right), 107, 196

MAINZ: Historisches Museum 291

MALMAISON: Musée du Château 58–59

MARBACH: Schiller Museum 311

Mary Evans Picture Library 240, 250, 262, 273, 274

MEISSEN: Porcelain Museum 140 (bottom left)

MOSCOW: State Russian Museum 263 (bottom)

W. Christian von der Mülbe 22–23, 36

MUNICH: Alte Pinakothek 206

National Trust, Waddesdon Manor 103

NEUCHÂTEL: Musée d'Art et d'Histoire 189 (bottom)

NEW YORK:
Frick Collection 120
Metropolitan Museum of Art, George Delacote Fund 191 (top); Bequest of William K. Vanderbilt 203

OXFORD: Ashmolean Museum 76–77

PADUA: Museo Civico 141

PARIS:
Bibliothèque Nationale 40, 100, 183, 185 (top), 187
Musée Carnavalet 42 (right), 62 (right), 70, 96, 114, 236, 246 (left)
Musée Cognac-Jay 126 (bottom)
Louvre 39, 46 (right), 49, 97, 104, 204–205
Private collection 21, 34, 57, 67, 158–159, 241, 256, 290

REGENSBURG: Walhalla 31 (top left)
Photo Robert Raith

RMN, Paris 97

ROTTERDAM: Museum Boymans-van Beuningen 161

ROVERETO: Accademia degli Agiati 268

ST PETERSBURG: Hermitage 12

Scala 141

SÈVRES: Archives of the Porcelain Factory 63

STOCKHOLM: Nationalmuseet 119

STOKE-ON-TRENT: Wedgwood Museum 105

SYDNEY: State Library of New South Wales 128–129

VENICE:
Cà Rezzonico 190, 194
Galleria Orsini Stampalia 190

VERSAILLES: Château 149

VIENNA:
Albertina 220 (both), 272 (bottom)
Galerie Gilhofer 224 (both)
Heeresgeschichtliches Museum 212
Historisches Museum 19 (bottom)
Josephinum 269–270, 271
Kunsthistorisches Museum 227
Schloss Schönbrunn 208–209

Wellcome Trust 113, 272 (top), 273 (right)

The Royal Collection, Her Majesty Queen Elizabeth II 257

WOLFENBÜTTEL: Herzog August Bibliothek 28, 174

Werner Forman Archive 136, 137, 134

YORK: City Art Gallery 135

ZURICH: Kunsthaus 201

Index

Page-numbers in *italic* indicate illustrations